Richard Tregaskis
Classics Collection

Invasion Diary

Richard Tregaskis

Invasion Diary

Published by JMFdeA Press

For information address:
JMFdeA Press
P.O. Box 235737
Honolulu, HI 96823
www.jmfdeapress.com

Paperback ISBN: 978-1-956695-11-3
E-Book ISBN: 978-1-956695-12-0
Audiobook ISBN: 978-1-956695-13-7

JMFdeA Press chose to keep the content and punctuation in the Richard Tregaskis Classics Collection as RT originally wrote it. We feel RT's flavor would have been diluted by making changes to adhere to modern rules. There are certain words RT used that will show the reader the era in which RT lived. Richard Tregaskis was a kind, generous, big-hearted man who continuously put himself at great peril to tell the stories the world needed to know. He used some terms that are not acceptable today. Richard meant no malice. He was writing about his enemies. JMFdeA Press did not alter RT's works out of respect for him, and to also show how far as a society we have matured *some*. On Sept.18, 2021 there was a rally "Justice for J6" in Washington, D.C.. Have we really evolved in today's time to be a more tolerant society?

"As a young boy, I enjoyed reading about the heroes of our Nation. In reading the Landmark book version of Richard Tregaskis' *Guadalcanal Diary*, I was inspired by the courage and sacrifice of the Marines and sailors who fought and persevered in that very difficult battle—the first land offensive of the US in WWII. It inspired me to serve later in my life, but more importantly, taught me about the importance of exhibiting will, courage, and resilience when things were hard. Thanks RT for telling the story of these great Americans and so many others over the course of your life and career."

Robert B. Neller
General USMC retired
37th Commandant of the Marine Corps

Contents

About the Author

After graduating from Harvard *cum laude* in 1938, Richard Tregaskis became a journalist and a staff member of the International Service. RT was anxious to get to the heart of the action to be able to tell the heart stories of the valiant men putting their lives on the line for our country. He was sent as a correspondent to cover operations of the Pacific Fleet at the outbreak of World War II. His experiences in the South Pacific became his first book. He wrote about war in a unique way and *Guadalcanal Diary* earned him a permanent spot in American literature and set the genre of war correspondence. It continues to be essential reading by U.S. military personnel.

Tregaskis was also with American forces in the European theatre following the Allies of the invasion of Italy. While there he was hit by German shrapnel. A piece went through his helmet and part of his head, and out the other side of his helmet. After learning how to speak and use his right hand again, he continued writing. In short time, came *Invasion Diary* and *Stronger Than Fear*.

In 1947 he journeyed for two years around the world. He spent most of that time observing the Nationalist-Communist war in China, from which he barely escaped. From those amazing experiences came *Seven Leagues to Paradise*, *Last Plane to Shanghai*, and *China Bomb: A Novel*. RT was compelled to write about the dangers of indirect insurgencies, and why they are successful. Since WWII, we had constant emerging enemies who brought new kinds of war. Tregaskis wrote about all of them.

RT felt compelled to pen *X-15 Diary: The Story of America's First Space Ship*, which describes the full story of the X-15 hypersonic manned rocket ship, first of its kind in the race to space. There are the many stories of the men and women who worked tirelessly in this great chapter of American history.

Vietnam Diary, another seminal war correspondence book, was the first definitive eyewitness account of this new style of guerrilla combat. Tregaskis spent four months in the thick of the war to gather the compelling stories of courageous men fighting in these vicious battles. Due to his special skills and extensive travel in Vietnam, RT was contracted to write about one of the largest war-time construction efforts in history. His book, *Southeast Asia: Building the Bases The History of Construction in Southeast Asia* was an incredible undertaking which only he, with his talent and expertise, could write. It covers every major construction by the U.S. Navy Construction Battalions (Navy SEABEES), and other military and civilian engineers and their stories as the events of the war evolved.

Amidst writing for motion pictures and television, RT delved into fictional biographies. *The Warrior King: Hawaii's Kamehameha the Great* was created out of his love of Hawaii after he made it his home. It is an exceptional historical story of the legendary leader of the Hawaiian Islands. Tregaskis transports the reader back in time to when the Hawaiian Islands were under the rule of many kings and the events that transpired to create a one Hawaiian Nation, governed by one ruler for the prosperity of all of the Hawaiian people.

RT left behind a halfway finished love story, *The Secret of the Taj*, about Mumtaz Mahal who inspired the creation of the Taj Mahal. It was out of his passionate love of his wife, Moana, and their assignments to India, that this manuscript came to fruition.

In 1964, Richard Tregaskis was awarded the George Polk Award for reporting under hazardous conditions for the book that became Vietnam Diary. The helmet he wore in 1943 in Italy when a shell fragment pierced through it and into his skull is on display at the National Museum of the Marine Corps, along with a copy of *Invasion Diary*. Although RT had challenges with Type I diabetes, he never complained and it never stopped him from telling the important stories of the times as they were happening. During his life Richard Tregaskis clambered in and out of jeeps, fighters, bombers, trucks, and choppers while carrying his pack and notebook into the battles of nine wars. He was a special war correspondent who was able to sense the problems of the men in the heat of battle, while having an extraordinary ability to understand the strategy of war.

Foreword

Flint Whitlock

Richard Tregaskis was a giant of a man, both literally and literarily. When, in mid-1942, the six-foot-seven-inch reporter was assigned to cover the war in the Pacific, a friend joked, "You'll be some target for the Japs, Dick. They'll capture you and use you for an observation post."

Although he went in with the first wave of marines to hit the beach on Guadalcanal in August 1942, and spent seven weeks under fire there, the twenty-six-year-old came through without a scratch—and without being used as an observation post. It was his first assignment as a war correspondent, but it would not be his last.

Tregaskis was born on November 28, 1915, in Elizabeth, New Jersey. In 1938, after majoring in English and being a member of the school's championship swim team, he graduated cum laude from Harvard and got a job reporting for *the Boston American*. With a working knowledge of Portuguese, he was selected by International News Service to be their correspondent in Lisbon; when the Japanese attacked Pearl Harbor on December 7, 1941, his assignment was changed to the Pacific.

Tregaskis's experiences on the tropical killing ground of Guadalcanal—first in the form of newspaper dispatches from the battlefield, and then his first book, *Guadalcanal Diary*—were eagerly grabbed by an American public hungry for positive war news. Within three days of receiving his manuscript, completed on a B-24 Liberator bomber over the Pacific, Random House accepted it for publication. It was snapped up a few days later by the Book-of-the-Month Club and became an instant bestseller. Stopping in California on his way back from the war, he helped turn his book into the screenplay for the hit movie of the same title, which came out in late 1943. Overnight Richard Tregaskis leaped from obscure war correspondent to literary sensation. He could have safely retired on the fame and fortune that came his way, but war correspondents seem to have a built-in magnet for danger; soon he was leaving the glamour of Hollywood and heading toward another war front—the Mediterranean.

Thrust into a two-front war, President Franklin D. Roosevelt and his advisors concluded that Japan could be contained in the Pacific; the more immediate danger lay in Europe, which the Germans had been ravaging since September 1939. England stood defiant against the Nazi's aerial blitz, but everyone expected that it was just a matter of time before German dictator Adolf Hitler would send his armies swarming across the English Channel.

But then Hitler made a fatal blunder. In June 1941, after postponing indefinitely the invasion of Britain, he instead sent a force of three million men into the Soviet Union, with which he earlier had concluded a mutual nonaggression pact. This attack, which plunged deeply into Russia, nearly to the gates of Moscow, gave the British a reprieve. It also gave the United States time to recruit, train, and equip an eventual twelve-million-man fighting force.

While the Soviet Union's leader, Josef Stalin, held off Hitler and pleaded for Britain and the United States to come to his country's aid, Roosevelt and British Prime Minister Winston S. Churchill demurred. Due to the strong isolationist sentiment that had arisen since the end of World War I, the United States had badly neglected its national defense and was still a second-rate military power; Britain nearly had been bled white by its defiant but costly stand against Germany. Both the United States and Britain were painfully aware that it would take years of slow and steady buildup before the Allies would be able to launch a successful invasion of the European continent and battle their way into Germany. Churchill was understandably reluctant to invade Europe, for the 300,000-man British Expeditionary Force that had been sent to France in September 1939 had been driven into the sea at Dunkerque in May 1940. The British did not return until August 1942, when a 5,000-man probing force, consisting mostly of Canadians, met with disaster at Dieppe on France's English Channel coast.

The situation looked bleak. Unless the British and Americans could relieve the pressure on the Soviet Union, Stalin's forces might very well collapse, allowing Germany to unleash all of its resources against Great Britain and the United States. Another way would have to be found to distract the Germans from their drive to take Moscow. The most likely place to insert American troops into battle against the Germans and their partners in crime, the Italians, was with an invasion of Morocco, at the northwest corner of Africa. Not only would such an invasion bolster the British, who had been battling first the Italians and then the Germans in North Africa since September 1940, but it would give the growing-but-green American army some much-needed combat experience. Just as important, it would prove to the British that the American fighting man was every bit as tough as his British counterpart. It would also provide senior American commanders (such as Gen. Dwight D. Eisenhower) with valuable lessons in the tactical and logistical workings of a large-scale amphibious operation that would be required later, during the invasion of France.

On November 8, 1942, a force of some 107,000 Americans landed against weak opposition from the German-controlled Vichy French, who governed Morocco. Although the Americans stumbled badly in their initial engagements against the Germans, Lieut. Gen. George S. Patton Jr., new commander of II Corps, soon whipped the inexperienced Yanks into shape; with the British they eventually overcame enemy opposition and utterly defeated the Germans in North Africa by May 1943. It was time to proceed to Phase Two of the Mediterranean campaign.

Many heated, high-level discussions followed the cessation of hostilities in North Africa. Stalin was still demanding a "second front" on the continent, but Churchill and Roosevelt insisted that the time was not yet right. The one way Britain and America saw they could help, however, was by drawing German forces away from the Russian Front with a threat to the Third Reich's southern fringe: first by invading Sicily and then Italy. Churchill viewed the region as "the soft underbelly of Europe," but Lieut. Gen. Mark Clark, who's U.S. Fifth Army, would have to fight for every yard of Italian soil, termed it "a tough, old gut." In the end Clark's assessment would be more accurate for, once Sicily fell in August 1943, the mountainous spine of the Italian peninsula would prove to be a haven for the German defenders and a nightmare for the American and British attackers.

This was the situation that Richard Tregaskis found when he arrived in Sicily in July 1943. A series of dispatches from the front that he later assembled into this, his second book, showed firsthand what a tough, old gut Sicily and Italy proved to be.

Tregaskis, like all war correspondents, was always in search of a good story. Since those "good stories" happened at the front, he placed himself there, with the men he wrote about, where danger and death lurked around every corner, or came screaming unannounced out of the clear blue sky in the form of an artillery shell or enemy aircraft. Written in the same chronological, diary fashion that made *Guadalcanal Diary* so compelling and immediate, *Invasion Diary* helps readers feel as though they are sitting at Tregaskis's side or peeking over his shoulder as he scribbles notes in his journal. Much of his prose is almost poetic: "A searchlight beam, leaning against the sky, snapped on, then off." Tregaskis takes us on bombing runs over Sicily and Rome and under a fearsome enemy barrage at Salerno. He describes his observations and feelings with great detail yet with a remarkable economy of words. Thousands of GIs have tried to describe what being under fire is like. Few of them were professional, gifted writers like Tregaskis. Even fewer had the ability and craftsmanship to bring the terrifying experience to life. Indeed, his description of being on the receiving end of numerous artillery barrages has seldom been equaled. His reporting makes war seem at once both romantic and repulsive, courageous and senseless, a grand adventure and a great human tragedy.

Invasion Diary is a wonderful snapshot of an era gone by, a grain of history encapsulated in a drop of amber. It is easy today for us to forget that no one at the time knew how the war would turn out, or how long it would take, or how many casualties would ultimately be suffered. Captured in that drop of amber too is an innocence and uncynical attitude that has all but faded from today's society and certainly from today's news reporting. Although he had been with the marines on Guadalcanal and had already seen death close up, Tregaskis still had a schoolboy's fascination with war or perhaps something like an alcoholic's addiction to it. His eagerness to get to the front lines and his fear of "missing the action" is obvious. The eagerness for battle expressed by the officers he interviewed is obvious too, as is their unabashed glee at the profession of war. To anyone brought up on post-Vietnam antimilitarism, this joy at seeing cities bombed and men killed will be, no doubt, a shock to the system. But that was the way it was back then. Patriotism for the cause was running hot. There was a war on, and virtually every red-blooded American male wanted in on it. Although much of what Tregaskis wrote was for home-front consumption—in order to put a good face on a bad situation and show the folks back home that American boys "could take it and dish it out"— he conveyed the prevailing sentiment of the time: that Americans were the good guys and the Germans were the enemy who needed to be killed, wounded, and/or taken prisoner so that the war would come to a swift and victorious conclusion.

Tregaskis is invariably compared to the other great American reporter of the Second World War, Ernie Pyle. Both were more concerned about chronicling the lives and exploits of the common soldier than they were about grand strategy and the movements of armies. In terms of their styles, some feel Tregaskis was the better writer; Pyle's sentence structure was often quirky, while Tregaskis's was more polished. But whereas Pyle concentrated primarily on what the soldiers he interviewed were doing, Tregaskis focused mainly on what he, the war correspondent, was doing in relation to the soldiers.

Invasion Diary is really about the life of the men who covered the war for their newspapers and wire services, a small corps of intrepid journalists who braved enemy fire just like the troops but who, in other ways, lived a privileged life. The "C" (for "correspondent") armband they wore often gained them certain perquisites, such as dinners with the top brass and better living accommodations than a damp hole in the ground. They were often briefed by officers and subsequently learned more about a coming battle or operation than did the men who were required to fight it. Their uniforms were that of officers (without insignia), and they enjoyed officers' privileges (without saluting). If the action became too hot, some correspondents could, if they wished, absent themselves from the front lines and write up their stories until it was safe to return. Not Richard Tregaskis or, for that matter, Ernie Pyle. To accurately report the war, they felt they had to be in the thick of things.

But bullets and bombs did not discriminate. They were equal-opportunity killers. They did not know that correspondents were noncombatants. They could not care less that the reporter carried a notebook and typewriter, not a rifle or machine gun. From a thousand yards away, a German or Japanese soldier could not tell that the fellow in the olive-drab helmet and field jacket was a writer, not a warrior. The "C" armband was not a bulletproof vest. It did not deflect torpedoes or shield planes from deadly flak. It provided no immunity from anything. Plenty of reporters were killed or maimed during the course of the war. Almost all of them had close calls.

War correspondents often had a curious effect on soldiers. Individual soldiers and even whole units seemed to fight a little harder and better when Tregaskis or Pyle turned up in their midst, hoping the reporters might mention their names and hometowns in their stories.

Like an infantryman with a narrow view of war from the confining perspective of his foxhole, Tregaskis restricted his reporting to a correspondent's-eye view. Seldom does he refer to the broader issues of the war; instead, he gives readers a sense of what the average soldier experienced—the heat, the cold, the wet, the fear, and the joy at simple pleasures (a bath, a hot meal, a night without an artillery barrage) . By reporting his own experiences, Tregaskis became Everyman, evidently feeling readers could extrapolate and realize that the soldier—somebody's son, husband, brother, uncle, or nephew—was going through virtually the same thing.

Some readers may become initially frustrated with *Invasion Diary*. Too often Tregaskis's view of the action is hidden by a hill or obscured by foliage. Too often he arrives on the scene only to find that the battle is over and the troops have moved on to the next objective. While this may be somewhat maddening, it also gives a true picture of what actually did happen in battle. In this sense, *Invasion Diary* is similar to Stephen Crane's great Civil War novel, *The Red Badge of Courage*, in which the protagonist, Henry Fleming, hears the distant sounds of battle but always seems to arrive too late to take part in the action he craves. Many times in *Invasion Diary*, Richard Tregaskis is Henry Fleming, left to report only the aftermath of battle, to silently stare at badly wounded men, and to describe the detritus of war without observing the action itself.

Tregaskis's war—and nearly his life—came to an abrupt end near Venafro, Italy, on November 22, 1943, when he became "the badly wounded man" after a chunk of German shrapnel tore through his helmet and shattered his skull. His descriptions of his reactions to being wounded and his long recovery are a polished, if painful, gem of war literature.

Tregaskis could not stay away from war. He authored seven more books, including one on the growing conflict in Vietnam in the early 1960s. His *Vietnam Diary* won the Overseas Press Club's George Polk Award in 1964. Ironically, on August 15, 1973, fifty-six-year-old Richard Tregaskis, the strong collegiate swimmer and war reporter who had cheated death so many times on the battlefield, drowned off the coast near his Hawaiian home.

As a realistic, one-man's view of war in the Mediterranean theater, *Invasion Diary* has few equals. Think of it as a time capsule. Inside are small treasures to be savored, details long forgotten to be inspected closely, old emotions to again be dusted off and strongly felt many of Tregaskis's paragraphs are like precisely painted Dutch miniatures, rich with finely crafted brushstrokes.

They don't write 'em like this anymore.

Introduction

It's a miracle RT was alive in 1944 to write *Invasion Diary*. After he wrote *Guadalcanal Diary* at Pearl Harbor, he left the Pacific to the European theatre. The size fourteen boots Marines called his PTs, for "Patrol Tregaskis," went along. Eventually, luck deserted him. In a battle in Italy, on a hill called Mount Corno near Cassino, RT was hit by German shrapnel. A piece went through his helmet, a part of his head, and out the other side of the helmet, leaving a gaping jagged hole. Somehow, he staggered to the lines of the American 38th Evacuation Hospital, dragging along the helmet. There, managing to convey the word "diabetic" to a doctor, Major William Pitts of Charlotte, N.C., who performed the tedious, massive surgery.

Within a few months, RT had learned again to talk. He read poetry to practice speaking. After a time, he again learned to use his right hand, and was right back to duty. RT wrote about the war in Italy in along with the stories of the soldiers who were in the thick of battle in *Invasion Diary*. And right after that he wrote *Stronger Than*

Fear, which is a fiction about a day in the life of a soldier who loses himself and then finds himself again. Never did he think about not returning to the field. He was set on his mission as a journalist and a writer.

RT did not just want to write about war. He wanted to go to where the thick of the action, for there were the greater stories—the ones that have a dire need to be told. He could not relax for our freedom was at great peril. As Rich so aptly wrote "time and determination and persistence will perhaps restore this mutilated world to a semblance of order and intelligence once the evil powers which wreaked this horror are crushed. If only we do not forget, when the time comes . . ."

The helmet he wore that fateful day in Italy sat on his desk for many years. He told me how it was a reminder that if he could achieve the impossible, anyone could. After his death, I donated it along with a copy of *Invasion Diary* and are now displayed at the National Museum of the Marine Corps.

While RT was having these life-altering adventures in WWII, I was a teenager. We conserved everything we could and had a victory garden. It was needed to save supplies to build arms, planes, and boats along with uniforms and medical supplies. I was proud to do my part at home—we all were. I remember a Japanese friend I had a school named Anne. She was taken away and I never saw her again. She went to an internment camp. I missed her and still think about her from time to time. I was too young to realize what horrors all soldiers go through in battle. It wasn't until I went with RT to Vietnam when I saw it first-hand. I felt, like RT, it was my mission to tell the stories of what was happening to the rest of the world.

The fear of communism in America started right after WWII. There was a heightened sense that communists were infiltrating America and converting people. That led to hysteria and many false accusations and blacklists, which was fueled by a political power struggle. Once Senator McCarthy was censured by the Senate in 1954, this upheaval started to quiet. But great damage was done. And at the same time, the Cold War was amplifying.

RT needed a change of pace. He was dedicated to report realistic lives of soldiers and their experiences. Yet it was time for something different. RT traveled around the world for True Magazine in 1948 for two years. *Seven Leagues to Paradise* was the book he wrote from that big adventure. On his travels, he discovered that Russians brought leaders of Third World countries to Russia for indoctrination. They then returned to their homeland to spread the values of communism. It worked by what he called the remote control method. There were few actual Russians living in those countries, so they could not be blamed for interfering. The conflicts that were created were by their own people, not the Russian army on the surface. The communist ideals seemed appealing with talk of equality for everyone. In reality, it doesn't work and is oppressive for the masses while government leaders enjoy the life of luxury. Freedom of expression, choice of career or being able to decide how many children to have are controlled because everyone has to be shoved into the same box. It doesn't matter if the person doesn't like it—they have no say in the matter.

RT wanted for the US to adopt this successful method to share our American values. After foreign leaders lived in America for a while, they would see how the US lifestyle is better than the communist way of life. They would return home and spread American ideals, not Communist propaganda. RT had other astute ideas to copy the methods of communist propaganda for the spread of American principles. He wrote *Last Plane to Shanghai* over five years as a result of these concerns that would not let him go. RT said that fiction was a way to sweeten a harsh message. He was stunned how these dangers seemed to amplify as he wrote the book.

In 1955 the US became official supporters of South Vietnam. Although their paths did not cross in the Solomon Islands, a man he knew in college days was at sea in the waters of Guadalcanal at the same time RT was on the island. This man became President John F. Kennedy. While President Kennedy was in office, RT wrote *John F. Kennedy and PT-109*. The President loaned RT his personal logs and notes for research. At Harvard, RT and Jack Kennedy were swimmers, and close friend Torbert MacDonald captained the Harvard football team. At competitions for the varsity swim team backstrokers, RT trounced Kennedy for a slot on the team; it was a special year—they beat Yale. As press secretary Pierre Salinger took RT into the Oval Office, the first thing the President said was, "Pierre, RT beat me out for the Harvard Varsity Swim Team." RT replied, "Sir, if I'd known you would be President, I would have let you win." Amidst the laughter, one could note that neither President Kennedy nor Congressman MacDonald ever forgot that competition.

RT also delved into the race for space with *X-15 Diary*. He was fascinated with the execution of the plan to go into new territory.

He covered the entire process of the US inaugural flight to space; the good and the bad—all of it thrilling. Both *X-15 Diary* and *Last Plane to Shanghai* were published in 1961. The same year President Kennedy added additional support in Vietnam.

In 1962 I was introduced to RT at the beach by my neighbor. The next day, I started working with him as a secretary. He was already researching *Vietnam Diary*. I took a photography course and traveled with him to Vietnam many times to cover the war. This was almost like art come to life, for in RT's book *Last Plane to Shanghai* (which was published before meeting me), he wrote about a male journalist meeting a female photographer. Against many odds, the characters fell in love and covered a dangerous assignment in the midst of the China Civil War. RT considered Martha a worthy literary achievement.

Together, RT and I tackled the communist regime in *China Bomb: A novel*. RT felt a great urgency to share how such indirect insurgencies happen and why they are so successful. Set in the near future, it explored what every American in the late 1960s feared—China building a nuclear bomb. Americans were all war-torn with Vietnam continuing, and here was an enemy emerging with a new kind of war with more dangerous weapons. It was vital for people to understand the importance of this instead of being lackadaisical, despite our weariness. I am including an outline in this edition as well as correspondence. There are other tidbits for you to get a sense of what was being taught to people across the globe. It influenced them to see Americans with "imperialist" ideals in a certain light. They viewed Americans as a threat to world peace while we perceived them as a threat to world peace.

RT and I went to many places and had innumerous adventures while writing books, magazine and newspaper articles, and screenplays. A scrupulous taker of notes, meticulous researcher, and diligent questioner, RT shared in the ordeals of the men he chronicled. While participating, he was uncommonly brave, and two generations of American fighting men accepted him as a member of their team. They talked about him, angular and tall, a bit over six foot six, soft-spoken and very thin, always writing, watching, questioning, and taking photographs at the height of battle. In addition to these traits crucial to the military historian, RT brought another quality to the battle lines—it distinguishes the great in both soldiers and civilians—he cared deeply about the affairs of the everyday man. I was never happier than I was with him, even in the uncomfortable bush being eaten by insects with the enemy nearby.

Over our many trips to India, we went to Agra. RT became enamored with the woman who inspired the Taj Mahal. He wrote a complete outline and half a manuscript of a fictional biography called *The Secret of the Taj* about Mumtaz Mahal, but did not finish it.

In 1964 RT and I were on an assignment in an area called Ladakh. It is the famous roof of the world where the Himalaya and Karakoram of India nearly meet the Pamirs of Russia. It is a high, cold, desolate moraine. Indian soldiers peered through binoculars at Chinese soldiers who peered in return over their own sandbags. We flew over the Karakoram in an unpressurized Indian Air Force plane, with oxygen bottles, then landed at the lowest elevation—11,000 feet.

We carried RT's insulin kit and an odd assortment of food and drugs. He acquired a blister on his foot from a faulty stirrup adjustment. We flew immediately to Kashmir. There, in an Army hospital, the gangrene set in. He went into a 4-day coma and his foot turned black. The doctor told me there was no diabetes of this severity in India. I thought – I know, they just die. I never left his room and helped my husband. They evicted me, but I went right back anyway. He recovered—I believe due mostly to that RT will-power that was so powerful. He immediately returned to writing.

RT and I had a rare, special relationship. We learned to play out our minds back and forth and the mental stimulation was exhilarating. I was grateful to always be in synch with my husband. RT was a man of courage and he inspired me to travel on assignment with and without him to cover the 1971 Indo-Pakistani War.

One of his favorite books to write was The *Warrior King; Hawaii's Kamehameha the Great* for he was much taken by the story of Kamehameha. RT was thrilled to share more about his home, beloved Hawai'i. He needed to exercise for his diabetes. Hawaii was ideal to do his daily exercises of swimming. Who wouldn't want to swim in the warm Pacific Ocean with the Hawaiian trade winds tickling you every day? RT went to Grey's beach and liked chatting with the regulars. In the tropics, he loved wearing as little as possible at home because the temperature rarely dipped below 66°. Living in Waikiki, we walked almost everywhere because everything was centrally located. Often, we visited Don the Beachcomber who was my first employer in Hawai'i. Friends constantly stopped by our home at any time. Once John Steinbeck spent the whole day with us lounging on our large lanai with a mural of a beach although we were two blocks away from the real thing. Those years were truly special.

In 2000 I reprinted some of his books. In 2016 a publisher approached me to turn a few of RT's books into e-books and audio books. It was a great success. Now I am thrilled to introduce The Richard Tregaskis Classics Collection through JMFdeA Press to share his complete legacy in audio and digital format as well as print while providing new personal stories and memorabilia. Look for *The Secret of the Taj* as well, for I am trying to finish it for my love.

RT was one of the few civilians to receive a purple heart for bravery in combat. He was a courageous man who made it his mission to share the reality of war as it was happening with details that was not normally covered. In 1964, the Overseas Press Club presented Richard Tregaskis with the George Polk Award for first-person reporting under hazardous circumstances for the book that became *Vietnam Diary*. In 1973, Marquis' "Who's Who in America" asked for a quote; RT sent these words: "Reverence for truth, thank God, continues to be a great American ideal. Beauty makes life most pleasant, and humor cushions the worst moments. But courage remains the most valuable of all. My life in many wars has shown me that America has ample stores of all of these values in the face of the most severe mortal dangers."

I want to extend my deepest aloha to the American Heritage Center at the University of Wyoming where the Richard Tregaskis Papers are housed. I have sent them a large part of RT's correspondence and research. They provided me scans of some of the memorabilia I am sharing with you. It is my hope to have his entire collection scanned to aid researchers with their work.

Please visit the estate's website about RT at richardtregaskis.com to learn more about this fascinating man who I loved deeply and his extraordinary books. Visit jmfdeapress.com to add to your collection of his compelling historical works.

Much aloha,
Moana
June 2021

Sept. 12, 1969

FOR MY UNDIMINISHED SHAKTI,
ON THE SIXTH ANNIVERSARY

Six years, and woe is Rich., he didn't even buy Mo a house,

And in the line of watches, was unable to dig up a Micky Mouse.

Strange that the six years should seem, to me at least, a blink,

Though I'm sure that to Mo, it'd be closer to say:"600 years
           with a fink!"
To me at least, to be married to such a streamlined and supercharged
           Mata Hari,
Is usually like a dream of Paradise, to her maybe Hari Kari.

Especially when her difficult husband decides to give birth to a book.

Bad enough, to put up with old Lanky bear who under normal circumstances
           is quite a malemuke.
But for her to have to play midwife to one fiction and one non-, and
           two stillbirths
In six years, that's worse than copying a dozen War and Peaces or
           Good Earths;
And that's at least what she had to do for her incorrigible Scribbler-
           mate,
Who in birthpangs is more of a bear than Beethoven; a wonder she
           isn't filled with hate,
But instead, most of the time she is actually able to smile that
           beautiful smile,
And she manages even though most of the Terrain of Time these days
           seems like The Last Mile.
Let Mo, the indestructible and the ever young, forever keep that trim
           figure and that dynamic zip;
And if I might temporarily soil my immortal verse with a current phrase,
           I'd say resoundingly: "Man, she's really Hip!"

Lotions of Love
Intoxicated Swain

Photographs & Archives

¶

The first shell of the barrage hit
me--- and then when consciousness came back,
and I knew I had been badly wounded, I
came to realize something I had long
suspected:

That there was absolutely no sensation
of pain. It ~~was~~ was
like a movie without sound.

Often I had seen badly ~~wounded men just~~
wounded men--here and there in the Pacific---
and it had struck me that their eyes had been
filmed over by some barrier to the contor-
tions by pain.

That barrier was the fortunate mercy of
the wounded soldier.

Now I knew that shock had ~~broken their~~
dimmed my perceptions, just as I had seen
other men cut off by shock, ~~from all except~~
~~the most primitive animal reactions.~~

But though all my senses were dulled
I knew that I must catch up with Col.
Yarborough(Lt. Col. William P. Yarborough of
Stanton, Va.), if I wanted to get off that
mountain, that night.

Col Yarborough and Capt. Frank Tomasik
of New Bedford, Mass., had gone a little ahead
of me, on our way back from the top of the
mountain. I had ~~stop~~ stopped off for a few
minutes to round up a ~~success~~ successful day's
notes. Then I had been bit.

To get a wounded man off the hard rock
slope ~~of~~ of Mt. Corno, west of Venafro,
I knew it would take a crew of eight to carry
me down the ~~mili~~ virtually impassable slope
to the nearest jeep trail, nearly a mile away.

Since I was all alone, it ~~stem~~ did not
seem likely that I

more

3

would be able to find eight
people to help me. The
The thoght
of self-preservation came strongly through
my shock.

Blood ran warmly down my
face but I half sat up and tried to shout
at two soldiers who were running
at a crouch a few feet away.

My own voice rattled
faintly like a broken
gramophone , and realized
that the words didnt make sense.

Surprised, I tried again
and another time to make words: I
had lost my power of speech.

A shell was coming: I
automatically grabbed the
ground and listened
But this time too I heard
the familiar sound muffled as if it were
rattled nearly off the sound track, as if
my whole head were joggling. The usually
frightening soubd of an approaching shell
and the explosion were
ghosts of themselves, almost comic.

A frightened soldier had skinned
his way into the rocks next to me during the
the arrival of the shell and I tried to talk,
fumbling over the words, trying to
say "Can you hehp me?", coming
out finally with the words "Can help.?"

Another shell burst farther down
the slope and then the soldier
fear-hollowed face was
looking back as he running away and saying:
"I can't kelp you I'm too scared."

4

Then I realized that my chances of
getting off that night depended
on my GETTING AND UP AND WALKING.
Blood still ran down my face and I
k ew I was bad;y hit. I saw my helpmet
lying on the ground, a hole like an open
mouth in the front of it and another
in the side. My glasses had
miraculously been blown off
but mot broken. I put on my
helmet and glasses unsteadily with
my left arm because my right ar, had been
knocked out of action. It felt like a
board by my side/ I stpod and began to
stagger down the rocky trail .I dropped
my helmet and stooped to puck it up
and thought that it would be a good
souvenir if I survived---probably that
was the on;y extran-
ous thought I remember except that I
felt my pockets to make sure that I
had my notes.
Then a shell was coming and I heard
the same ragged, distant distant whist;ing
of the movement and the rattling,
loose explosion. I was on the .
ground for a little time and the n I
found a medical soldier wrapping my head in
a bandadge and
saw that he had stuck my right arm with
a morphine surette but I was not aware of
the prick of the needle. I
picked up my right arm in my left hand and
if felt like a foreigh body and when I
dropped it fell inertially .
Then the me lic was gone and I begame
again consciously aloee and
helpless

page 5

I got to my feet again and stumbling
dropping my helmet time after time picking it
up with my left hand and dangling my right
dalking my ape-jargon and and with my
blood running down my glasses, I must have
been a grotesque sight.

But in this peculiar way I was
sti;; trying to catch up with Col.
Yarborough . That was the focus of my
stunned mind and even the
arrieal of each
rustling and rattling shell halted me
only temporarily while I hit the
rocks. Once the shell burst was so
close that I felt I could have touched it
and it towered over me like a geyser, but
I was not frightened but
only at its proximity.

Then there were ,ore shells fallowing
me and I found a small cave which
a German had evidently had dug a fe t
days ago against this sort of
danger when the Germans held the
area. I began to wonder
whether I wound be able to cautch
up with Col. Yarborpugh after all of
whether I would stay the night
in the mountain, in which
pase I wou;d probably
die, Meanwhile the bursts in a frusl ing
orocession hit close below my little
cave. I felt something like
relief about being wounded
even though I might die tonight . It seemed
just somehow that after so many
close ones my luck should at last catch up with
me.

but the mechanism of shock made the thought seem unimportant.

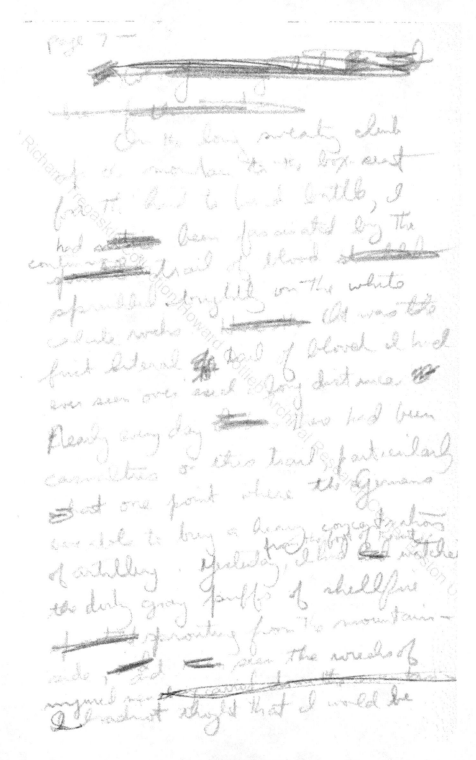

contributing some of my own blood to this
crimson trail.

However, here I was in the cave, badly
wounded through the head and I thought also
through the in the arm.

Thinking back over the time, I
remember however
that I singularly unconcerned
about my plight. I seemed
vastly good-natured and nothing seemed to
disturb me-----but the automatic force of me
self-preservation seemed to be telling
what to do/

When the shells slacked off
I climbed to my feet again, dropping my
and retrieving my souvenir helmet several
times. Then I staggered dowb the
rocky trail. still impelled by the force
which pushed me in the direction of Col.
Yarborough.

Like a mechanical creature I wavered
and unsteadily on my feet under steady
directional control

Like a robot unsteady on his feet but
controlled directional control I stumbled
stumbled over the rocks and fell automaticall
each time I heard the fuzzy sound of the
approach approach of a shell,
got back to my feet and went ahead.

Time did not seem
to be moving fast or slowly; time seemed to
be in neutral gear, but I knew that the
distance I walked was long.

more

Page 9

Around a bend of the trail I saw
Col. Yarborough, bending over a bleeding
enlisted man who sat on the ground.
With Yarborough was Capt. Tomasik,
and I felt a surge of pleasure at seeing
them again, like a dog wagging his tail
at the sight of some familiar
person. Then I knew that somehow I would
be able to get down the mountain
that night, because I had found Yarborough.
Fortunately, for me, Yarborough and
Tomasik had stayed behind to care for one
of their men whose arm had been blown off a
minutes ago.

From then on, down the long
trail, Yarborough helped
to support me, and the long haul
might have seemed like a nightmare if I had not been shielded by the
impervious barrier
of shock. As it was, this was not a
particularly unhappy dream.

It must have been about a half
an hour later that we reached a
peasant house, where the bare mountain
mass of Mt/ Corno stretches into
foothills. Here the jeep trail begins and
here I could lie down on the dirt floor
and wait for transportation.

Still I tried to talk, and uttered
apish, unconnected syllables, and lifted my
paralyzed right arm in my left hand and tried
to indicate that I thought it had been hit.
They stripped the sleeve from my arm and it
was untouched. Still the blood ran down my face
and coated my glasses.

Page 10

Across the room I saw a line of ~~certain~~ soldiers
~~standing~~ standing with that fascinated, awed
~~look~~ look written on their faces, as they
stared at me, the badly wounded man. ~~Th~~
It was a novelty to me to be in place of the
badly wounded man---and to ~~realize with~~
know that ~~those who~~ those ~~who could~~
~~Th~~ fascinated spectators ~~were who~~ felt more
imagined pain than I ~~could~~ did actually.
~~Th~~ Such it the power of shock, and the will
to ~~preservation~~ preservation.

More than a month later, when I was
recovering my ~~power~~ powers of speech and
the use of my right arms and a great hole in
the side of my skull was healing, I asked
the ~~doctor~~ doctor who was a patient in a
bed ~~next~~ next to mine, the question I ~~had~~
which had occurred many times ~~to~~ to me
~~many times~~ since I had come through
the experience of being nearly wounded.
The doctor said that he believed that almost
all of the men badly wounded feel no pain,
~~at the time~~ at the time.

That, I think , is the only owrth-while
bit of information gathered in that otherwise
~~introduction~~ unpooductive ~~day of~~ day of
news-gatheering , November, 22.

end

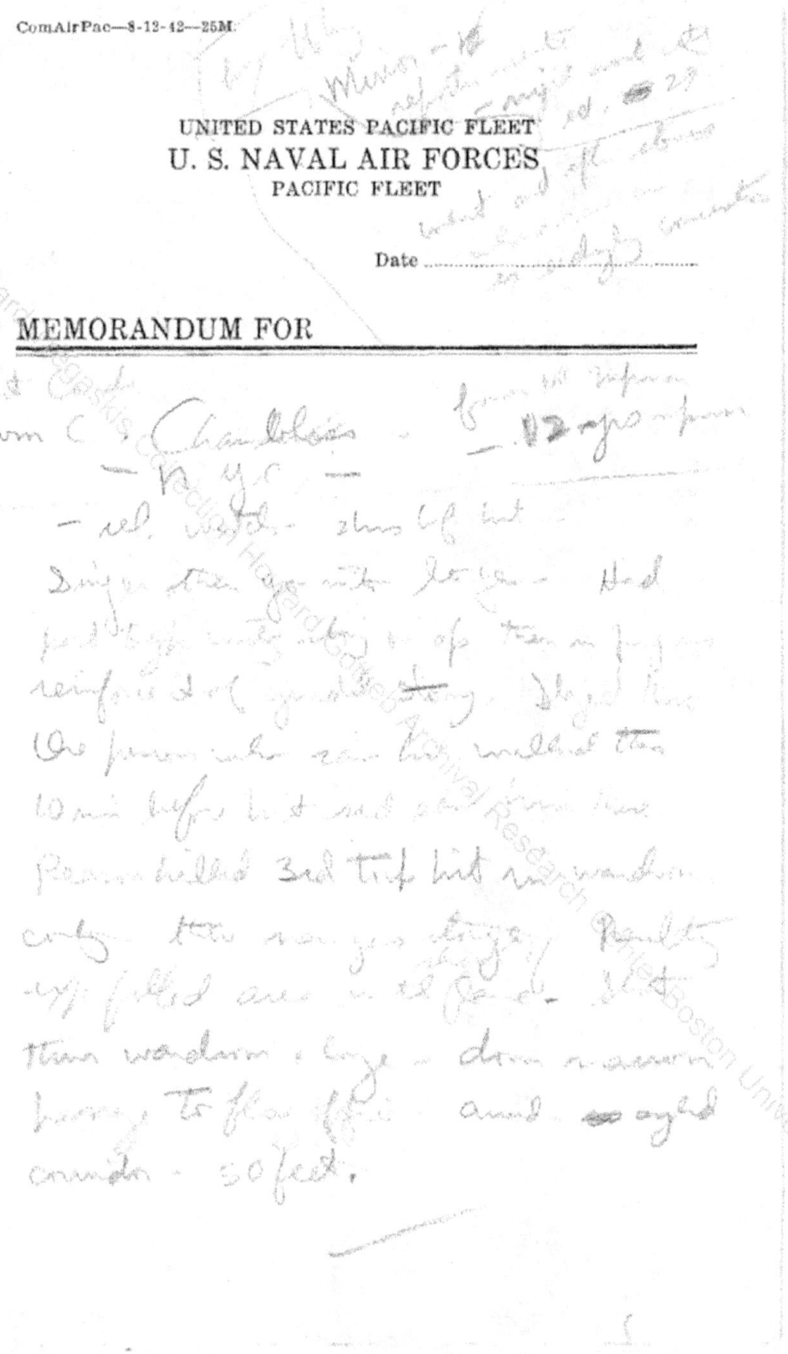

ComAirPac—8-12-42—25M

UNITED STATES PACIFIC FLEET
U. S. NAVAL AIR FORCES
PACIFIC FLEET

Date ....

MEMORANDUM FOR

[illegible]

Sept. 14 -

notes for stories -

settings 1. 57th squad
- bar, Louis XVI furniture,
etc. at
Sentini

2. Manly -
ward - room etc
top deck with guns

3. Marrakech -

4. London.
- 35. S. Audley
- Mac's apt
- Savoy
- Mt. Royal
- Piccadilly
- Deanery

Red Cross
Marie

5. 301 Bomb group -
Chateaudun

6. Algiers - mess
Red Cross - aletti cafe
- Palm Beach -
gov

7. Tunis -
beach at Salammbo
aquarium

8. fighters etc

9 - Kairouan -
    - Paratroop camp -
    wirehouse
    lt. girls in hospital

10 - Sousse
    - gal at corner.
    swimming -

11. Sentini - fighters group nearby

12. Hill 1189 -

13. Centuripe

14. Scalatta with Commandos.

15. Airfield at Catania -
    for love scene.

16. Licata at time Italy fell -
    Red Cross gals.

17. Palermo -
    Excelsior -
    Palms
    Job.

18. El Djem - coliseum.

19. Messina - cave.

20. Beach at Noumea
    Camp Barnes - waves, none.
    Marine camp. Camp Goettge.

21. Auckland - Kia Ora.
    Royal
    Now ~~Dominion~~ -
    New Criterion
    Star -

22. Wellington. St. George
    New Occidental
    -

23. Espíritu Santo - French girl
    time of Jap street.
    raid - ~~press~~ movie
    path by harbor.

24. Guadal - C.P. with live out at
    Tenaru.

25. Pearl - girl out window at
    quarters -

26. Moana - fat lady + daughter.

27. Pacific Club   - Dillingham girls
         Curt Fairman

28. Cibron Field - Girl's quarters

29 - Rec'd a [...] Waikiki
(Alexander)
30 - Young Hotel - fried eggs into chief
yolk

31. Feet on Seaside Ave.
Wagon Wheel, Beach - corner
32 - Marian's home at Coco head
33 - Eileen's Juis home Kai Mukee.
34 - Sears, Roebuck in Honolulu
35. Betty Mac Donald's home.
Honolulu -
36 - Puiis on Chief Pt Road
37. Park near Diamond Head
aquarium -
38 - Kanhan intra, near Kendallah.
dark woods where lovers walk

Stories

1. coming back from Guadal to Noumea —
   from honesty, freedom — to red tape;
   inefficiency, chaos — longing to get
   down there, from guadal — longing to
   get back again — after was out of
   ~~words~~
   who too busy with ~~front~~ to do
   anything — N.Z. waacs; Not
   War, Not Peace.

2. Otter with plans for attacking
   Jap — "Bougainville experience" —
   I never could figure out Otter
   went to dance at 83 Cavalry
   but he not interested —
   wanted get back to ship —
   Finally achieved purpose —
   Yes — could never understand Otter,

she efficient, keeps tight

3 — ~~Got~~ Marion Forbes with
husband. She interested in keeping
everything as it is — keep
things home. But he home drunk
every night, and especially
that one night when she had
party ~~drunk~~, she let her go
generous occasion — gleefully, he
into Army. ~~But~~ ~~Stationed~~ Bellows
Field. (Soon she grew so tired of him
~~that~~ would hold you away, and
arrived happily ever after — at
least for several years.)

never together — ... had recorded — ...
until this ... implied, or ...
... hawk-nosed · American
of himself — Hard to check on mad,

4. / Gal whose husband away — on this.
Kairouan, with American — Eye
Harry her. Crete, N. Africa —
not enthusiastic young American, at
fence. She romantic girl. Other
other side of fence would be greener.
Knows ... Jim 3 days — he tried,
good-looking, ~~f~~ ... serious. Should
she go over fence into greener. ~~But~~
Decided not try and Jim very tired about
it. ~~They just leave~~ stayed ... ~~To find~~
~~my letters~~ ... ~~hey husband or ...~~ ...
~~...~~ ~~he just came out of whorehouse~~
he
died in Kairouan, was feeling unfair. ~~...~~
where ~~...~~ letters ..., ... dimly.

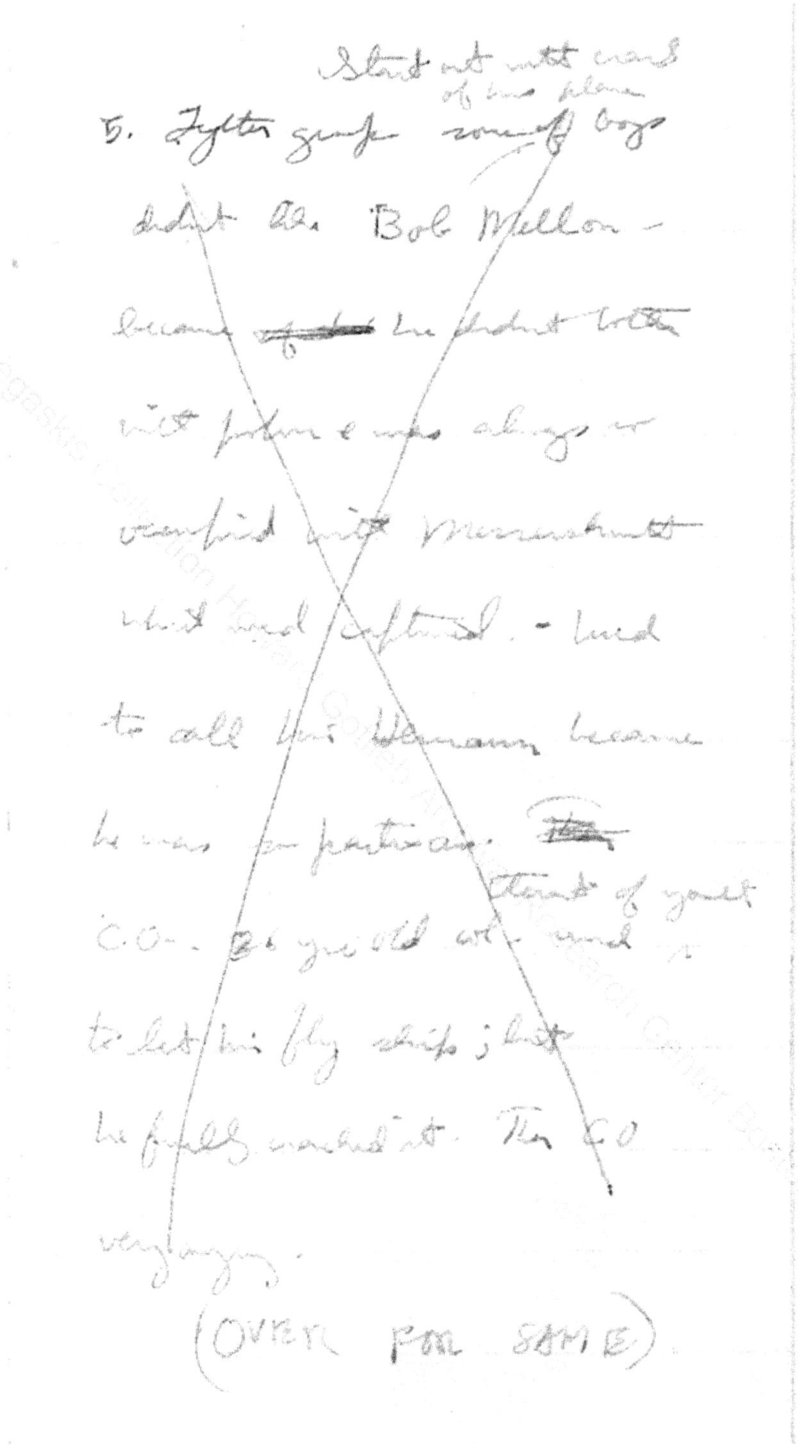
Start out with crash of the plane

5. Fighter group — some of boys
didn't like Bob Mellon —
because he didn't bother
with planes & was always
occupied with measurements
which [illegible] captured. — Lead
to all this [illegible] because
he was so particular. [illegible]
[illegible] of youth
C.O. — Bob [illegible] old [illegible] [illegible]
to let him fly ships; but
he finally worked it. The C.O
[illegible].

(OVER FOR SAME)

visited, he recounted his famous

stories of

6- ~~[illegible]~~ I

always forget that drawn

glamorous female spies were

mythical, until got to Derby

Club in London. There met

gloriously Teutonic girl- first

took her for Russian.

I decided investigate. She

mysterious. Finally, found

out after making many enquiries

that she only a waitress,

in the Polish restaurant on

Oxford St.

~ mid aft   2 00

c 100 Jap planes fighters + d. bombers equally
att ship area off Koli Pt — between Koli + Tulagi
engaged by large number fighters henderson
21 Jap fighters } downshot
6 bombers

(Jap ← scored hits number small craft

ships' AA accounted 5-6 d. bombers
hellova lot airplanes B da Kahili reconnaissance.
Jap losses ratio 1-5 –

marine –
sgt of guard – }

Moana Tregaskis donating the helmet that saved RT's life to officials at the Pentagon

Invasion Diary display at the Pentagon, which is now housed at the National Museum of the Marine Corps.

Richard Tregaskis, the tall guy on Guadalcanal by Jim Stovall -
https://www.jprof.com/2020/11/28/richard-tregaskis-the-tall-guy-on-guadalcanal/

In memory
of my beloved sister
MADELINE

Waiting

July 9, 1943

I HAD JUST FLOWN INTO ALGIERS FROM MOROCCO AND WAS walking down the sun-bathed main street, Rue Michelet, feverishly searching for the Public Relations Office, when I met Pete Huss, the International News Service manager at Allied Headquarters. We shook hands, and then he immediately led me to his room in the Aletti Hotel. He knew, without my saying, that I was hot on the trail of the invasion.

I had been running fast, struggling, cutting corners to get down here to the Mediterranean theater in time for the big excursion into Europe. I followed Pete into his third-floor hotel room, and he shut the door behind us.

"Is it Sicily or Sardinia?" I asked him. From various indications in London I had guessed that it would be one or the other.

"That's right—Sicily," said Huss.

"When's D-day?"

"Probably tomorrow."

I would have realized as much if I had looked down from the balcony to the blue, white-capped water of the Bay of Algiers. There ten or twelve troop transports, the rails colored khaki by lines of troops, were even then weighing anchor. Some of them had begun to move and I knew that I had missed the landing. It was too late to get aboard this task force.

"And they're only reserves," said Huss. "The main force left about a week ago." He grinned at my crestfallen expression. "But you can still catch up. There'll be plenty of fighting left to cover."

July 10

At 4 A.M. a telephone call summoned us to the Public Relations Office. There was no moon, and it seemed a good night for the invasion. In the press room we found the correspondents assembled for the expected announcement.

The British Col. McCormack, wearing his brilliant red staff officer's cap, stepped up to the front of the room, cleared his throat, and said, "British, Canadian and American troops began landing operations in Sicily early this morning."

The copy—the small amount of it that was permissible—was passed in, and a deadline of six o'clock was declared for the release of the story. It was getting light, and on the balcony outside the press room I saw Hugh Baillie, President of the United Press, looking down into the silent Rue Michelet. "Well," he said, "I guess plenty of our boys have gone to glory by this time."

July 12

This morning I received word that I would be able to get air transportation to Tunis, first step on the way to Sicily.

July 13

Gen. Eisenhower arrived from Sicily. We correspondents piled into our jeeps and made a journey of some distance to a villa near Tunis where the general's Headquarters had been set up. It was a spotless modern house with beautiful mosaic floors. A few minutes later, "Ike" breezed into the room, looking fresh and cheerful. He wore a tropical worsted shirt and trousers, with four silver stars sewn on his collar, his only decoration. He is a good-looking man, with regular features, a balding crown, and notably pale blue eyes. Most striking is his quick, agreeable manner. He seemed to sense the implication of every question quickly, and answered with concise phrases. He said that we are facing 240,000 to 260,000 Italians. They are probably coastal divisions, he said, adding, "They have no stomach for fighting."

The campaign has been so far very successful, said the general, and tanks and supplies have been put ashore without any difficulty. More than 500 tanks are in Sicily, 6,000 Italians have been captured, the enemy resistance is negligible, our casualties "far lighter than expected." The general said, "A decision should be reached in about two weeks, if our present good luck continues. We effected considerable tactical surprise. Evidently the enemy had expected that our attack would be based from Pantelleria, and had prepared for an assault against Northwestern Sicily."

July 14

Five days have gone, and still no arrangements for my transfer to Sicily. The swimming at Carthage is wonderful, but, under the circumstances, every pastime is sheer waste. I want to get going.

This afternoon I went to the summer palace of the Bey of Tunis, now an American Army billet, to see Col. Elliott Roosevelt and try to arrange at least a look at Sicily. The photographic reconnaissance group under his command had made twenty-four flights over Sicily yesterday alone. He had flown with the most recent night photo reconnaissance himself in an A-20, and would go over again tonight. I asked him if I could go along and he consented.

"It's a wonderful sight," he said, "You can see explosions everywhere on the island. You can even pick out the bomb flashes when the bombers are making a raid. The ports are taking an awful beating. Messina looks as if it had been wiped off the map and Palermo is the same way."

I asked the colonel how soon he thought the fight for Sicily would be over, "I'm not a military expert," he said, "but my impression is that it will be over quickly, maybe inside of two weeks. The pressure is on day and night, and the aerial bombardment is terrific. Come along and see for yourself."

July 15

I was at La Marsa Airdrome at 1:30 A.M. Outside the Operations Tent, Col. Roosevelt said, "Are you all ready?" and pointed toward the B-25. It was the same type of two-engined, double-tailed, medium bomber which the Doolittle flyers had taken on the historic attack on Tokyo. Mechanics were working in the half-light, hoisting parachutes and other equipment into the trap-door opening in the belly of the ship.

I put on my Mae West, struggled through the bottom hatch and tried on my parachute. The colonel took the co-pilot's seat next to

Capt. George Humbrecht of St. Louis. From the small compartment directly behind the pilot's and co-pilot's chairs, I could look over their shoulders and through the wide strip of windshield.

It was 2:07 A.M. when we took off. We could see the wrinkled mountain mass of North Africa in the growing moonlight. Cape Bon, a rocky point reaching out toward Sicily where the Germans had staged their final evacuation in North Africa, lay to our right. The Mediterranean seemed ghostly still, like a sea of fog in the moonlight. Col. Roosevelt's duck-billed cap bobbed as he looked over the water, and the crossed straps of his parachute harness seemed white and distinct. An orange beacon winked on our port beam from the misty plain of the Mediterranean.

Through the astrodome, where the navigator takes his sights, I could see stars strewn over the moonlit sky, and Cassiopoeia, the queen on her chair, pointed toward the North Star. We were heading northeast.

I crawled through the narrow tunnel to the bombardier's compartment in the nose, the "greenhouse," where he operates his machine gun and bombsight. It was noticeably cold in the compartment, for we were climbing to the zone of lower temperature. The bombardier, Lieut. Everett Anthony, of Hartford. Conn., was concerned about a light from the toggle switchboard, which seemed to be out of commission.

The moonlight was brighter and the sheen of the sea more lustrous. Only the top of the propeller arc shimmered above the shadow cast by the wing. The colonel was rubbing his hands in an attempt to keep warm. He looked back over his shoulder and smiled. We were approaching Sicily.

The strip of beach, green in the moonlight, like a scar between the sea and the mountains, was now behind us. The ridges of the high mountains, white icing in the moonlight, incrusted the dark background of the land mass.

Suddenly I saw embers of fire, another fire beyond the first. From the detached distance of the air, they appeared mere bonfires. The closer fire, on the right, proved to be a disorderly group of large blazes, like strewn coals against the land. The farther fire, beyond and to the left, magnified by the binoculars, was revealed as a huge U-shaped double row of houses, burning brilliantly. In this one group there must have been thirty to forty large conflagrations, and the even spacing and arrangement indicated they were the buildings of an ammunition dump or a factory.

"They're firing at us over there, on the right," said the colonel. White flashes of gunfire pricked the darkness of the ground. A searchlight beam, leaning against the sky, snapped on, then off. Another beam of light swept the sky ahead of us. The colonel and the pilot were shouting at each other. The canvas back of the colonel's chair came loose. There were more flashes of anti-aircraft firing, closer on our right.

We were maneuvering violently, attempting to stay clear of the anti-aircraft fire. As we passed over the U-shaped mass of fires, we saw a large orange explosion near by, and felt the lifting blast of the concussion. It might have been a bomb dropped on the ground by some plane we had failed to see, or perhaps a fresh fire in the munitions dump—if munitions dump it was.

I looked at my watch. It was 3:23 A.M. Now the fires were fading into the distance behind us, and we were coming near to our objective, Palermo. The moonlight was paling, the land growing misty, and the horizon had become a line of cloud just below the moon.

"We are to the west of Palermo," said the colonel. "We'll try to find out through the overcast just exactly where we are."

We continued to descend, and passed over a shore line, with a mountainous mass on the right, and circled again. We had overshot our target.

The pilot looked down nervously and said to the colonel, "Dawn is breaking at 4:15. We don't want to get caught up here."

The weather grew increasingly misty. "We'll have to go back," said the colonel. We swung southward. We could not drop our flash bombs.

At 4:30, a searchlight probed the sky to the left. There were more glowing coals of fires to the right. We were still over Sicily.

The fires and searchlights faded, and there was no more anti-aircraft firing. I buttoned my jacket around my neck, squatted on my parachute and began to doze. When I woke up we were landing at La Marsa Airfield in North Africa.

We rubbed our hands, shivered and stretched our creaking joints. I asked the colonel about the route we had followed.

"We passed over Sciacca, then Palermo and Castelvetrano. The large fires were probably in Sciacca." He yawned and added, wearily, "Not much of a show. Come back again sometime and we'll have another try."

I worked on the story until late in the morning. The flight itself had been a failure, but I had learned, at least, that the President's son was not afraid to share danger with his men.

July 16

I am trying desperately to make arrangements to go to Sicily. The details of getting transferred by the P.R.O. progress with tantalizing slowness. Col. Joe Phillips, head of the P.R.O., assures me that my assignment will be coming soon, but it is a full week since the Allied forces landed in Sicily. If the predictions of Gen. Eisenhower and Col. Roosevelt come true, then the campaign is already one-third finished, and there remains little time for me to see any action.

July 17

Maj. Max Boyd, of the Air Corps, dropped in casually and let it be known that an air mission of considerable importance was impending. His quiet approach made the whole matter so much the more mysterious. When he said that any of us who wanted to go along should report to Air Corps Headquarters tomorrow, my interest perked up. Anything to distract me from the annoyance of waiting was welcome. The campaign in Sicily might well be over before I set foot on the island. In any case, I might get a good story out of this mysterious mission, and still be back in time to catch a boat for Sicily. I had nothing to lose.

Raid on Rome

July 18

AT ALLIED AIR FORCE HEADQUARTERS WE WERE MET BY Brig. Gen. Laurie Norstad, second in command to Maj. Gen. Carl Spaatz. Slim, blond, clean-cut Gen. Norstad greeted us soberly. Less than thirty-five years old, he is the ultra-modern officer.

General Norstad drew some photographic prints from a file and passed them out to us. They were aerial pictures of cities and other bombing targets. We waited for the explanation.

"Our job is to cut the enemy's communication lines," he began in his precise manner, choosing his words carefully. "The photo reconnaissance unit photographed our raids in Sicily. It seems that we did a lot of damage. Our emphasis is now shifting to the mainland. We have made two attacks on Naples—probably the most concentrated to date."

There was a pause. Gen. Norstad seemed to be measuring his words. "I think we have demonstrated that we bomb for military effect. We do not bomb to scare people. We've now reached the point where it is necessary to cut the enemy's supply lines. We must achieve the destruction of enemy aircraft and bases.

"Bombardment from the air is a precise instrument. We are using it with precision methods. That is done in all cases. Precision bombing reached a peak at Pantelleria. We checked it every day. We checked it coldly and scientifically. We found that we were even a little too conservative in our claims."

The general waited a moment. We looked up expectantly.

"You people may participate in a flight which will be very interesting," he began.

Now we were going to get it.

"There may be an air attack on Rome very shortly." He spoke almost casually. An electric silence filled the room. It was broken when Gen. Norstad continued in his meticulous way.

"It is very important in this mission that not one of the religious institutions should be damaged. We have selected our crews with the utmost care. When the city is attacked, it will be attacked only by those units which have indicated that they are capable of bombing with great accuracy."

It developed that some 250 heavy bombers and nearly 300 mediums would attack marshaling yards and similar installations.

Norstad gave out confidential photographic mosaic maps of Rome.

"You will notice that I have marked the Vatican and the other religious monuments with this legend: 'Must on no account be damaged.' Here is the St. Paolo Basilica, less than five miles from the San Lorenzo yards. There is the St. John Lateran. That too must be given a wide berth. The closest of all the buildings is the St. John Lateran, about a mile and a half away.

"If any cloud formation exists which might make bombing inadvisable, we will not do it. Those are our orders. We have been preparing for this mission literally for months. But when we do it, when we go out to destroy something, we should really destroy it, go out and bomb the hell out of it."

The precise, handsome young general had made all his points. The talk was over.

Eight of us correspondents were chosen to make the flight over Rome. A C-53, two-engined transport plane had been chartered to take us to the air bases where the attack on Rome would originate, and afterwards to Algiers to write our stories.

As the last remnants of sunlight were fading over the bare, almost grassless African plain, Herbert Matthews, of the New York *Times*, and I reached the camp of the Heavy Bombardment Group to which we were assigned. Already the chill evening winds had begun to blow through the tent camp. From across the company street came the sounds of a reed organ, and voices singing a hymn. Chaplain Harold T. Whillock, of Springfield, Ill., who was passing, volunteered the information that singing was quite common here on Sunday night. The chaplain said that church attendance had been very good today—the day before the Rome raid—and that he had conducted three separate services, one for Protestants, two masses for Catholics.

A yellow harvest moon hovered on the sharp horizon, and the evening star was brilliant on the blue shoulder of the night. The quartet in the briefing tent across the street, which did double duty as a church, shifted into another hymn, and from the yellow triangle of light which was the door of the neighboring tent came the sounds of a squeaking phonograph, giving out the swing version of "Don't Sit under the Apple Tree with Anyone Else but Me."

July 19

This morning at six o'clock, carrying our armful of paraphernalia, which included oxygen masks, earphones, Mae Wests, and field glasses, we joined the group of crew members being "briefed" by Col. Fay R. Upthegrove, CO. of the outfit. Most of the pilots—the "grapevine" of underground information was usually rapid in any aviators' society—knew in advance that the mission was to be directed against Rome.

Nevertheless, as he stepped onto the little wooden platform in front of the large black briefing board, the colonel announced for the benefit of those who had not heard the news, "This morning we're going to bomb Rome. There is need for great accuracy in this job. I don't want any God-damn individual bombing. If you have to salvo 'em, why, salvo 'em—but get 'em out over the target."

The colonel looked tired. The sound of airplane engines on the field made it difficult to hear him. But he was assertive and conscientious. Standing under the garish glare of a naked electric-light bulb, holding a sheaf of notes in his hand, he glanced up at the large cellophane-covered map of the target area on his left. He repeated himself vehemently, "If there's any doubt in your mind, don't drop."

With a long wooden pointer, the colonel indicated a point about fifteen miles from Rome. "You come into Italy here," he said, "and turn on a wide angle. That'll take you right on to the target. The squadrons will javelin down and echelon to the left. The target is only 1,500 feet wide, so you'll have to watch your bomb interval and get your bombs away fast. The deflection will be taken care of by the lead bombardiers. Those elements that have got to string along on the inside of the turn, don't switch out." He sneezed, and continued with the thought, "That's your position. That's a good thing to remember. Any of you that straggle, just get on the God-damn horn and tell somebody."

The pilots and crew men shifted nervously. There was a mist of cigarette smoke in the tent. The noise of airplane engines stopped, and the colonel talked on.

Then, without any climax, the colonel was through. The meteorologist had a brief report that the weather was "generally good, with low clouds and low winds over the target." The bomber crews trooped out of the tent toward their planes. I stayed behind to meet Capt. Robert F. Elliott, of Richmond, Cal., the pilot who was to fly the ship in which I was a passenger; the navigator, Lieut. Ben W. Jones, of Washington, Ga.; and Lieut. Warren S. Douglas, of Atlanta, Ga., the bombardier.

I asked Elliott what he thought about the mission, and he said cheerfully, "It should be pretty good."

In a jeep, we rolled up to the ship, which bore the bright letters "Queenie" on her nose, and a row of yellow stenciled bombs below the pilot's window, indicating the number of bombing missions which she had completed. I swung up into the bottom hatch and attempted to find a comfortable place amidst the litter of belted. 50-caliber ammunition flares, oxygen bottles, masks, hosing, and the other impedimenta in the midst of which airmen must always move.

With the oxygen mask, my glasses, the collar of the Mae West around my neck, the case of my field glasses dangling on my chest, the separate strap of the binoculars themselves, my map case, my canteen belt with a sheath knife, plus my parachute and the goggles which I would have to put on in some way if I had to jump out of this plane, I was an airgoing assemblage of junk. I had difficulty sitting down without gouging my spine on the corner of an ammunition box.

"Do you have much trouble with flak these days?" I asked Jones.

Jones glanced slyly at me and allowed that flak was considerable these days. "The closest I ever came was when a piece hit into the nose, right there, hit the bombsight, and took a chunk off it. It didn't hurt me, but it scared hell out of me." He pointed to a ragged hole, covered with a metal patch over the center of the nose. Somehow the sight of the hole made the danger seem much more immediate.

The motors of the big plane roared, one by one, as the pilots tested them individually. Then we were moving forward, with squealing wheel brakes, as we swung into the runway, and taxied down before the wind, following the huge tail of the leading B-17, with little else visible, except the tail itself, because great clouds of dust whirled up from the propellers ahead of us. The particles of dust and gravel rattled against the transparent circular window in the nose of the ship. Then we swung into the wind, the engines filled the plane with sudden power, and we began to move. The tail was up, we were accelerating, and then, looking back, we could see huge triangular clouds of gray dust rising from the field where other planes were taking off. We were airborne, and on the way to Rome.

The element leader and several other Fortresses were forming up below, and to the side. In a few minutes we rode over the convoluted mountains of North Africa, and we were above the Mediterranean.

The earphones on my head buzzed with some interplane conversation. Somebody in the rear of the ship was reporting that an oxygen line had blown out. There was much talk about the check valve between the bomb bay and the pilot on the right side of the fuselage. I gathered that something was out of order, and began to fear that if an important part of the oxygen system was out, we might have to turn back. But Douglas said that it was only one of the trunk lines, and there was an alternative.

A faint mist still drifted over the Mediterranean. "Misty as hell," I commented to Douglas, and he said, "Yeah, it will probably burn off by ten or eleven o'clock. One good thing is that Rome is about forty miles inland."

Across the blue water came a convoy of ships homeward bound from Sicily to Africa. They were arranged in six straight lines, like the buttons of an abacus. They were strung on narrow white wakes, with the six or seven parallel strings making a nearly symmetrical square against the sea.

We swung in a gentle turn around the convoy, and Douglas explained, "We give them a wide berth, even though they must know we are their own planes. No use taking a chance."

The earphones rattled into my auditory nerves. It was a warning from Capt. Elliott, the pilot. "All gunners, all gunners, we're off the coast of Sardinia. You'd better get on the alert. You might pick up a plane or two here." Douglas wriggled into his parachute harness. Jones checked his Mae West.

We were climbing steadily, and if I wanted to talk to the other members of the crew, I would have to hurry, before we reached oxygen level, at about 12,000 feet. From then on, I would have to stay fairly close to the oxygen tap, in the nose.

I crawled to the pilot's compartment and talked to Capt. Elliott and his co-pilot, Lieut. Julius Horowitz. Horowitz was wearing new shiny second-lieutenant bars. He wasn't as nonchalant as the other crew members.

"Your first trip over?" he asked me.

"Yes," I said.

"Me, too!"

Capt. Elliott picked up his oxygen mask, and said, "We are starting to climb." I thought that I must get back to the greenhouse, so that I could don my mask. And to myself I said: "We've got to get to the target some time."

I struggled into the elaborate paraphernalia of the oxygen mask, screwed in the large tube from the oxygen system, and checked the deliberately rising and falling red rubber ball in the respirator. In their masks, Jones and Douglas were no longer individual American boys, with likable features, but only expressionless, goggle-eyed, gray cogs in a larger machinery. Looking at the uniform snouts I read on the blunt metallic end of their new faces: "Type A-10-STO." On every such mission as this, every American flyer has of necessity to become an automaton labeled: "Type A-10-STO." War certainly is the assassin of personality.

I noticed that the two "Type A-10s" were craning their snouts toward the greenhouse front, and had apparently spotted an object below. That would be Italy, a strip of green amidst the flat islands of cumulus clouds. The navigator extended the folded map, bearing the penciled line of our approach to Italy, and nodded. I looked at my watch. The time was 11:10.

We turned sharply to another leg of our course. Now we could see clearly the curving blue arc of the shore line, which was Italy. Rising from the mist to the south, a geyser-like knout of black smoke towered into the sky, and farther to the left a plume of white smoke. Rome must be down there, more than sixty miles away. The waves of bombers preceding us had done their job well!

That last village over which we had passed was evidently Civitavecchia, on the coast north of Rome, and ahead of us lay the flat blue saucer of Lake Bracciano.

We passed over the shallow blue plain of the lake, and I craned into the nose of the greenhouse trying to make out the white, gull-like shapes of Italian seaplanes anchored on the surface. The seaplanes appeared to be motionless, and we could have destroyed them, but the target of the day lay ahead, and we would have ignored any other objective.

The great mushroom-cloud to the right marked the fires rising murderously from the San Lorenzo marshaling yards. Down there in the midst of the clouds of smoke I could visualize the twisted sidings of the yards and the blown-up buildings of the steel factory and workshops in the area.

The planes ahead of us, dots against the flat-floored mass of cumulus clouds, were winging over the etched rows of streets and buildings which were Rome. Anti-aircraft fire was rising to meet them. There were black smudges, puffs which smeared into foul little clouds, to the right and left and ahead. The first puffs of ack-ack directed toward us sprang into life. Suddenly everything seemed to be happening at once, as had been my experience during the minutes of the approach to a bombing target in every attack I had witnessed in the South Pacific. It was 11:25, and the voice of the bombardier squeaked in the interphone: "Bomb bays open." The buildings in the tiered rows of streets in the city of Rome began to grow larger. A crawling thrill of excitement electrified my brain as I spotted the gray, winding tape of the Tiber bending like a worm through the heart of the city, curling into Rome!

Douglas, his head pressed tight against the rubber eyepiece of the bombsight, moved nervously. His right hand, expertly, with the graceful movements of a symphonic conductor, adjusted the little metal wheel, lining up his salvo. Automatically his mind must be running over computations familiar to the modem master of destruction, the bombardier: the tables of windage, altitude, bomb interval, and weight—all the factors in drawing his pattern of explosion and death and damage. Jones, his work of navigation to the target done, stood up, a hunchbacked figure in the bulk of Mae West, seat-pack parachute and oxygen mask, and unhooked the cable which supported the portside machine gun in the nose. This would be the time when enemy fighters might make their most determined bid to knock us down.

Puffs of anti-aircraft filled the sky ahead and a straight line of bursts broke into the air directly in our path. But any deflection from the line of the attack would have cost us a miss or two. In a bombing run, the pilot must always hold to his course, although he may have to fly through hell to get to his objective. Soon we went, and the ack-ack bursts, first concentrated and dense, expanded into sooty clouds that seemed to drive directly into our vision. The view from the greenhouse was smothered by the passing smoke. I was astounded to see the man-made cloud slip over the smooth surface of the wing, like water, apparently without any damage at all to our machine.

The planes ahead of ours had passed the target, and their bombs had fallen into the far-spread city. I saw the mushroom-cloud of smoke, where the previous bombs had fallen into San Lorenzo, bubble and regurgitate with hundreds of new bomb explosions.

We were coming on the range ourselves. I saw the silvery wedge of railroad tracks and sidings which marked the location of the yards. My field glasses clattered against the vibrating plexiglass of the greenhouse while I tried to pick out the Vatican, the St. John Lateran Basilica and the Basilica of St. Paolo. I could spot none of these buildings, but even in the excitement of the moment, I knew that the Tiber lay between the target of the marshaling yards and the Vatican. We were on course.

Jones was turning his gun, and I wondered if he had seen an enemy plane. At that moment I heard the rasping voice of the bombardier and the cry: "Bombs away!" I looked at my watch. It was 11:39. The anti-aircraft was increasing in violence and still we passed through salvos of black clouds. I wedged myself into the very nose of the greenhouse and watched the flash and puff of the bomb explosions below springing into being like a living carpet of flame and smoke. I looked carefully to see whether the bombs had over-ridden their target and might have fallen near the Lateran and St. Paolo basilicas. With my photographic map in one hand and my field glasses in the other, I tried to measure the distance between the yards and the church monuments. It seemed that there was room to spare.

"An enemy plane at middle-low altitude at 11 o'clock," said the bombardier, and both he and the navigator bobbed nervously from one side of the nose to the other. The fighters were coming in. Douglas turned his gun swiftly and a thin trickle of smoke drifted from the breach. The nose of the plane shivered under the shock of firing, and a cascade of empty shells tumbled onto the floor. His two hands, grasping the gun grips, vibrated under the impact of the recoil. To the right side, a white dot streaked across our vision, passing at terrific speed in a direction opposite from ours. It was an enemy fighter plane, and Douglas followed the swift motion with continuous fire. We saw the bright streaks of the tracer bullets arching toward the enemy. But he was gone and far away in a few seconds, apparently unharmed.

Another plane had passed on our left, and Jones was firing at him. The nose of the ship was filled with smoke and the acrid smell of powder. Empty shells clattered on the floor, and I pushed them aside so that I could sit in relative comfort.

There must have been another enemy plane on the left side at that moment, because Jones continued to fire, and the shells cascaded onto the floor.

We were turning now, the whole formation swinging wide to avoid further anti-aircraft fire. We had done our job and the only remaining task was to return to our base. There was the usual feeling of relief, even though the danger was not over. The wheels of our plane had been lowered. I shouted over the roar of the engines to Douglas: "Why wheels down?"

"Straggler," said Douglas, and he indicated a low-flying B-17 which dragged behind the elements of the formation. I wondered if the plane had been hit by anti-aircraft fire, but the pilot, speaking into the interphone, cleared up that mystery: through a mishap one of the plane's life-rafts had been blown out of the fuselage and become entangled in the tail surfaces. It was an unromantic accident.

Douglas pointed to the lowered wheels of the other elements of the formation, and I knew that the whole group had deliberately dropped their landing gears in an attempt to reduce their speed so that the lone straggler would not fall behind. Such a deserted cousin would be easy meat tor enemy fighters.

We had passed over the Italian coast and were flying over the Mediterranean.

We were safely on our way to our North African base. In the pilots' compartment, I asked Lieut. Horowitz, the young co-pilot who was making his first flight over enemy territory, how he liked it, He said, "It's fun. If they're all like this, it'll be all right."

I was curious to get the reaction of Capt. Elliott. I knew that his religious beliefs were Roman Catholic. He did not seem perturbed as he looked back at me and said calmly, "It's all right."

Sicilian Front

July 20

THE DAY FOR WHICH I HAVE BEEN WAITING SO LONG HAS come. We took off this morning from Maison Blanche Airfield and, I hoped, Sicily. When I checked in at P.R.O. headquarters at Tunis, Col. Phillips told me that arrangements for a boat ride from Bizerte, the amphibious center, had been made. I am on my way at last!

July 21

The docks at Bizerte were lined with towering, squarish LSTs, the great 300-foot landing barges which are doing the bulk of the work of ferrying troops and supplies to Sicily. Trucks were climbing into the open maws of the ships. The figures of men moving up the thick steel platforms were tiny under the shadow of the giant barges.

We trudged up the steel draw of the ship to which we were assigned and looked down the long line of ramps, a hundred castle doors drawn up at the dock.

We passed into a shadowy, high, rectangular cavern as spacious as a subway station. The floor of this particular hold was now empty, save for a few trucks, tiny in the far end, where the light trickled down to them from the open hatches above.

We passed through long galleys of canvas cots on iron frames and neat and antiseptic washrooms. We heard the sound of swing music coming from a public-address system. I walked by the officers' galley, ship's style, full of steam and the sound of rattling dishes. The Negro messboys, in their white coats, were cleaning up. This was the de-luxe way to travel to battle.

Up on deck, in the cloudless twilight of the Mediterranean summer, I picked my way through a tangle of equipment which had been lashed for the trip. A large part of the deck space was covered with half-track ammunition carriers and trucks. They were part of an armored force, moving in to Sicily to support tanks which had already landed. The loading crews worked into the night amidst the forest of steel: the crooked arms of davits, the steel tree trunks of winches, the squat stumps of deckhouses. They were stowing tangled piles of canvas-covered boxes of ammunition and sacks of gear.

July 22

We backed away from the dock this morning and took our place in the single file of LSTs heading down the narrow harbor of Bizerte. I watched the wreckage of the town slipping by the rail. From the water, as from the land, Bizerte remained the most completely destroyed city I had seen in North Africa. In the wardroom we found a mimeographed newssheet announcing the capture of Enna in Central Sicily. The radio said, however, that Gen. Eisenhower revealed that the British Eighth Army was advancing slowly against heavy resistance.

July 23

In mid-morning a misty blue land mass rose on our beam and we traveled northward along the coast of Sicily, until we reached the curving harbor of Licata, where the 45th Division had landed in the original invasion on July 10. Steep, rocky hills towered over the small cluster of houses that marked the town. There were light-colored stucco buildings, but all seemed intact, except one at the center of the town where a patch of roofing had been blown away. The soldier standing next to me at the rail stared and then said simply, "It looks just like Africa."

The bay of Licata was spotted with the angular sails of fishing boats, their lateen rigs white as sharks' teeth against the blue water. But the smell of the town dispelled the illusions of romance. As we came inside the arms of the breakwater, we could see that the little fishing boats, so pretty in the distance, were smeared and stinking at close range.

American landing barges were ranged in the lee of the dock. The concrete surface was lined with precise rows of yellow artillery shells like soldiers in their ranks, and there were piles of the familiar clover-leaf-shaped black cartons for howitzer ammunition. A lighthouse stood at the end of the dock, and on the side of the building next door, which was conservatively lettered in Italian "Stazione Piloti," a GI sign-painter had splashed in glaring large letters "Army Gear Room."

A big sergeant had already assumed the proper imperial attitude as he shepherded a bunch of tattered Italian dock workers. They were engaged in picking up the yellow shells and piling them into a truck. The Italians chattered genially, regarding their plight as a huge joke.

The sun was setting as we started up the gray dusty road from Licata into the mountains. The winding road was almost deserted.

We passed a shattered concrete house, an Italian truck lying on its side, shredded by shell fragments; an Italian motorcycle with one wheel off; a bridge with the center span blown out, so that we had to detour down the steep side of a ravine; another overturned truck, burned and blackened, evidently by the fire of a strafing plane.

And then we saw a beautiful silhouetted Greek temple atop a ridge, and we knew we were nearing Agrigento. We reached the town before all the light of the evening had faded, and saw the first considerable evidences of fighting in Sicily. Along the boulevard which was the main street of Agrigento, on a towering hill overlooking the Mediterranean, shells from our naval vessels had struck into the best buildings and smashed them with great hammer blows.

In the Italian Automobile Club in Agrigento, where the Public Relations Office of the 7th Army had set up, we found one of the correspondents, Charlie Corte, who had just come back from Palermo. He said that Palermo had been occupied by American forces. Our troops had passed through and were going ahead rapidly.

July 24

This morning, while we were waiting for a truck to come and take us to Palermo, I learned that Gen. Patton had returned to Agrigento. We found him in the large concrete mansion which served as his temporary headquarters.

The general stalked into the room and smiled. His eyes seemed very blue in the bright morning sunlight, and he was strikingly attired in faultlessly tailored whipcord shirt and breeches, and shining cavalry boots. On one hip he carried a pearl-handled revolver.

The general leaped into his subject. "We had about 200 miles to go over crooked roads to get to Palermo. Our drive was faster and over rougher ground than anything the Germans ever did. We didn't give them a chance to dig in."

He gave us the figures: about 44,000 enemy had been captured, most of them Italians; around 6,000 Italians killed and wounded; 190 enemy aircraft destroyed; sixty-seven guns, 25-millimeter and up, captured.

Back at the P.R.O. headquarters, the truck was standing by. An Italian was trying to sell beer for $6.00 a case. Another, who could speak the language which some Americans had already learned in North Africa, French, was trying to peddle cheap wrist watches for $80.00. Americans had already caused a slight inflation in prices.

We were off, bouncing about on the rear platform of a truck, and the Sicilian laborers were still shouting, "Cigaretta! Americano!" and giving the "V" sign, which, we decided, served not only as a morale builder but as a charade indicating they would like to smoke an American cigarette.

The road from Agrigento to Palermo was more heavily marked by the signs of battle than the stretch from Licata to Agrigento. We passed a half dozen black baby tanks, two of them knocked off the road and down hillsides, the others evidently surrendered by their Italian crews. There were motorcycles discarded at the side of the road, and several field-pieces of about 88 millimeters, forcibly knocked out and burned; larger fieldpieces, of a howitzer type; and in the fields rolling from both sides, there were occasional areas scarred and brown-pocked where shells had been laid down in barrages; there were blackened and twisted wrecks of trucks, and dead horses by the roadside. But even in this stretch of road, where the intensity of the battle had evidently increased, the marks of war were lost in the peaceful groves of olive and almond trees, the gray craggy mountains, and the terraced vineyards of ancient Sicily.

We reached the water-front district of Palermo, where buildings were smashed into the street as far as one could see. Façades and pieces of roof and splintered lumber dripped from the structures like sad veils. We found one relatively undamaged hotel, the Sole. We entered the front door through a massive bomb shield of concrete blocks. The clerks of the hotel smiled sheepishly, but they pointed out that the price of a room would be seventy lira.

July 25

It was time at last to get a look at the Sicilian front. The road led along the sheer cliffs of the northern edge of Sicily, high over the white-edged sea.

We reached Cefalu, swung through the town and followed the coast road along the cliffs. Suddenly shells banged sharply ahead, and off a point of land, at the next bend in the road, two or three waterspouts of white foam sprang from the blue water. We had reached the front.

Our driver suffered a definite change of complexion with the arrival of the German shells. "I don't want none of this," he said. But it seemed worthwhile to venture another half mile to get a better look at the tunnel at the bend of the head-land. We reached the tunnel; just then two more German shells burst; and the driver refused to go another foot.

At that moment a jeep, coming in our direction, passed through the tunnel from the far side and was headed for the rear when we stopped it. The driver was a major from the 180th Infantry, named Joe Cathey, from Ada, Okla. "We've been in just about the same place all day," he said. "The Germans are interdicting the road about a mile away, beyond this point. We can't get much observation, as long as we're working on this coastal road. Some of our troops are trying to get into the high ground inland. If they can weed the Germans out of this high ground, we can go along the coast more easily. This is the first resistance we've had since Palermo."

As he finished, the German guns spoke again farther down the coast: bum bum bum. A jeep, carrying a wounded man on the rear seat, came back from the tunnel, and I noticed that despite the firing, the barbed wire and possible mines, three or four naked soldiers were sun bathing on the beach.

We decided to go back to the Headquarters of the 45th Division to get an over-all picture of the military situation. In the warm afternoon sun a young G-2 major indicated our present position on a large cellophane-covered map.

The major pointed out the disposition of American troops in Sicily. "We're here on the northern coast. On our right flank is the First Division, and beyond them are the Canadians. The First Division is trying to take a road net near Nicosia, to cut the enemy's lateral communications. That'll force the Krauts to fall back, and make it easier for us to advance on the north coast. For the present we are canalized here."

I asked the major if I might possibly get a ride to First Division Headquarters. A colonel named Sutherland, of Philadelphia, happened in at that moment from the First Division and offered to provide transportation. Sutherland said that he had bad news about his Division sector. The German counter-attacks were hitting back east of Gangi.

The colonel and his driver, who were covered with the characteristic white dust of Sicily, helped me to get my belongings into their jeep, and we were off.

Two hours later we came down a steep valley and the colonel pointed out two of our tanks sitting desolately by the roadside, blackened by fire. There had been a tank battle here a few days ago.

We were coming near to Gangi and the First Division Headquarters. Within a few minutes we saw the town rising beyond the next valley. We heard the heavy bombing of cannon, saw the blast of the firing from the Long Toms. We stopped and trudged into an olive grove, where a large stone building had been taken over as Headquarters of the First Division.

In the bare living room of the house we discovered the characteristic clutter of an array office in the field. A brisk, pleasant lieutenant colonel explained the situation of the First Division on the front beyond Gangi. "We had some hand-to-hand fighting today, the closest yet," he said. "This morning the Germans knocked our outposts off their positions. We counter-attacked. They attacked again this afternoon. And we drove them off. It's been pretty bloody."

The colonel showed me the positions of the forward regiments of the division. The 26th Regiment, at the very front, had moved forward about a thousand yards. The 16th and 18th were moving up behind. Tomorrow, said the colonel, will be a day of reconnaissance; there will be a meeting of the General Staff—and the following day the Division will try to get to Nicosia, about six miles, and en route will have to take Sperlinga. As the colonel spoke we heard heavy thudding of cannon from the valley, and the house rattled and shook.

"The last few days have been tough," said the colonel, "because the men are tired. They are going on their reserve. They've been marching at night and fighting in the daytime, because Gen. Allen is trying to conserve their combat efficiency."

He spoke matter-of-factly of casualties. "In the last two fights we've been having heavier casualties. More enemy mortars and guns. Instead of withdrawing, when it looks as if we're going to engage them, they counter-attack, and withdraw under the cover of their counter-attack."

Tonight, wearily, I spread my blankets on the thinly strewn hay of a barnyard. I lay awake listening to the crashes and watched the bright blasts of the Long Toms in the valley. The firing went on insistently, and along the road winding through the valley to Gangi and beyond, squads and companies and battalions of men slogged on steadily in the dark.

July 26

A long mess table was set up behind the stone house. I sat with John Hersey, of *Time Magazine*, an old friend whom I had met in the Pacific campaign. We waited for the food, which John assured me was good. Even in a battlefield the fame of a good kitchen travels far and fast. The food was excellent: prunes, Spam fried with care in powdered egg batter so that for once it was palatable; hot cakes and crisp biscuits. It was all a pleasant change from lukewarm C-ration or granular powdered eggs or Vienna sausage usually offered at field kitchens.

A smiling little man with a crew hair cut and bright blue eyes took his place at the table. He was Brig. Gen. Theodore Roosevelt, second in command of the First Division. He spoke enthusiastically of the coming attack on Sperlinga and Nicosia. "This is going to be one of those jolly nights when we go without sleep," he said, energetically. He did not seem at all disturbed by the thought.

A lieutenant colonel named Stone took his place at the table, greeted us with, "Well, gentlemen, here's the news we've been waiting for. There's a report from Rome Radio that Mussolini has abdicated. Interesting, if true."

"Maybe Hitler'll get an idea," Hersey suggested.

"There is no confirmation from London yet," Col. Stone warned.

After breakfast, Hersey and I cornered Gen. Roosevelt, and asked if we could accompany him tonight. The general said, of course, he would be delighted to have us come along—if we didn't mind rough riding, because he was in the habit of striking out across rugged country where there were no roads.

Hersey and I started out with Gen, Roosevelt and his aide, Lieut. Marcus Stevenson. The general outlined the strategy of the attack toward Nicosia, The 26th Regiment, which had been bearing the brunt of the assault for the last few days, would be relieved by the 16th and 18th Regiments. The 16th would push along the south side of the road from Gangi to Nicosia; and the 18th on the north side.

Our jeep drove through Gangi and went down into the next valley and stopped at a large Italian house. It was the CP of the 26th Regiment. Lieut. Col. Clarence Beck of Daytona Beach, Fla., second in command, received us with an offer of chow. This was the first step in our progress to the active front line.

Gen. Roosevelt greeted the officers of the 26th Headquarters with his customary cheeriness, called them by their first names and slapped them on their backs. He quickly unfolded his maps and began talking briskly of the night's business. Col. Beck confirmed the news that Hill 937 was now in our hands. The general asked for the exact disposition of the three battalions of the 26th, referring to them in the usual way as Red, White and Blue. His flood of interested questions continued and occasionally he would say, as he rushed around the room, "That's good. Very good." There was something in the rapid movement of his short legs, in puttees which nearly reached his knees, like the twinkling walk of the sandpiper on the beach. He added to the illusion by constantly slicing the air with his small cane.

Their business done, Col. Beck said, "General, I haven't talked to you since this Mussolini thing. How do you G2 that?"

"I G2 it this way," answered Roosevelt. "Italy is getting out of the war. It's simple."

At the mess table in the back yard of the house, we dined on Spam and cheese. It was pleasant in the early evening light. Guns were booming behind us near Gangi and occasionally we heard the sound of a shell passing over toward its German target.

Col. Beck was sitting next to me. "This is almost as good as El Guettar. We had twenty-two days of continuous marching and fighting. Here in Sicily we've had only seventeen."

An officer wearing the silver cross of a chaplain sat down at the table. "How's business?" somebody asked him.

"Picking up," said the chaplain.

When night fell we bundled into the jeep again and started for another sector. Batteries of 105s and 155s banged behind us and we heard the gentle rustling of the shells as they passed over our heads in quick succession. Finally we reached a stony slope, dismounted and looked over the terrain occupied by the Germans. Ahead of us in the dark, where the enemy-held ridges lay, we saw the flashes of the exploding shells. And on our left, there were German time bursts blinking like orange signal lights in the sky. I heard the quick rattle of a distant machine gun somewhere in the valley.

"That's Hermann," said a soldier next to me.

Behind us we heard the grinding of a radio generator and the muted voice of the radio man calling for fire, mechanically, "Correct 443, 300 left, 200 short. Hurry, hurry!"

I asked, "What's the target?"

"Infantry," he answered in the same mechanical voice.

We piled into the jeep again and bounced through several more plowed fields until we reached the Nicosia Road. We climbed a practically vertical slope of huge boulders to reach the stuffy little oblong tent which served as the 16th Regiment's CP on the side of a mountain. From information I had been able to gather in the day's travels, I had decided it would be best to move up with one of the rifle companies of the 16th in the push toward Nicosia. Hersey and I could join the troops in the field in the morning.

The Road to Nicosia

July 27

IT HAD BEEN A COLD NIGHT; I HAD SLEPT IN TWO SUITS OF heavy woolen clothing with three extra blankets—and shivered. Periodically during the night there had been eruptions of sound from the batteries of 105 and 155 howitzers.

Hersey and I started up the steep slopes, toward headquarters of the 2nd Battalion, 16th Infantry. Beyond a certain point, even jeeps could not go; and after we had reached the top of a bumpy mule track of stones worn smooth by centuries of use, we started on foot. First we had a cliff side to climb, and we had to haul ourselves up the slope with the utmost labor, slipping and sliding in the short grass, falling in the thorns, jumping from one rock to another.

Finally we reached the top of Hill 1333, where our infantry had established the highest observation post in the vicinity.

At the triangular tower atop the hill, in an outcrop of rock, we found Lieut. Col. John Mathews, of Bridgeport, Conn., battalion commander. He said that it seemed surprisingly quiet up here today. He wondered why the "Krauts are not firing at us up on this beautiful OP."

We looked down on a bald-headed knoll, and just beyond it a steep-sided ridge, with a long scar of sandy earth on one side, where shell bursts were rising in irregular sequence. "That's Hill 1139," said the colonel. "The Germans are dug in there right now. If you look down with your binoculars on that bald knoll you'll see our people have dug in—down there by that patch of wheat." I spotted the patch, flax-colored in the sun. Just beyond it on the higher slope of the hill, I could see the foxholes, little pockmarks on the relatively smooth crown of the hill. The figures of men showed very little movement, and were difficult to distinguish from rocks and bushes.

The colonel studied Hill 1139 with his glasses, and said, "Betcha a nickel we'll get through today."

He explained the general plan of attack on this section of the front. "Once we get on to 1139, we'll be pretty well on the way to Nicosia. But we'll have to work down beyond 1139 to that lower hill, that wooded nose, where the shells are exploding now. That's Hill 841, and from there on it will be downgrade to Nicosia."

We heard the sounds of rifle firing, and in the valley plumes of smoke rose in a little group from the woods. The clouds merged and drifted over the area in a white, persistent fog. "Smoke shells," the colonel explained.

"That G Company," said the colonel, indicating the few figures on the bare hill this side of 1139, "stood ground with tanks coming right through them, back at Gela. They knocked out two with a bazooka. They're a veteran outfit—did a good job in Tunisia, too. Capt. Wozenski commands the company." I asked the colonel if I could get down to G Company, and he said, "Sure."

Just then, two figures topped the rise leading to the OP where we were sitting. One of them, a bedraggled, dirty man in a torn uniform, wore the visored cap of the German infantryman. He staggered, and his head sagged on his chest, but the American soldier with him kept him covered with a rifle. The German's drawn cheeks were stubbled with a red beard; but the worried look in his eyes made them the dominant feature of his whole face. Private Weiherman, the interpreter, explained the hunted look in those pale eyes; after a few words of conversation with the German, Weiherman translated that the Nazi had been told he would be shot if captured. The German's face relaxed when the interpreter assured him that he would not be killed.

The German looked at us with those fatigue-ridden eyes and asked if he could have some water. He said, *"Danke,"* and nodded gratefully when we gave him some C-ration biscuits. He said that he had been a member of the German machine-gun squad on the hilltop where we were now standing.

There were only about thirty men left in his entire company, Weiherman translated for us. There had been no warm food for three days. His last food had been sardines and bread—two days ago.

We noticed that a long irregular scar covered one of the prisoner's cheeks. The scar was a large dark area under the right eye, trailing into a narrow red line down the side of his jaw. Weiherman asked if it was a wound, and the German replied, yes, it had been received at Bryansk in Russia, thirty-five kilos from Moscow. "Two of my toes were frozen. I didn't lose them; but I can hardly march."

This man was thirty-seven years old and had one child. He was a machinist by trade before the war, and he came from Hanover in Northern Germany. Now he repeated his wonder that he was not going to be shot.

There was a pause while the circle of American faces studied the German intently. Someone asked Weiherman a question which was, I suppose, in all our minds: "Ask him what he's fighting for, anyway."

The German looked down at his shoes, then glanced up at us with tired eyes. He said in German, "We're fighting for Adolf Hitler"—and there was something slightly sardonic, but cautiously noncommittal, as he added, "I guess."

An officer had come up from the rear with more troops. He was Lieut. Melvin Groves, of Lawrence; Kans. Groves' men, the colonel said, were going to pass through G Company and push on to the wooded ridge of Hill 841. They would probably be the first troops to enter Nicosia. The colonel said that if I wanted to, I could go down with Groves.

Groves, a clean-cut young man with a thin and determined mouth, studied the enemy position with his field glasses. He said sharply, "I saw some of the smoke of firing down there. Just a wisp. Right there in the white triangle on the side of the hill."

"O.K.," said the colonel. And to the forward artillery officer, "I think it might be better to go over on this side of the hill." The officer replied, "200 short, all batteries."

The shells began to fall in the wooded area around the light triangle on 1139, and one of the men, peering through the artillery scope, said with some excitement in his voice, "I saw a man running in that light spot."

And the colonel said, "Good. They're getting in there."

More and more men were arriving near the top of our hill. That would be Lieut. Groves' company, Company F, preparing to push along to the bald knoll.

We crossed the rim of the hill and started down the slope across the short ferns moving in the wind. It was hard to keep our footing as we passed down the steep decline over the slippery stubble of wheat. There were stones and boulders occasionally which helped. But many times I lost my balance, skidded and sat down, often sliding along for a foot or two in a sitting position. John Hersey did better than I, for he wore rubber-soled and -heeled shoes. Sometimes I virtually skied down a particularly slippery incline, and landed with a bump at the bottom. But we pushed on, passed through the valley and the sweet-smelling thorn-bushes that reminded me of musk. Suddenly a shell screeched overhead and burst with a crash about 150 yards ahead. We hit the ground; since there were no more, we decided that it was one of our own shorts.

Beyond the rocky valley, we climbed another grade, passed through a tall wheat field and, sweating and panting, finally came to a stony, bare area near the top of the knoll. Here figures in olive drab were scattered, some in foxholes, some simply lying on the side of the incline. Lieut. Groves headed for a large foxhole in the center of the area, where three or four men huddled near a telephone. We flopped onto the ground beside the foxhole. A broad-shouldered captain with a blond mustache and the harassed look of a man who has been living close to death moved over to make room for us. He was Edward Wozenski of Terryville, Conn., commanding officer of G Company. He talked quietly, as if he wanted to expend an absolute minimum of effort on unessentials. Still, there was enough energy left for a smile; he had even white teeth and there were deep patterns of wrinkles at the corners of his eyes. He spoke with good nature, although his voice was not wholly free of nervous tension. "Our point" (foremost outpost) "is pinned down with machine-gun and sniper fire and mortars. We figure about fifteen or twenty casualties."

A young lieutenant named Charles Martin, of Nashville, Tenn., who sat next to Wozenski in the foxhole, added, "We tried to get onto that hill up there. The snipers waited until we got by and then shot two of my men from the back." The lieutenant looked gaunt and his hand shook.

Wozenski said, "There's one sniper right over here." He waved a hand toward Hill 1139. There was a loud metallic crack, followed by a buzzing sound, as the bullet ricocheted over the hill, and we ducked flat to the ground. "There he is now," said Wozenski.

Within a few minutes we found out that the bullet had struck a target. Later a soldier limped along to our foxhole, sitting down periodically to rest. One pants leg had been torn away by first-aid men, and the upper leg was wrapped with fresh bandage, with a large crimson stain on one side. As we looked up at him, someone remarked that the bullet had pierced his canteen. The bewildered private held it in one hand. "Too bad you lost your water," said Lieut. Martin. We all laughed.

Our foxhole lay below the crest of our hill, so that we were shielded from the direct fire of the snipers on 1139 beyond. But a shell or bullet gives no advance notice, and, when others nearby are being struck down, you have the jittery feeling that somewhere, from some point of the compass, an unseen enemy is preparing your personal destruction; that your next moment may be your last. The alto singing of our own artillery shells, passing just over our hill, continued. The earth shook with each explosion and our ears were filled with crashing concussion.

"That artillery must be falling all around 'em," said Capt. Wozenski softly, "Guess they don't know when to get out."

Suddenly a rifle cracked and the bullet made a fuzzy whistling sound as it ricocheted over our heads. "That's him again," said Wozenski. A few minutes later, a sergeant, who had a pronounced Brooklyn accent, came up wide-eyed. "You know that shot you heard," he stuttered. "Well, it killed that fella named Crumm—that tall dark fellow, that private. Hit him right in the middle of the head—dead center."

Wozenski philosophized as our artillery smashed into the German positions. "Some places along the line you go ahead without any opposition, particularly; but you meet spotted strong resistance—some place that the enemy wants to hold on to, for instance." He smiled. "Like this."

I talked with a staff sergeant, Robert J. Kemp, of Fenelton, Pa., about the seizure of this knoll where we were lying. "It was last night. I was with the platoon that had the point," he said, matter-of-factly. "We crawled up as close as we could. We got picked up by the enemy at about 300 yards. They kept firing, firing, bullets whizzing all over the place—lots of 'burp guns'—machine-pistols. We closed in to about twenty-five yards. Then we jumped up, and gave a whoop, yell and holler, threw grenades, ran in and hollered some more. We killed a few of them—I killed one myself with a tommygun—and all the rest took off and ran in different directions, all confused. That's the way you usually make a bayonet charge."

"Want to get a look at the Krauts?" Capt. Wozenski asked Lieut. Groves. I followed, and, working our way at a crouching run, we reached the very rim of the hill, a skirt of deep dry foxholes. We crawled the last thirty feet. Then we fell into a large hole, and Wozenski warned us to stay low.

I lifted my head cautiously above the earthen edge of the foxhole. In that one glance I saw a stretch of stubby grass, the declining slope of the hillside, and, beyond, that great sandy scar in the side of Hill 1139. There were no Germans to be seen.

"They're in pretty good positions," Wozenski was telling Groves. "I don't think they'll budge unless somebody comes in behind 'em."

Groves nodded. "I can have a hell of a barrage laid down and go in. That right flank is going to be tough to take down. It's a rough, rugged son of a bitch!" He studied a map for a moment. "Yeah, we'll send two platoons over here on the right, and two down there."

It would be a regulation flanking movement, in miniature, just as the whole envelopment of the objective, Nicosia, would be a flanking movement on a larger scale.

We crawled back to the headquarters foxhole—to the field telephone and radio. Groves passed on his plan to his platoon leaders. They worked out details of the movement: timing, supporting fire: When should the mortars open up? Should the machine guns start firing as soon as they got into position? Then Groves called Headquarters on his field phone, and "suggested" the plan. Actually it had already been worked out in every detail.

There was a lull in the firing. This battle-scarred knoll became as quiet as a picnic ground. Capt. Wozenski was picking wheat kernels from the tall stalks. "You know, this wheat is pretty good," he said. "Especially if you haven't got your rations. It's damned hard to get rations over these mountains, when we can't even get the jeeps over."

Then the German artillery began to fire at us. We heard the screech of the approaching shell, but it was so quick that we did not have time to hit the deck. I saw a splash of earth forty or fifty yards away, and then the blast of the explosion came almost directly over us. I felt the concussion and must have shut my eyes. By that time I was lying down and I found myself next to a sergeant. Almost immediately we heard the crying of a wounded man, a bubbling sort of attempt at "Help, help," which had the strangely liquid sound of a voice under water. I had heard similar cries of the wounded in the Pacific.

A man hobbled down the hill with his hands over his face, blood running down his shirt. The sergeant called out, "Jimmy, you hit?" Jimmy nodded, made no sound. Another man sat on the ground, one hand holding his back. The captain called, "Medics here!"

I suddenly realized that the burst must have gone off just over my head, for two men had been hit, one on each side of me, neither more than fifteen feet away. Then I, too, began to feel the increasing breathlessness, that almost unbearable tension of waiting for the next shell.

Then it came. We heard the rustling of a shell suddenly swelling into a screech, then bursting with a blast that shook the air and filmed our vision over with concussion. Again there was the breathless moment of waiting for the cries of the wounded, wondering if you, too, had been hit, thinking that you should look and see, not daring for a moment to make the effort. Again the wounded screamed, and we looked up higher on the hill where, apparently, the shell had done most damage. Up there someone cried out, "Medics, medics!" It was the same desperate sound I had heard on Guadalcanal, only there the word was "corpsman." Soon two men carried a litter, close by me, down the steep hill, and I saw the blood running down one bandaged foot.

There was no telling how soon the next one would come or how close. The Germans really had our range. They must have direct observation, I thought. And the shell came. I ducked my helmet against the ground, and waited. The rending crash seemed to tear the very innermost part of my nervous system. That one was close, less than 100 feet away, but, miraculously, no one had been hit.

I had the feeling of being naked and helpless on the side of this hill, with nothing to do but wait, no place to take shelter except in the stubbly wheat. There was nothing like the cloaking underbrush of the South Pacific islands to lend you at least psychological comfort. Here there was only the hope that one of our observation posts, looking down on these craggy mountains, might locate the fire of the enemy batteries.

Now we heard a clear and distinct "ping," coming from somewhere in the vicinity of Hill 1139. It was a familiar sound—the discharge of a mortar, an enemy mortar. We waited a few seconds, and the shell landed in our midst with a loud "carrumpp!"

I began to work my way toward the headquarters foxhole, which looked comfortably deep. I made the final dash and was dismayed to find three prostrate figures already occupying the hole. However, Wozenski crowded over a bit and exposed a small area, into which I crammed myself.

It was none too soon. "Ping" went the mortar, and we glued ourselves to the bottom of the foxhole, waiting for the "carrumpp" which might bring jagged icicles of steel into our bodies.

A flight of planes came over, like dots of ink suddenly spattering the clouds. It was impossible to tell whether they were theirs or ours, and, under the present circumstances, much too great an effort to look. But anti-aircraft guns, Axis or Allied, began to thud all around us, and we heard the rapid "whoomp-whoomp-whoomp" of the ack-ack bursts somewhere in the sky. The pale ceiling of the sky was smudged with antiaircraft puffs, trailing the planes. But before they disappeared, obviously seeking a more important target than a few troops on a hillside, we heard the pinging of the German mortars again, the "carrumpp-carrumpp-carrumpp."

The wounded who could walk were gathered together to make their way to the rear. Bandaged and bloody, they were a sad collection of halt and lame. One of the group was the man whom I had seen staggering down the mountain with his hands over his face. He was blind. Hersey offered to escort them to the rear, even though he would probably have to pass through a zone covered by snipers. He and two enlisted men led the little column down the slope, and disappeared into the ravine.

The Germans were pounding us again with artillery. We heard the screeching sounds, like a car being driven around a corner, and felt the shells thudding into our hill, the explosions jumping into our little field like dark-brown giants. We hugged the ground until the storm might pass, if it ever would.

Wonderfully, there came a lull; such pauses always come when least expected and, to the target, most unaccountably. Perhaps the Germans manning the particular batteries which were firing on us had been spotted.

Sgt. Betancourt, who had been lying beside me when the first shell went off, now crawled up to our foxhole, peeked over the rim, stretched out a shaky hand, and said, "Anybody got a match for a nervous sergeant?" Lieut. Martin complied, and Capt. Wozenski said, with a wry smile, "Anybody got a cigarette for a nervous officer?"

Suddenly a single shell screamed through the air and crashed into the side of the hill above us. Silence. Then we heard a bubbling cry, like a fountain of discordant sounds. It was a human voice, and we saw the stubby form in Army olive drab, head bowed, arms dangling like an ape's, short legs swaying and slipping like rubber things as the little figure stumbled down the side of the mountain. "Oh . . . ah . . . oh . . . ah," gurgled the voice, and we saw the shocked man staggering past us, tears running down his cheeks, and a dull look of pain and frustration in his face.

Two men seized him by the arms and sat him down on the ground. The strain of the fighting on this knoll had been too great for one man on this day. "Shock," said Sgt. Betancourt. But no one said anything more.

Sgt. Betancourt was lamenting the loss of men this afternoon: "If we keep on like this, we won't have any platoon leaders left."

Capt. Wozenski said, reminiscently, "I remember the time at Mateur when we had thirty-three men left in the company out of 195."

We waited for the next enemy shell, but none came. Now the firing of our own batteries resumed, and picked up in volume. The shells were falling on the top of 1139, and on the left and right slopes, like a living tiara of fire. That barrage, during the lull in the enemy firing, was comforting. It made the situation seem less desperate.

Lieut. Groves had gathered his officers and platoon leaders around him at the foxhole. The time for the assault on 1139 was nearing. I heard Groves giving his men instructions: "The barrage will lift just before we start getting up on the hill. . . . I hope to Christ we can get in there without machine guns holding us up." Groves said to Lieut. Zbylut, who was leading one of the platoons, "If they put up a lot of resistance where you are, just fix bayonets and give it the old Indian yell."

Two more enemy artillery bursts smashed into the air over our heads. The Germans were using deadly time fire with fuses set to explode at a certain height over the target, showering fragments of high explosive over a maximum area. I heard our own mortars firing in the din, and the "carrumpp, carrumpp" of the explosions, smashing into 1139 seemed unusually loud.

"Alert the Second Platoon," said Groves. "Seven minutes to go."

The Germans had not been firing for a few minutes, when we heard the screech of an approaching shell, and ducked flat. The projectile landed on the edge of our wheat field, and, from the explosion, a tall cloud of pure white leaped up, then sat like a column of fog on the hillside. It was a smoke shell and, as we sat and watched it, silently, a soldier summed up what we were thinking. "Now we're going to get it." This peaceful cloud, marking our position so that some German observer could correct the range of the fire against us, was a prophecy of the hell of bursting shells which would probably soon fall upon us. I was glad that I had decided to go with Groves' company on the attack against 1139. It would be better to get into that attack, even though Groves said it would be "pretty damn rough," than simply to sit here and wait for that next German barrage. The men of Wozenski's company did not look too happy about the prospect as they dug their foxholes deeper into the ground.

"About a minute to go," shouted Groves.

I slung my map case, binoculars and blanket roll over my shoulders. From the other side of this knoll, I heard the sudden rattling of a German "burp gun."

"Get ready," said Groves. And he shouted to the telephone wireman, "O.K., hook on there, and, boy, let's have a good one!"

We were moving out through the wheat field, brushing through the tall stalks. We had reached the edge of the field, when rifles began to crack behind us. We hit the ground, thankful that, for once, we had ample cover, and wondered where the German marksmen might be. It is hard to locate the origin of a sound in echoing mountains. While I thought about it, there was a sound exactly like the whir of a bumblebee, and an object plunked into the grass within two feet of my head. It was a ricochet, possibly fired from the other side of the hill. But the rifle shots had sounded close.

I had started to get up when the loud rattle of a German machine gun drove me to the ground again. Bullets cracked overhead, and Groves indicated we had better get out of here. Now the Germans atop 1139 were able to fire directly at us.

Crouching and running, we pushed toward a ravine where we were considerably more protected. We saw the American mortar battery which we had heard firing a few minutes ago. As we passed the line of up-angled tubes, a telephone operator relayed directions to the crews, "Range 450. Fire one round." The loader at each tube obediently dropped a bomb-shaped projectile into the instrument, and blurs of motion rose from the muzzles as the mortars "pinged."

"Guess they spotted the son of a bitch," said Groves.

We had halted for a minute, as the barrage directed by our artillery against Hill 1139 increased in violence. "That should soften 'em up," Groves said hopefully. And he motioned the column forward farther into the ravine, toward the bottom of the valley through which we would move as we swept around the flank of Hill 1139.

Groves waited for the point of his column to pass, and occasionally shouted encouragement to one of the group. A blond, tumble-haired corporal was carrying a Browning automatic rifle over one shoulder. He was Willard E. Donne, of Tiona, Pa., and Groves shouted good-naturedly to him, "Donne, I want you to keep that God-damn B.A.R. talking tonight."

"Don't worry," Donne grinned. "If the son of a bitch'll go, I'll be working all right."

The column of soldiers struggled to carry their ammunition, rifles, and machine guns down the steep slope. As usual, I felt sympathy for the lad with the forty-pound steel machine-gun tripod on his back and a heavy case of machine-gun ammunition in one hand. It was hard enough to go up and down these precipitous hills in Sicily without such extra burdens.

The slope grew steeper as we progressed into the bottom of the valley. I was following along with the heavy-weapons platoon, while Groves had gone on ahead with the point. Ahead of me, a man, carrying the long barrel of a bazooka over one shoulder, slipped, skidded, skied down the slippery incline, as I had earlier, and sat down with a thud. He picked up the bazooka barrel and lifted it again to his shoulder, rubbing one hip with the other hand.

I hurried ahead and caught up with Groves. It was difficult to distinguish one man from another in the twilight, but the tall whip of the portable radio was a clue to the location of headquarters. Groves had reached the rocky bottom of the valley, filled with heavy, irregular boulders, and the sweet-smelling thorn-bushes.

We peeped out from behind a boulder and Groves pointed out the same diamond-shaped scar of sandy earth which we had seen from the top of the hill, marking the spot where the Germans were entrenched. In the twilight the scar seemed pale, like moonlight, and very peaceful, although I thought that somewhere around it must be the German machine gunners, riflemen and mortar crews who had been firing on us during the afternoon. Probably also the OP from which the Germans had been directing artillery fire.

Our barrage of artillery was still smashing into the sides of the hill. As the light of the day faded, the explosions of the shells flashed brilliantly against the dark mountain mass. But in several places, fires had started and were seeping through the fields of harvested wheat. The dry tinder burned vigorously. I began to fear that the light of the flames might give away our position, although we were attacking under cover of night.

The barrage was over. We waited for a few minutes, while the only sounds in the dark ravine were the occasional whispered words of soldiers, and the static of the radio. The time had come for us to get up and move on toward the mysteriously silent objective. We tried to move quietly. But in the darkness, we slipped and fell and skidded over the irregular boulders.

I found myself with the weapons platoon again. I heard Groves' hoarse whisper, as he said, irritably, "We're losing contact. Why don't you close up? You're strung all over the God-damn ditch."

The men moved silently down the gully, with only an occasional grunt of discomfort. The radio continued its zany chorus, like a chattering macaw, "Diddiddittidda," so loudly that it seemed inevitable that the enemy, up there on top of 1139, would hear us. And they did.

"Brrdddt-t-t-t." The sound came suddenly out of the darkness, quite close. Single rifle shots followed quickly. Streaks of light zipped over the gully, not more than three feet from us. A ricochet zoomed into the rocks near my face, making a phosphorescent streak between my head and the feet of the man in front of me. Then there were more streaks lighting the night above our ditch, more ricochets whining amongst the rocks.

No one was hit. The steep sides of the creek bed had shielded us from the direct effects of the firing. And, as abruptly as it had begun, the shooting stopped.

I wondered what would be next. Certainly now, the Germans knew that we were attacking. Would they mow us down as we climbed the sides of the hill? As I moved forward along the valley, another fact added to my concern. The flames started by the American artillery in the underbrush of the hill had spread in a broad arc along the lower slopes. The crackling fire shed a glare brighter than moonlight over the whole valley.

I found Groves sweating and cursing about the job of holding a company together in the middle of the night. He, too, was concerned about the German firing, and, through his radio, was trying to get into contact with the point of our force, somewhere in the lower slopes of 1139.

"Zbylut" (Lieut. Zbylut, leader of the point platoon) "is out of touch," said Groves. "I'd like to know what the situation is up there. The sons of bitches are too quiet."

"I'd like to know where that firing came from," I said to him.

"Me, too. Zbylut got one message back, that there were six or eight firing from the top of the hill. He wants to know if he can get some mortar fire on the Krauts, to get 'em out."

But there was no word from Zbylut. So we made our way along the creek bed, trying to re-establish contact with the rearmost elements of Zbylut's platoon. Soon we came to a point at which the platoon must have left the ditch and started up the lower slopes of 1139. We halted there, contemplating the gentle incline at the upper end of which a fringe of fire crackled. We would have to cross that almost level spot in that bright, revealing glare—so bright that our moving heads cast dense black shadows in the underbrush of the ditch. Should we risk it, charging across the field, or wait until we had word from Zbylut? For somewhere beyond those flames, Zbylut's platoon had vanished.

The ailing radio revived sufficiently to convey the information, from somewhere beyond, that Zbylut was moving up the hill toward the objective—and there was something about snipers on the top of the hill. Then the radio refused to function.

Groves motioned us out of the ditch, and we started across the burning wheat field, now as bright as day with flames. We trotted across the field at a half crouch, watching the dark beyond for the sudden flash of a rifle. We hurried up a gradually steeping incline, uncomplaining; shortness of breath was the least of our worries at the time.

We skirted the brightest of the flames, and passed beyond them into sudden darkness. The enemy had not fired a shot. We halted at the foot of a steep cliff, and we had to advance one step at a time, using the burned tufts of grass for hand holds. But there were no sounds except the panting of the men, the scratching of their clothes against the bristly grass, and, behind us, the faint crackling of the flames on the lower slope.

We reached the top of the charred cliffside, and sat down to rest for a moment. Apparently the Germans who had been defending the peak had left.

Groves allowed an extra minute for rest, and then called to the men, "Come on, on your feet. We're sitting on our behinds when we should be digging in." The sergeant translated the order into his own lingo: "You f----------g eight balls get the f-----off this God-damn hill before I rap this rifle barrel around your neck!"

The men dragged themselves to their feet and moved out left and right along the top of the ridge. Actually we were in the middle of a saddle, with a peak at each end, the taller hill being 1139. On the slope, I found the white scar, which we had spotted as an enemy strong point. The area was not sand at all, as I had thought, but an outcrop of soft limestone. The Germans had dug caves under the surface of the limestone to afford protection during the day's barrage.

I sat next to a private, R. E. Gravitt, of Athens, Tenn., who had been one of the first to reach Hill 1139 tonight. "There must have been five—six—seven snipers on the hill, but they ran." He showed me a pair of spectacles, equipped with an elastic band to keep them in place, which had been left behind by one of the Germans. There were some clothes, too, a few newspapers, and a machine pistol, or burp gun, and two ·303- caliber machine guns on heavy tripods—with ammunition. "They must have left in a big hurry," said Gravitt.

Lieut. Ellzey, leader of one of the platoons, reminded me that the Germans might counter-attack at any time during the night. When our outposts had been placed, Groves, Zbylut, Ellzey and the others gathered near the German limestone caves for a smoke. The technique was novel. Two or three officers covered themselves with a blanket, so that the glow of the cigarettes could not be seen.

I unrolled my blanket and stretched out on the limestone outcrop. Groves and I talked over the advisability of sleeping in the German catacombs; then decided they were probably lousy. Ellzey lay down next to me and we "shot the breeze." It was relaxing to talk after the effort and tension of the day, even up here on the top of a chilly mountain peak where the Germans might counter-attack at any minute. Ellzey was telling me that he is only twenty-one, that he had a lot of trouble, at first, getting the men to do what he wanted. "But after Niscemi, it was all right. Now I say, 'Jump,' and they jump. The platoon call themselves 'the mad dogs,' and that's good. They grouse a lot, but they'll fight."

My clothes were still damp with sweat from the violent effort of the day, and the mountain wind was absolutely frigid. Groves, who had no blanket of his own, lay down near by and I offered to share mine. Even with the warmth of our bodies and the blanket tucked under us, we went to sleep shivering,

July 28

The Germans did not attack during the night, and this morning we realized that they must have withdrawn their forces from the area around 1139, toward Nicosia.

I had a look into the German catacombs, and examined a rifle and machine pistol which the enemy had left behind. I did not look at the clothing, which by in a pile, but Pfc. Henry Hovanik, of East Vandergrift, Pa., told me that he had worn one of the coats during the night when the air was so cold. "After I had it on all night, this morning I found out it was bloodstained," he said with a grin. And in the morning light I found that the area along this saddle and on the slopes of Hill 1139 was thoroughly sprinkled with shell fragments. Corp. Donne, the tow-haired B.A.R. operator whom his fellow soldiers addressed as "Punchy," showed me one of the German machine guns which had been blown apart, apparently by an American artillery shell. The butt of the gun was broken off raggedly, in the middle of an area which had been showered with American shell fragments.

We moved on to Hill 841, without resistance, and also, noticeably, without breakfast or water. We paused to look out on Sperlinga and Nicosia, the usual clusters of gray buildings. It soon became apparent why the Germans had offered a considerable fight for this high ground. We could look directly over the road winding through Sperlinga and from there to Nicosia, and even see such details as the movement of carts in the streets.

Sgt. John F. Plitcka, of Brownsville, Pa., who had been at an outpost during the night, said he had heard enemy trucks moving out during the hours of the night, "Just like I heard at El Guettar, when the Germans pulled out there." In Sicily, as in North Africa, the Germans' favorite time for withdrawal was shortly after midnight.

From a lower ridge beyond 841, Groves and I saw men in uniform moving along the trail toward Nicosia. They were Americans, from the 18th Infantry, which had moved along the northern side of the Gangi-Nicosia road while we swept farther south.

"It looks as if they're going to get in first," said Mel Groves, ruefully. "That'd be the 3rd Battalion."

"Well," somebody said sadly, "they've had a road to walk on, instead of these God-damn mountains."

Col. Mathews, who had joined us by this time, was still anxious that the 2nd Battalion of the 16th (he being the commander) should be the first into Nicosia. Still, the colonel cautioned, we must keep our eyes open: the chances were very good that there might be pockets of Germans all through this scrub wood.

We crossed a slight rise, and then several rifle shots cracked the morning stillness. We halted, looked down into the valley. Our point had stopped at the edge of a large ravine, and two of our men were shouting at us down there. We couldn't hear the words but we knew from their agitated manner that they wanted help. We hurried down the hill, keeping a watchful eye on every shrub. As we came closer, we saw that two other figures of men were sitting on the ground. They were wearing German uniforms.

Soon we recognized Lieut. Don Creelman, a Canadian who had been serving as an artillery observer back on Hill 1333. He and another man had captured the two Germans. "There's a wounded Jerry on the other side of this ravine," he said to Groves. "I shot him. I guess I better get over and have a look." I followed Creelman over the boulders and through the trickling stream, up the other side to the spot where the German was lying.

The wounded enemy, a corporal, had the same haunted look as the prisoner who had been interrogated on Hill 1333 yesterday. While Creelman dressed the bullet wound, through the fleshy part of the leg, the prisoner told us that he, too, had been wounded in the fighting in Russia. He had served during the campaign in France. His eyes had the prematurely aged look which I had seen in the gaze of the German yesterday. He said he was tired, that his squad had been left as a rearguard in that section; that the trouble with the fighting here in Sicily was that all the German planes and guns were in Russia.

A couple of soldiers, who had come up to see the excitement, told me that Creelman had made his shot—a single shot which hit the target—at a distance of 200 yards. I asked Creelman about it, and he said, "Pretty lucky, I guess. The Jerry fell down, and the others began to yell. I saw one coming out with his hands up, and I hollered my whole vocabulary in German: 'Kommen Sie her.' And they came."

We heard the sound of "burp guns" and the crunching of mortar shells from the direction of Nicosia. The troops of the 18th Infantry, which we had seen moving up the trail toward the town, were probably fighting in the town itself. A smudge of dirty black smoke puffed from one section of Nicosia. Then there were golden lines of machine-gun tracers from one direction, answering tracers of a paler color.

The colonel, looking down on the town and its obvious fighting, seemed depressed because, as he said, "Somebody else got there first." But, he added cheerfully, he was sure that his 2nd Battalion had done a damn good job. "Well, sir," he said, scratching his chin thoughtfully, "the more I see of it, the more I think that that little hill over there, that 1139 and 841, commanded the whole thing over on this side." Certainly when the troops under his command had made the German flank untenable, the center of the German defense had been forced to pull back.

Nicosia had now grown quiet, and the troops were pouring into the town. I decided to accompany the prisoners with their guards back to headquarters.

As we passed down the road toward Gangi, avoiding columns of supporting infantry moving toward Nicosia, we noticed many signs that the Germans had contested our advance in this sector. The fields along the sides of the road were spattered with shell holes, and we saw three burned-out skeletons of our light tanks.

A jeep picked us up, and the driver, Lieut. Dunlay, told me that despite the fact that three tanks were knocked out, the total casualties in the tank troop had been one man killed and one wounded.

I had heard some sporadic firing from the left during the last night, but had not known what was happening. Each little spearhead of a large attack is usually quite isolated from the others.

The Germans riding on our jeep were interested, not to say fascinated, as they had their first look into the American lines. It must have been impressive to them to see the assemblage of power moving up the road to Nicosia: an endless procession of new trucks loaded with troops, scores of half-tracks carrying ammunition (and each armed with the latest anti-aircraft guns), brand-new Bofors 40-millimeter ack-ack guns moving down the road. There were 105-millimeter howitzers already going into position, with truckloads of ammunition behind.

Back in the villa near Gangi, we sought out the officers at Headquarters, to get an over-all picture of the attack on Nicosia. On the second story of the building, in a bare room which Gen. Terry

Allen, commanding general of the First Division, had appropriated as an office, John Hersey and I interviewed the general.

Tall and slender, with a gentle and thoughtful manner which reminded me of the traditional Abraham Lincoln, he unfolded his map case and showed us the two curving arrows which he had drawn in crayon at the center of the map, pointing toward Nicosia. In the jaws of the trap, indicated by the two arrows, he had lettered a large "E," for "enemy."

"This is a good illustration of fire maneuver" (an attack of maneuvering forces supported by artillery). "The infantry cut off the enemy, which necessitated a quick pull-out.

"The 26th came up a few days ago to take Hill 937 and 962, and it was such a painful process that this maneuver plan was decided upon. Had we kept up just a frontal attack, it would have meant just a bloody nose for us at every hill."

We asked the general how the attack had compared with the others carried out by the First Division in Sicily. "We've been meeting the Germans—very few Italians—ever since we landed," he said. "This was about as stubborn as any resistance we've encountered so far. The fall of Nicosia probably means that the Germans will have to retire to their next road-net at Troina, Troina is the last road-net center before Mount Etna.

"The Germans realized this, and I think they intended to put up a stubborn, prolonged delaying action at Nicosia in order to permit the flanks to fall back. The enemy was unsuccessful in this attempt."

Outside the headquarters building, the column of trucks, half-tracks, and artillery pieces in tow—and always the long, substantial line of the infantry troops slogging along on foot continued.

Objective: Catania

July 29

I RETURNED TO THE P.R.O. CAMP ON THE NORTH COAST OF Sicily. There was a note for me from the office, asking me to move over to the 8th Army front. INS had no correspondent there; they were worried about the possibility of missing the story of the fall of Catania, principal city of Eastern Sicily, second only to Palermo in size. The message, dated five days ago, urged that I transfer "soonest," which, in cablese, means "something you should have done long ago."

Driving into Palermo to make necessary connections, we passed a long, irregular procession of rickety carts stacked high with beds, chairs, mattresses and other household items. The refugees who had left the city when our bombing grew heavy were going back to their homes and their shops with the few possessions they had been able to save.

Inside Palermo, we could see manifestations of a return to normal life. The metal window shields of many of the stores, rumpled and sometimes torn by the blast of bombs, had been raised, and merchandise, apparently buried during the German occupation, was being offered for sale again. On the street corners, newsstands displayed Italian magazines, most of them of Fascist vintage. New democratic magazines could not be printed overnight.

On several walls which we passed en route to the Hotel Sole, brightly colored Fascist posters still urged hatred of England and America. But already a conscientious AMG official had slapped up the proper counter-propaganda nearby. His poster showed a yellow-faced Prussian officer, a smirk on the severe, monocled, visage; and, reflected in the monocle, the image of a gibbet and a dangling corpse, with the legend: *"Ecco il nemico!"* (Behold the enemy!)

July 30

For two days in Palermo I have been trying to make arrangements for my transfer to the 8th Army. After hours of pavement-pounding, I have finally located the proper military authorities. There are no guide books to direct a stranger amidst the confusion of a city newly occupied by military forces. I will, I am assured, be able to move "within a day or two." The wait is made endurable by pleasant company: Quent Reynolds, Red Knickerbocker, Herb Matthews, of the New York *Times*, John Hersey and Demaree Bess, of the *Saturday Evening Post*.

July 31

This morning, at the magnificent palace of the ancient Kings of Naples, where the advanced CP (Command Post) of the 7th Army is located, we interviewed Gen. Eisenhower, just arrived from North Africa.

We reminded the general that he had said, on the 12th of July, that a decision might be reached within two weeks. "I'm a born optimist, and I can't change that," he replied with his characteristic sidewise smile. "But obviously it will take a little longer than we thought."

I learned this afternoon that I am officially "in the clear" to go to the British 8th Army—if I can get transportation. I will simply have to thumb my way—and hope to reach there before Catania falls.

August 1

I was awakened this morning by a metallic clattering sound in the dark. "Ping-ping-ping-ping," like the chattering of apes, amplified hundreds of times until it rattled one's eardrums and dinned into one's innermost senses. It was the high-pitched sound of fast-firing automatic weapons—20- and 40-millimeter anti-aircraft guns echoing eerily in the corridors of the city streets. In the bedlam of sound the building seemed to bump and thud under the impact of heavier concussions: the deeper-toned big guns going off with a periodic bang. Air raid, air raid!

Jumping out of bed I pushed back the blinds and saw the tracers streaking the sky, and three white flares shimmering in the dark like lights reflected in a millpond. They floated over the harbor, where the Nazis were apparently preparing to bomb shipping.

I dressed rapidly and stepped into the darkened hall. Excited Italian voices came from the stair well, and Americans in parts of their uniforms hurried in various directions. I bumped into Lieut. Comdr. Charlie Duffy, Naval P.R.O. for the Mediterranean theater.

"There are ten ships in," said Duffy, nervously. "A fleet of transports."

We found a well-placed window, standing back so that we would not be hit by flying glass or ack-ack fragments. Bombs were falling. We could not distinguish the sound of their explosions in the cacophony of sounds, but we saw the characteristic red glow of bomb bursts. The illumination spread farther in the sky than the flash of an ack-ack gun and lingered longer.

Suddenly a wide-armed blossom of orange fire burst in the darkness of the water front. Another tremendous explosion came almost immediately from the core of the first, shooting out a shower of sparks and starlike explosions into the high sky. Curving arches of fire, trailing strangely luminous tails of smoke, lingered in the black. That would be ammunition exploding, I thought. Perhaps an ammunition ship . . .

I looked at my watch. It said 4:30. Now we could hear the zooming engines of planes, directly overhead. The apish chattering of the automatic weapons and the bang of big guns continued. The tenor stuttering of a light machine gun could be heard now.

Each time the sound of planes came near—they had to sweep in a circle over the city to make their "passes" at their target—the firing of our automatic weapons and big guns mounted into a crescendo. We waited for the bomb that would land on *us*. I told myself, as usual, that it was all a matter of chance.

The fire in the harbor burned brightly, exploding again and again and tossing out showers of sparks. At about five o'clock another great flash erupted in the water-front section. It, too, tossed a geyser of sparks and tracers across the sky, and renewed itself with violence.

Now both fires, broad smears of ruddy flame, detonated within themselves, within the smoke columns which towered over them. The columns of rolling smoke glowed, grew brighter and burned more fiercely.

The firing of the ack-ack guns diminished shortly after five o'clock. A few automatic weapons still chattered in the streets, but there were no more sounds of zooming engines, no more bombs. Fragments of stray ack-ack shells tinkled onto the tin roof of a lower building outside our window, but they would probably be falling for several minutes. The raid, apparently, was over.

We went down to the front door and stood just inside the heavy concrete bomb shields which had been built along the façade of the hotel. A group of Army officers, soldiers and a few correspondents waited for the rain of ack-ack fragments to stop—just as one might wait for the last few drops of a thunder shower.

Still we could not be sure that the Germans would not come back. John Hersey, Charlie Duffy and I wanted to see the bomb damage, so we decided to risk a trip to the water front.

We walked close to the line of buildings to keep away from fragments, which still occasionally rattled into the street. Thousands of such fragments, slivers and jagged shreds of steel, now littered the pavement.

At the foot of the deserted street, an Army command car approached us and Hersey said, "That's Gen. Patton." We hailed the car, and it came to a stop. Patton was wearing his usual tall cavalry boots, whipcord breeches and pearl-handled pistol. He seemed to be very much at home in the atmosphere of yammering ack-ack guns and exploding bombs. We asked him about the damage to the water front, and he said, "I couldn't get very close—too hot. There appear to be at least two ships burning. And they hit the freight yards. But fortunately," he added with a broad grin, "they missed the transports altogether."

Hersey, Charlie and I made our way to a long pier, or breakwater, which formed one of the enclosing arms of the harbor. From there, in the shelter of a dingy water-front storehouse, we could see two ships, drawn up at the dock about a mile away, burning brightly. The nearest ship was a flaming skeleton, illuminated like the glowing remains of a Fourth-of-July fireworks display.

Walking along the water front, where the fires of the two ships and the burning of the railroad yards beyond still continued, we commented on the accuracy of the German bombing. Only two bombs had strayed into the residential section; but the others had hit their targets, the ships within the arms of the inner harbor and the railroad yards and sidings near the dock. Probably the Germans had been careful to avoid damage to civilian dwellings in this case, for they seemed anxious to preserve whatever pro-German feeling there might be amongst certain sections of the populace in the first attack on Palermo.

The first bomb had struck an ammunition ship tied up at the dock. Six British sailors had escaped somehow without injury when the vessel blew up. A seventh had been killed. They had been the only members of the crew aboard at the time. On the dock to which the ship was tied, 350 prisoners, mostly Italians, had been confined. "Those Ginzos just went crazy when the bombs went off," the officer in charge, Lieut. Thomas Rice, said with a wry smile. "I guess they had been figuring that the war was all over for them—until last night,"

Later in the day I went to the Palermo airfield and hitched a ride in a little Fairchild monoplane with two RAF officers who were flying to Cassibili, near Syracuse, on the British side of the island.

Cassibili was a dusty field with an old castle at the center, a good many miles from Syracuse, British Headquarters. There was no transportation going from Cassibili to Syracuse tonight. I would have to spend the night at the airfield. But it was interesting, at least, to find suddenly that I was living with Englishmen, and no American in sight.

I went to the medical tent, in an olive grove at one edge of the airfield, and begged some supper. The kitchen had been set up to feed the wounded who were waiting for transportation to the rear by air. Supper consisted of beef stew with potatoes, and tea, with jam and crackers—biscuits, the British call them. I sat with a group of wounded men and found their conversation similar to that of American soldiers.

The favorite subjects were food, women and mail from home. The food situation, which provided a meager beef stew, was a "f------all," not to say a "bloody f------all." "Why didn't the f---------g mail f----------g well arrive?" When was the particular soldier going to see this or that dame again? An Italian, holding a pretty young girl by the hand, wandered through the olive grove, and the girl attracted the attention of the Tommies. Surmising that the Italians didn't speak English, one of the soldiers said, "Eh, how'd you like to tuck that one in bed?" And then the conversation turned abruptly to the subject of the death of a favorite cricket player, who had been killed at the front near Catania. "Got a bloody machine gun right across his chest, 'e did."

Tonight I found a bed on a stretcher in the tower of the castle. A kindly corporal helped me to find the spot. "The walls 'ere are three and a 'alf foot, sir. They'll be good for you if there's any flak flying about, and some nights there's plenty. The Jerries go after Syracuse pretty regular."

The corporal, a sergeant and two other British Tommies stretched out on the floor of the same room. They said they were a bit tired of the war, you know, after four years. One of them was a South Wales coal miner, and he observed that he didn't mind the war too much, but he'd rather be mining coal any day.

I asked them what they thought of Americans as people, and one of the voices in the dark, in typical chopped, singsong English, answered, "They 'ave more money than our chaps and take the girls about. Yet," he added, "the Americans 'ave plenty of guts, as we saw at that tank battle at Djedeida."

August 2

I found the British P.R.O. camp this morning near Lentini, in the edge of an orange grove, and sought out Jack Redfern, of the London *Daily Express*, a friend who gave me a brief picture of the situation on this side of the island.

"We've captured a Jerry map," said Redfern, "which shows that they have set up three defense lines around Catania. Two of them are to the south of Catania. It's been decided that if we can break the lines on the flank, we can force a retirement. We took Regalbuto, a key to the first defense line, yesterday, and nearly succeeded in taking Centuripe, one of the important positions in the second defense line. Once Centuripe falls, Jerry will probably abandon Catania—if he follows his plan. And he probably will."

August 3

I decided to go up to Centuripe with tall, kindly Maj. Lewis Hastings, a British Broadcasting Company military commentator. We found that British troops had already taken Centuripe and were pushing beyond.

Now, even though the Germans were still dug in beyond the town and along the river in the next valley, the peasants were coming back to resume their work of centuries. Some of them, a little wealthier than the rest, were astride horses, returning to Centuripe and their farms on the terraces.

A few minutes later, in the little park in the town, we heard the whistle of a shell, and saw the puff of dirty brown smoke spouting in the valley below us. The German artillery had fired that shell from beyond the River Salso, where even now advanced British patrols were in contact with the enemy.

Beyond the Salso, and over the lower slopes of Mount Etna, we could see planes maneuvering, and a miniature forest of smoke puffs sprang into existence on one edge of the town. They were the tall gray-brown columns raised by bomb explosions, I could see with my field glasses. Adrano, the pivot of the last German defensive line south of Mount Etna, was being softened. The Allied command was making the most of our great air supremacy during the clear and rainless Sicilian summer. If we could soften Adrano sufficiently with air bombardment and artillery, and move in with numerically superior troops, then the prize, Mount Etna, would be ours.

A column of British Tommies, trudging in step along the grade, passed us. They were whistling a marching tune, in rhythm with their steps, and their strength and plodding patience were impressive. They were sturdy and sunbrowned, but short men by comparison with the Americans. I commented on that fact to Hastings, and he said, "The average Tommy is about a welterweight. But he is tough."

August 4

We arrived at the P.R.O. camp to find that the fall of Catania was expected this afternoon or tomorrow morning. In accordance with their plan, the Germans were apparently falling back from their defense position which pivoted on Centuripe, retiring to the last line of defense before Etna—a line swinging from Adrano on the west to a point a few miles north of Catania.

We bundled into our cars and started for the Catania front, anxious to be present at the collapse of the city.

The Catania plain is as fiat as the New Jersey meadows. The British had evidently attempted to use armor on these flat areas, but the Germans had foreseen this and built strong pillbox positions along the main road into the city. The pillboxes had been smashed, but the wrecked carcasses of tanks, one of them a Sherman with the turret ripped off, lay beside the road. And piles of round Teller mines (*Teller* is the German word for "plate" and refers to the shape of the mine) stood at the side of the road, where they had been dug up by British sappers. There were also many of the ordinary varieties of road blocks, which had been shoved aside by the advancing British: X-shaped frames of wood supporting barbed wire, pyramid-like blocks of concrete and concrete walls across part of the road, joined to sturdy pillboxes. These were the heavy German defenses which had slowed the British advance toward Catania to a halt, and finally forced the use of flanking tactics in the rugged mountains to the west.

Correspondents with the British Army usually travel with conducting officers. These officers led us to brigade headquarters of the infantry outfit which was moving into Catania. We talked to the brigadier, beside his radio truck, in a grove of trees not more than six miles south of Catania. He gave us a picture of the military situation. "We suspected last night that the enemy had pulled out," he said. "We noticed a good deal of signaling and Very lights, and the patrols observed that there was no machine-gun fire. Presently, we are only 700 yards south of the city on the right, somewhat farther south on the left. We're delayed by pillboxes." We heard the carrumpp of a mortar shell somewhere in our vicinity. "Also mortars," the brigadier added, with a smile.

He suggested that we return tomorrow. "The troops probably won't get into Catania tonight. So why don't you chaps just come back tomorrow?" That sounded, somehow, like an invitation to a cricket match, but it was the sensible thing to do.

August 5

With our conducting officers, we stopped again at the brigadier's headquarters south of Catania. He warned us, "We've got Bren carriers, and foot troops going through the town. I expect that you can drive in. But be careful. The place is lousy with mines. An Eyetie said this morning that the Germans had been sowing them for five days." He grinned at us. "But there are no decent shops." He knew that we were anxious to get into a large city with some semblance of civilization.

We passed the wrecks of buildings which had been the once-proud Catania airfield. The roofs of the hangars were blown in, the modern dormitory buildings were broken and pockmarked by flying fragments, and the field was spotted with the sad wrecks of fifty or sixty airplanes, some of them standing like rumpled birds in their revetments. The geometrically round circles of bomb craters ranged along the side of the road. Some of them contained pools of stagnant water, evidence that this effective bombing job had been done some time ago.

We drove in the center of the road, to avoid enemy mines, which were usually dug in on the soft margins. We passed one burning Bren carrier which had driven on the soft shoulder of the road and ignited a Teller.

A heavily wired area, further protected by stone road blocks, marked the beginning of the city of Catania. Most of the buildings had been struck by shellfire or bombs, and the least-damaged structures had been pocked by flying fragments. Many buildings had been broken into hunks of stucco and concrete, shoved into the street as if by some giant hand. At several places whole houses had been pulverized into heaps of rubble. Already I had seen enough of Sicily to expect that a city or town through which the war had passed would look like this. And the crowd of ragged Sicilians who watched our arrival gleefully were also a standard fixture. They clapped their hands and some showered us with acorns and almonds. Some shouted, "*Viva Ingleterra!*" and some of them, spotting the American helmets of two correspondents, seemed in doubt about the advisability of mentioning "*Ingleterra*" and shouted only, "*Viva, viva!*"

We went on to the center of the town and passed a squalling crowd who were banging at the metal shutters of a store in the shopping district. The establishment was a uniform shop, specializing in Fascist military clothing. Ragged Sicilians were carrying out bright banners, flashy nickel-plated parade swords and boxes of medals. Another jabbering crowd began to attack less legitimate targets across the street—women's clothing stores, dry-goods stores, and some of them were invading the kitchen of the Hotel Europa, where a caretaker stoutly defended the larder with a stick. Looting was a favorite Sicilian pastime. The ornate Casa di Fasci, the Fascist headquarters next door to the uniform shop, had been already given a thorough going-over. Sounds of breaking glass and furniture being upset mingled with the joyful babble of the vultures.

In the broad Piazza del Duomo, Cathedral Square in the city, we saw the jeep of the British brigadier, who stopped to survey the wreckage of the place. He showed us a message from the city authorities, a token of surrender. "The authorities and functionaries of the city of Catania are in the Caserma Carabinieri" (the police station) "in the Piazza Giovanni Verga, awaiting orders."

Two rows of carabinieri stood rigidly at salute in their splendid uniforms, outside the office of the chief of police. A carabinieri officer received the British brigadier. He spoke English with a suspiciously American accent and idiom. He told me later that his name was John Cassini, and that he had been a landscape gardener in San Francisco. His brother George, he said, still lived in San Francisco on Sadowa Street. The mayor, a slick-haired, very smooth Italian who also spoke English, bowed formally and affixed his signature with a flourish to a surrender document which he offered to the brigadier. This was a theatrical moment, important in the history of Catania, and like all the Sicilians whom I had seen, the Marchese di San Giuliano had a vivid sense of the histrionic.

The Marchese told me that relations between the Germans and Sicilians had been growing increasingly strained. "At first when they came, the Germans are saluting, laughing, and they are friendly. Later they are different. Now they speak bad of us Italians. They say, 'We are fighting for you, and you do not stand by us.' But we know if they had done it for our love, they would not have blown up our city.

"When the Germans have first come to Sicily, to see them drilling in the square was wonderful. I spoke with many officers who said that the war would be finished by July of 1941. However, later they insist to me they are meeting resistance which they had not expected in Russia. They assure me that they would never lose Africa.

"Now that the Germans are leaving, they treat us abominably. They come with machine guns. At my villa two nights ago twelve Germans have kicked down the door, knocked two ladies from their bed, only looking for food. Then they have stolen my car. A few days ago some of the Germans break into many homes. They have taken food and mattresses, sheets and blankets, and sell them to the population.

"At Mascalucia the Germans go to a stable where there are fourteen mules. They threaten to take them, but the whole population come down and say, 'We will not give the mules.' The Germans point their machine guns. The Italian soldiers come with grenades. The Germans fire and murder one or two people."

The mayor confirmed a report that the Germans had blown up the Hotel Corona and the Bank of Sicily. They had also, he said, mined the Palazzo di Toscano and the post office, the best public buildings in the city, to keep them from being used by the Allies.

Driving through the town, en route to the P.R.O. camp, we saw that the throng of looters was still at work near the Piazza del Duomo. The streets were now littered with sheets of paper and boxes which the looters had thrown away as they broke into new stores. A few carabinieri strutted amongst the peripheral rioters, and swung their clubs vigorously, but at the center of the throng the looters were still intent on their work. A ragged Santa Claus on the balcony over the door of one of the stores was tossing armfuls of packages to the people below. Equally ragged scavengers below clawed and struck at each other in the scramble. And with this pleasant vista, we took our leave of beautiful Catania.

Gateway to a Continent

August 6

THIS MORNING AT OUR DAILY CONFERENCE WITH THE Intelligence Officer we learned that an attack on Adrano might be made tonight. Maj. Hastings, Ned Russell, of the UP, and I decided to go along. The Intelligence Officer said that a tremendous artillery barrage had been "laid on" in support of the attack on Adrano. That should be interesting to watch.

We arrived at the abrupt ending of the bridge over the Salso, when a mortar shell burst less than 300 yards away, sending a cloud of dirt flying, and we heard the burp of a German machine gun. We decided to get some information on the situation of the front line before going farther.

We found the brigade major, a debonair chap who wore his clothes like an *Esquire* fashion drawing, in a radio trailer near a stone farmhouse. "Seem to be a few machine guns and mortars," he said crisply. "But we shall be going up tonight—not, however, until we have made all preparations. The barrage should be in by 3 A.M. It will be the real thing. We shan't be firing concentrations on one spot, but a rolling barrage that will move in ahead of the troops. Possibly 170 to 180 guns."

At eleven o'clock tonight, the British column materialized out of the darkness and tramped down the road toward the broken bridge over the Salso, through the dry river bed, then down again into the valley of the Simeto across a pontoon bridge. We hurried, stopping only to make sure that our companies kept together in the dark.

The Tommies were not talking, but there was a great shuffling of feet and the sound of scraping hobnails as we thumped along the road. The hobnails, the close formation and the old-style washbasin helmets of the British reminded me of accounts of the First World War.

After a long climb up the steep mountainside that led to Adrano, we stopped and waited for the beginning of the barrage.

Pinpoints of light sparked in the black mountains towering up to Centuripe behind us. We heard the booming of guns and the whine of shells over our heads, and far up on the hill where Adrano lay, we saw the quick white flashes of the exploding shells.

A veritable percussion concert was now going on. The booming of the guns behind us was continuous, like the rattling of a nervous drummer banging on kettledrums. There was a steady singing of shells passing over our heads, a heavenly chorus; and the sharp, metallic rapping of explosions on Adrano. Occasionally there came the twanging sound of ricochet shells. Our machine guns, firing at closer range, giving us a protective cover on the lower slopes of the mountain, added a rattling, wooden tone, like the clavé sticks in a rhumba band.

The bombardment had begun to stir up dust. Now the dust was drifting our way, a pale haze visible even at night.

The colonel stood at the side of the road watching the procession. In the dark, a tommygun strapped around one shoulder was distinct against the background of his lighter-colored shirt. The gun seemed huge in comparison to his small size.

An enlisted man approached from the dark and the dust, snapped to salute, and said, "We found a fort up the road, sir."

"A fort?"

"It's all right, sir, there's no one in it."

The percussion concert continued. The dancing stars of the gun flashes twinkled on the hills of Centuripe. The singing of the shells was almost a sedative. We began to surge forward again, and the line of the bombardment moved ahead of us. And so midnight came without a sign of German resistance.

August 7

At about 12:30 A.M., we were about half way up the escarpment. The barrage was lifting well over the top of the ridge, and most of the flashes, no longer sharp dots of light against the black hill, were now heat-lightning flashes coming from beyond the brow.

It seemed that every available gun had been thrown into the last artillery assault before the British troops pushed into the town. The guns behind us were booming in a steady basso rumble.

I looked at my watch. It was three o'clock. "That's the final barrage," said a young captain. "It'll be over at three-thirty."

We agreed that this was the most concentrated bombardment we had seen in Sicily. But, said Russell, the bombardment at El Alamein in Africa was much heavier; less spectacular, he said, because, with the flatness of the land, one couldn't see the flashes of the guns so distinctly as here. Hastings asserted that this couldn't compare with the artillery of the First World War. "I remember times when there were 6,000 guns firing at once," he said. "It didn't flash like this bombardment, for there were too many pieces firing at once. They made a constant light."

The barrage continued. In an effort to snatch a little sleep, I sprawled in a culvert. When the firing halted, the column began to move again. We reached a huge gap in the road where a bridge had been dropped into a chasm by high explosive.

Hastings, Russell and I forged ahead and began to scale the steep side of the valley, treading gingerly because in many cases the Nazis mined all paths around demolitions. We crossed the completely chaotic heaps of masonry which filled the bottom of the little stream bed, forced our way up the far side through a tangled grove of dwarf orange trees to a high wall which we had to scale. Fortunately it wasn't topped with broken glass, as most of the Sicilian walls are. And on the far side, we dropped into the yard of a house. We skirted the house and found ourselves amidst a scattered array of buildings, the outskirts of Adrano. Dust still filled the air. Almost every house had been hit. It was just another Sicilian town, smashed by our artillery.

There were no people to be seen in Adrano: no Britishers, no Sicilians. It was a ghost town, and the foglike dust stirred by the shells still drifted sluggishly between the houses. The chill mountain air blew through our thin clothing. The acrid smell of high explosive, the loneliness, gave the place the smell of death. We decided to retire to the rear. It was unhealthy to be this far in advance of the British point, even though the Germans had apparently abandoned the town.

It was five o'clock, and the sky over the mountains to the east was colored by the first light of dawn. As we wandered back through the valley and onto the road, where a sentry challenged us, sharply, we must have been a bizarre sight: Ned Russell, in a battered military cap and shorts; Hastings, also in shorts, and wearing a black beret over his bushy red eyebrows; and I, in a shabby American fatigue uniform, and the usual American helmet, which, to the Britishers, looked so much like the German coalscuttle. It was no wonder that the sentry summoned the lieutenant, and that the lieutenant asked to see our credentials.

We hitched a ride down the mountainside and through the valleys of the Simeto and the Salso. We slept most of the way home to the P.R.O. camp. But I remember the major saying, "Remarkable how many of these mountains are taken by small parties of infantrymen—a few companies or perhaps a battalion—with tremendous artillery support to push them into place." We agreed that it was very fortunate that the Germans did not have artillery strength to compare even remotely with ours.

August 8

This morning we heard that, with the collapse of Adrano, the Germans had withdrawn all their forces from the southern slopes of Etna. Santa Maria, Paterno and Biancavilla, along the lateral highway from Catania to Adrano, had fallen to us.

We were given for publication a copy of a German field order issued to the Hermann Goering Armored Division. The order said that all vehicles not absolutely necessary in Sicily should be transported to the mainland. The document specified the numbers of ferries which would carry the vehicles; and it announced that Lieut. Gen. Heiderich had been appointed to command troops in Southern Italy. The German evacuation of Sicily was being accelerated.

August 9

"From now on it seems to be a question of who can walk back the fastest," the Intelligence Officer said this morning. "The Germans are definitely getting out everything they can. Aerial photographs again confirm the arrival of empty ferries and their departure, loaded.

"Jerry is putting up a terrific cone of flak at the Straits of Messina—makes it a bit difficult for our aviator chaps. It's the heaviest ever encountered in the Mediterranean—heavier than 'flak alley' between Bizerte and Tunis—greater than the inner artillery of London, I'd say."

With Jack Redfern, I started for the American 57th Fighter Group which had been working with the 8th Army. Their rickety old P-40s, specially equipped with bomb racks, had been harassing German evacuation boats loaded with enemy troops disengaged from Sicily to the Italian mainland.

We drove into the dust of the fighter strip and stopped at a tent for directions. We realized that we had found Americans when we heard the strains of a swing version of "Baby, Won't You Please Come Home."

In the radio trailer which was Group Flight Operations Headquarters, we met slim, tow-headed and young Col. Salisbury, CO. At twenty-six a full colonel, he had the undefinable air of responsibility.

"There's quite a lot of flak over the Straits of Messina—the Straits being so narrow," he began. "Some of our boys have been shot down, but we've been getting in occasionally and sinking some of those Siebel ferries. There's been a lot of motor transport carrying troops to the beaches, and we've been strafing 'em,"

The colonel suggested that we talk to some of the pilots, to get a first-hand account.

Lieut. Herman Goodman, a Jamaica, L. I., pilot, told how he had knocked out a ferry a couple of days ago. "It was a big square thing with a stern paddler, like a Mississippi riverboat. I went in and dropped my bomb, and it just blew the thing apart. You could see the water and pieces flying around all over the place. It looked just like it was raining."

Maj. Glenn Reich, of Tripp, S. D., said that the Germans were using E-boats to protect the ferry traffic across the Straits. "They put up a hell of a lot of flak. I caught two E-boats near Milazzo. They were zigzagging to beat hell, shooting at me with their 20s. I could see that old string of pearls coming right up at me. The son of a bitch made a left turn and I dropped the bomb. Then he sure stopped quick. It just seemed like the butt end of the boat had been blown off."

The Group had suffered considerable losses while they were inflicting such heavy damage on the enemy. Capt. Gilbert O. Wymond, of Louisville, Ky., who had been shot down by enemy flak in strafing a truck column, but had escaped with only a few scratches when his plane crashed, put it this way, "Whenever you strafe—or bomb, for that matter—you lose. My squadron lost two out of twelve planes yesterday."

"And I lost two wing tips," said another flyer.

"And I lost my tail wheel," added a third.

But at least, the pilots agreed, they did not often have to contend with enemy fighters. The German fighter strength, such as it was, had been withdrawn to the mainland; the few ME-109s which our flyers had seen in Sicily had been disinclined to fight.

Back at 8th Army Headquarters we heard that the Americans were making rapid progress along the north coast of Sicily. An amphibious force had landed near San Marco. Held up by the

Germans along the narrow road of the north coast, Gen. Patton had swung his troops in a bold flanking movement. Landing from boats, they had come in well behind the German rear and cut off a pocket of enemy troops, 300 of which had been captured.

There seemed to be good reason for supposing that the British forces would try a similar maneuver on the east coast of Sicily, south of Messina. Their forces driving toward Messina would be more severely channeled along the east coast than were the Americans on the north.

August 11

This morning we drove south to the 15th Army Group Headquarters, near Cassibili, for an interview with Air Marshal Sir Arthur Coningham, second in command to Air Marshal Tedder. Coningham trumpeted the glory of the Allied Air Forces, giving them a major share of the credit for driving the Germans out of Sicily. He asserted that American Flying Fortresses had been largely responsible for establishing the complete and absolute air supremacy of the Allies in Sicily. "There's no doubt about it, the Fortress weapon is an absolute killer. Nobody foresaw its effect. We didn't, and the Germans certainly didn't." As a result of the severe bombing administered by the Fortresses, between 250 and 300 enemy fighters were destroyed in Sicily. The better part of these were knocked out on the ground. "The effect of the Fortress combined with the fragmentation bomb was devastating. Where a large bomb might miss a building altogether, one of the smaller frag bombs would burst inside the building."

Coningham, brisk and dynamic, with the appearance of a successful American businessman, answered our questions directly.

In the matter of casualties, the air marshal said flatly, "About 20,000 casualties in the two armies. A large proportion dead.

"Where is the Luftwaffe? It is outed—absolutely done. The heart is out of it, everywhere, I should say roughly half of the remaining planes are occupied on the Russian front. About half in Europe.

"The invasion of continental Europe? I call this the Mediterranean year—where we exploit our advantage. It's obvious we must try and do something—and go on. . . . The German is playing for time now. He's holding us up while he's building up back here." And he pointed to Italy on the large map.

We asked about the significance of the first raid on Rome. "I think the Rome raid ended the Mussolini party. The timing when the commanding officers did that was brilliant. It was magnificently done, a most perfect job of work."

Tonight at P.R.O. headquarters near Catania, a German air raid came without warning. We watched the green flares shimmering in the sky, the red and white and green trellis work of the tracers, the bright stars of anti-aircraft bursts. A ruddy glow spread over the horizon to the north where a fuel dump must have been hit. We heard the zooming engines of the planes—they were circling over our camp between passes at their targets. All around us, ack-ack fire banged and chattered. The heavy thuds of bombs shook the farmhouse from which we were watching. Coningham certainly picked a great day to give his interview on the demise of the Luftwaffe.

August 12

Another captured German operations order was released today. It urged that the troops should save as much equipment as possible. "The passport to Italy is a gun," the manifesto said melodramatically. "Carry as much ammunition as you can." For the first time, it was specifically stated that the Italians must not be allowed to impede German progress. "The Italians are to be ruthlessly thrust aside," said the order. "Italian heavy weapons and motor transports are to be thrown off the road if they get in the way. The only Italians to be allowed passage to the mainland are those under German command." And the I Officer commented in typically British fashion, "Shows quite a catastrophic state of affairs."

About eighty craft of the Siebel ferry type and the F-boat type (self-propelled lighter) could be spotted through aerial observation in the Straits, the officer said. They were protected by 180 heavy guns and 120 lights, totaling up to the heaviest concentration in this part of the world. It was difficult for our aircraft to break through the flak screen.

August 15

German demolitions have seriously impeded British progress along the coast road to Messina. The British command has decided to send the amphibious landing force we have been expecting. I heard about it this morning. Another correspondent, Evelyn Montague, of the Manchester *Guardian*, and I have been given permission to go.

We reported to a colonel of the 4th Armored Brigade—which, with a group of Commandos, will make the assault. The colonel's headquarters were located in a seaside villa with a broad concrete terrace overlooking the clear blue water. In the modern living room a group of officers from the brigade were having tea from a china service borrowed from the owner of the villa.

The colonel told us that the brigade, equipped with General Sherman tanks, tank destroyers and a few field pieces, would land shortly after the Commandos, who would secure the beachhead.

We drove down to the British naval offices on the Catania water front. The harbor had already been cleared of mines and was in operation as a military port. A line of LCTs of American manufacture lay alongside one section of the dock. The tanks and "Priest" tank destroyers (so called because the high open cockpit gave the effect of a pulpit) were being loaded through the lowered ramps in the boats' bows.

In the office of a former Fascist functionary, we were briefed by a British naval commander. "D-day, 16th," said the commander briskly. "Military force commanded by Brig, Currie embarking in LCT 387. Intention: to land a force of 400 men with tanks and artillery in the vicinity of Cape Galli." Cape Galli is a point of land about fourteen miles south of Messina.

Evelyn Montague and I boarded LCT 387, the brigadier's ship. Tanks and scout cars were jammed into the ship's open hold. A young lieutenant was briefing a little group of men next to a small field piece. They were the gun crew. He illustrated his lecture with a map.

"The enemy is retreating at bloody great speed. The only way we can make sure of holding them up is to land here" (he pointed to Cape Galli, near Scaletta) "and cut them off."

A chunky Tommy commented with a guffaw, "Sounds like a damn bad show for Jerry. Hope he takes a lenient view of it."

Half an hour later, the landing craft next to us began to back away from the dock. The soldiers lining the rail jeered at us. One of the Tommies bellowed, "You're on the wrong boat."

But in a few minutes our engines were vibrating, and sailors tossed off our bowline. On the raised deck at the stern the sharp-faced, slender brigadier waved his cap toward the shore. And the soldiers began to sing lustily, "We're Shovin' Right Off."

August 16

I had been asleep since ten o'clock, sprawled on the hood of a scout car aboard LCT 387. At 2 A.M. I woke up. My mental alarm clock told me that I had at least an hour of grace before the landing.

We were heading north along the narrowing Straits of Messina, hugging the shoreline.

Brig. Currie came out of the little deck house and stood in the moonlight, watching the shore with his field glasses. Our miniature fleet of LCTs slipped quietly through the slick water.

The brigadier asked if I had been on one of these landings before. I told him I had.

"Stimulating, isn't it?" he said cheerfully.

We were far enough north now so that we could see the mountains of Italy rising on our right over the shimmering water. On our left, against the cliffs of Sicily, a light suddenly glowed bright yellow. Near by another startling flash punctuated the dark land mass.

"They're demolitions," said the brigadier's executive officer. "Jerry's just making sure that we don't use the road along the coast."

I went forward and passed a pleasant hour chatting with the RAF liaison crew, three enlisted men in the scout car which would serve as mobile headquarters. One had been an automobile salesman, one an office boy in a stock brokerage, the third a clerk in a store. Their names were Adlington, Fincham and Bowles.

We were late. My watch said 3:25—and we were still heading north. The line of road along the cliff was now clearly visible, and on the road a thin black streak moved north, it seemed to me. Adlington confirmed my thought when he looked through the binoculars.

"Looks like a Jerry motor transport," he said.

Our LCT was turning slowly toward the beach at reduced speed. The Commandos had already landed and were at work: a terrific explosion splashed against the Sicilian coast. From it a far-spreading phosphorescent shower of fire curved in many directions. I guessed that an ammunition dump had been blown up.

A small, fast landing craft bounded toward us in a smother of spray. Through a megaphone a voice boomed, "No landing for tanks yet."

From the south we heard the quick clatter of rifle and machine-gun fire. The tail end of the German motor-transport column had run afoul of our Commandos.

We were close in shore now. In the first rays of dawnlight we could see the buildings of a village. A signal light winked at us. "Send one LCT in here."

We proceeded cautiously under the guidance of blinking green lights on the beach. The boat gained speed and we ground up onto the sand.

Our heavy ramp clanked down with a thud. A small group of Commandos came down the beach, escorting a crowd of Italian prisoners. I talked to one of the Commandos, a captain, who told me that there had been only three British casualties in the landing; that the explosion had been caused by a Commando grenade which hit an enemy ammunition lorry on the bridge at the town, killing five or six Germans.

"Those Eyeties" —he indicated the prisoners who had been brought into the boat—"were artillery. Had some 50-mm. guns up at the end of the beach, but they were just waiting to surrender."

At that moment another great explosion shattered our nerves. High up on the hillside above the beach a cascade of rocks was falling. Debris splashed into the water, and a cloud of smoke rolled down over us. The ammunition was still exploding. Brig. Currie said, "It's the wrong beach. Tanks can't get up from here."

We backed out and moseyed along the shore. The sun was coming up. Far out in the Straits of Messina, our destroyers were moving rapidly, trailing a smoke screen to cover our maneuvers. We heard the sound of big guns booming from the mainland of Italy. We proceeded along the shore to the south, seeking a landing spot. Now we knew the Germans had observed us. Two shells puffed up clouds of smoke on the cliff off our bow. Two more cracked as they struck the water between us and the shore, sending up miniature geysers.

The other LCTs swung into the beach in echelon. Ahead of us an LCT had struck the sand and its ramp was being lowered. Two shells flung dirty columns of sand from the beach a few yards away from the ship. Another shell threw up a spout of water off the stern. Then one burst directly on the hull of the ship, covering the stern with smoke. We could see the figures of men, running.

We too hit the beach and the ramp clanked down, with incredible casualness. Farther down two more German shells exploded, near the busy column of men and machines, pouring from the open bow. It began to look as if we were really in for it, as if we had blundered into a nest of Germans.

I came ashore on the RAF scout car. We stuck hub deep in the gravelly sand. We were trying to budge the car, when two projectiles crashed, "Carrumpp! Carrumpp!" into the sand a few yards away.

We shouted to a tank destroyer which was clattering up the beach, asked for a tow. We hooked the scout car on to a rope. A mortar shell smashed into the ground near by. Another was on the way. We heard a short screech, and ducked. And then, at last, the scout car budged. Noxious fumes whirled up over us from the stern of the tank destroyer which towed us, but that gasoline reek was perfume to us.

The British mechanized column passed over a bridge and into the near-by town of Scaletta. I transferred to the scout car of the forward observing officer (FOO), a bespectacled young man with skinny knees. He was heading north to get a look at enemy positions.

The FOO directed the car through the little town, where Sicilians were shouting, "*Viva Ingleterra!*" and up the hill beyond.

The FOO stopped his car, and he and I went forward. We had taken only a few steps, when suddenly we heard the screech of approaching shells, and over our heads great black clouds burst. Fragments whizzed through the air around us. There were one, two, three, four and five; we waited a few seconds, breathless, for the next one to burst; and then, scrambling to our feet, we dashed for cover. We knew it would be only a few more seconds, probably, until the Nazi guns would fire again, and I hoped we would have time.

We reached a stone wall, scrambled over it, and discovered too late that there was a ten-foot drop on the other side. I slid and skidded down the rough surface, scraping the skin from my arms, happy to escape from the unprotected road above.

We fell in a heap at the foot of the wall. Then, working forward toward the top of the hill, we heard more artillery coming. "Crrackk, cr-rack-k, cr-rash!" Air bursts were exploding over the road again, battering our ears. Two more shells crashed into the air above us, and the fragments clipped branches which fell in a shower at the foot of the wall.

Farther up the hill we climbed over the wall and back into the road. Air bursts still exploded occasionally behind us. At the top of the hill, we found a castle-like structure dug into the high bank on one side. It had been an enemy pillbox, and here, relatively secure behind the two-foot walls, Tommies were resting. The British point should be less than 200 yards ahead. A short distance from the pillbox we saw souvenirs of the blown-up German ammunition lorry.

The only traces of the lorry itself were a few dented, charred scraps of metal. Exploded artillery shells littered the surface of the street, and the edge of the road was blackened by fire. At one side of the road, part of the charred body of a British soldier lay, a grotesque parody of a human form sculptured in charcoal. On the other side the body of an enemy soldier sat doubled up, with the knees clutched nearly to the chest. The eyes seemed to be starting from their sockets, and the whole face was frozen in a stare of terror.

Two other corpses, bloody and battered by the explosion, lay near the enemy soldier. They wore the summer uniform of the German Army. Next to them lay three wounded Germans. Two of these had already been bandaged.

A Priest tank destroyer was moving into position at the curve of the road, and preparing to engage enemy artillery. As the 105-mm. gun whanged away, and the empty shell casings clattered to the pavement and rolled down the hill, I knew that the firing would bring retaliatory measures from the Germans. I was sitting in a scout car at the side of the road when the first German shell burst with a terrific crash at the top of the bank above the pillbox. Pieces of masonry and shell fragments clanked down from the top of the pillbox and showered the street. I heard a metallic crash and saw a huge fragment, five or six inches long and jagged, bounce from the floor of the scout car. It was still hot when I picked it up. And a young British lieutenant examined it curiously. "There seems to have been a slight mistake," he said. "I thought they were using mortars. This looks like a 17-centimeter." I examined the thickness and the rifling of the fragment, and agreed. Despite the evidence that the Germans had withdrawn heavy forces from Sicily, the gun which fired this was no pea-shooter.

I walked along the top of the cliff, absorbed by the sight of Italy just across the Straits. The atmosphere had cleared and, with binoculars, I could make out the spreading white buildings of Reggio, with the gray alluvial fan of the Saint Agata River at one side, and the level plain of the Reggio airfield near by. It was startling to realize that we were now so close to the mainland of Italy that we could see individual buildings and streets and rivers.

But the Germans interfered with my reverie. I hit the ground automatically, and that was fortunate, for again the bursts were right on top of me. The earth shook under my body, and the air sizzled with the sound of fragments zooming by like hornets on the prowl. My hands shook. I counted, one, two, three, four bursts. Then came the moment of decision. In a split second I made up my mind that I should move, that these four shells constituted a group, that there would not be a fifth shell for a few seconds. Then I jumped up and ran for the abandoned Italian pillbox on the top of the hill.

The Priest tank destroyer was still firing furiously from the road. A General Sherman tank had come up to supply extra fire power, and there was a great welter of cardboard shell containers in the street. Abruptly, German shelling stopped.

I hitched a ride back to Scaletta, to the railroad station, where Brigadier Currie's headquarters had been set up. Somehow, the Germans had discovered the location of the headquarters, and put a concentration of shells into it. A blond private told us that "about twenty" people had been killed or wounded. One shell had landed right next to a Priest tank destroyer near the station. It had killed five out of seven of the gun crew outright, and wounded the sixth man so badly that he was not expected to recover. The private showed us the Priest, which did not seem seriously damaged. But I noticed quickly that the vehicle was spotted with wads of gore and smears of blood. The private looked away and it occurred to me that he might have been the one who escaped injury. "I was," he said.

Around the corner I found our friends, Adlington, Fincham and Bowles. They looked nearly as depressed as the blond gunner with whom I had just talked. Adlington said, "I was just passing H.Q. when the Priest blew up." He looked helplessly at his hands. "I was trying to get the stench of the dead from my hands with kerosene. I can't. I tried to help one fellow who was lying with his insides scooped out, his chest all gone. Two other gunners had been blown in half. There was one fellow lying there with his hand over his eyes. He said, 'Can I have a bit of water? I pulled his arm aside and his eyes didn't move. He was dead."

The brigadier's headquarters had been moved away from the main street of the town, to the side of a hill. Currie appeared no more nervous than usual as he strode to the center of the circle of officers sitting on the ground. He called on a captain for a report of the condition of the road ahead. The captain said that two bridges in the next town to the north had been blown up.

"Well, that's all very good," said the brigadier. "We'll get around along the beach somehow."

The brigadier told us that reconnaissance parties, trying to establish contact with the main body of the 8th Army behind us, had been unsuccessful. The Germans had blown out the coast road in several places. One crater measured 100 yards across. It seemed unlikely that we would be able to establish contact for several days. But at least, there were apparently no large groups of Germans to our rear.

"As you know," he said, "we've been under artillery range all day, from that mountain inland from Tremestieri, the next town north of Scaletta."

He paused and squared his jaw.

"Our intention is to advance north and capture Messina."

Brig. Currie told Montague and me that Lieut. Col. Churchill (I learned later that he was a distant cousin of the Prime Minister), the C.O. of the Commando detachment, would lead the first troops in the advance to Messina. The tanks, Priests and other armored forces would follow. The brigadier gave us permission to go ahead with Churchill.

The Commando C.P. had been set up on the steep hillside near the beach. The captain who took us to Col. Churchill was imbued with a devil-may-care attitude. "We had some fun this morning," he said, talking about the explosion of the German ammunition lorry.

The colonel, a sturdy man with a raggedy blond mustache and yellow hair, was lying in the sand. He had been sleeping when we approached and he nodded pleasantly and told us we would be getting under way at eight o'clock. As we talked, German artillery began to fire, and the shells screamed past and exploded harmlessly in the water. The colonel casually proceeded to eat his messkitful of soup. He suggested that I should get hold of a British helmet during the advance, since some of the men might mistake me for a German if I wore my American headgear. The captain said there were ho British helmets available—the hats of all the soldiers who had been killed today had been reissued. "Except," he said, "that one up the road." I finally took that charred helmet formerly worn by the Tommy who had been burned to death. The discomfort of wearing it was preferable to the prospect of being shot by a Commando.

It was dark when we began to move. I rode in a huge captured German truck with our sappers. We paused for a moment at the top of the hill where I had been so heavily shelled during the day. We passed over the hill, around the curve and down the far slope without being spotted. In the bottom of the valley, our column of vehicles came abruptly to a halt. I jumped down from the truck and walked forward in the moonlight to the head of the procession. Fifty yards beyond the leading truck the road terminated abruptly, the thick tarvia surface broken off like a piece of peanut brittle. The Germans had blown up a bridge; the entire bridge lay at the bottom of the valley.

Brig. Currie, wearing the red-banded cap of a staff officer, strode up to have a look at the demolition. He conferred with an engineer officer, who agreed that the column could make a diversion along the beach and back to the road on the other side of the valley. A tank, rattling and clanking, waddled up to one of the retaining walls at the side of the road. For a moment the monster strained its might against the resisting object, engines roaring, a cloud of smoke rising from the rear, and the tread squeaking against the stone. Abruptly the wall fell away, and the tank backed off, leaving a gap. The sappers were coming up with small beehive mines to finish the job. Then the German mortars opened up.

The Nazis had waited until traffic clogged the road. The first shell landed with a crunch in the valley; the second smashed into a house near the bridge, causing a cascade of tinkling glass. But the sappers had begun the job and they were going to finish it. The demolition men set up a beehive. It went off with a terrific crash. Everyone lent a hand. Even the slender brigadier, in his anxiety to get the job done, tugged at a rock. The mortar shells crashed into the buildings in the valley, and our Priests began to bark back. Great flashes of fire bloomed from the mainland of Italy, and the shells landed with heavy thuds to the north. From somewhere in the darkness of the Straits of Messina, ships were firing, British monitors blasting at the Italian shore batteries.

Meanwhile a detour had been carved to the beach and the column of vehicles was moving at last. Jumping onto a Priest, I rode across the seaward end of the valley. It was nearly midnight.

August 17

With a great grunting and rattling, the Priest began to move on, until, at the end of the little village, Commandos on foot waved us down. "You're now on the bloody front line," said one of the men.

I went forward, sometimes walking with the point elements, sometimes riding in this or that vehicle. There was no firing, until at three-thirty, as I slept in the rear of a truck amidst a pile of infantrymen, I heard the stutter of machine guns ahead. The bright light of an amber flare suddenly appeared, burned noiselessly for several seconds. Possibly it was a signal to batteries on the mainland of Italy. In any case, the big guns flashed from across the Straits of Messina, and we heard the shells sighing through the darkness and landing with a distant thumping sound, somewhat inland.

There was no more firing from Sicily. It began to look as if the Germans were making one of their midnight withdrawals. We had heard no mortar fire since the concentration in the valley north of Scaletta, and the Commandos, heading our attack, had not run into any pockets of resistance, or, until this last burst of machine-gun fire, heard a single shot from German small arms.

It was about four o'clock.

I rode on the sapper truck inching along the road to Messina. I slept when I could amongst the tangle of equipment and humanity. Each time I sensed that the vehicle had stopped and the sappers were piling out, I climbed down to watch the proceedings.

The sweepers went quickly to work. Each man walked cautiously over the suspect ground with his "Hoover," so called because of its resemblance to the well-known vacuum cleaner. Whenever one of the electric mine-locators detected a buried explosive, the man, falling on his knees, scooped the earth away from the lethal instrument. Then he lifted the bomb gently from its hole with bare hands, trusting to the responsiveness of sensitive fingers to warn him of booby traps.

The blond Commando colonel rolled up in his jeep. He said vigorously, "We're going to hook trailers onto the tanks so that all the troops will be lorry-borne. That will step things up a bit. We've got to get to Messina." He unfolded a map and waved a hand at the road indicated along the coast. "We've got five valleys to get through; that, that, that, that, that."

I climbed back on the truck and we moved along the road to Messina. As we neared the village of Tremestieri, we saw signs of recent German evacuation. On the beach, strung with barbed wire for defense against a possible Allied landing, we spotted eight large German artillery pieces, each carefully covered with canvas. A little sapper sergeant waved happily toward them. "All ready to knock 'ell out of Italy," he said.

The people of Tremestieri were out in force, lining the streets to see the *"Inglesi"* coming into the village. They swarmed up to us and lambasted us with bunches of grapes, pears, nuts and even melons. We had never heard such recriminations against the Germans anywhere in Sicily. "The *Tedeschi*," said the Italians, "stole everything, shot people, took their food." I stopped to talk to a Sicilian who spoke English with an American accent, and he said, "The Germans come into the houses, they take what they want. Yesterday they shot a boy, about sixteen-seventeen years old. He wouldn't give them his car."

When were the Germans last in this town? I wanted to know. How far were they from here?

The Sicilian said nervously that the *"Tedeschi"* had departed last night. As if to contradict him, we heard an explosion ahead of us, and saw a huge cloud of smoke rising. Evidently the enemy had not yet left the island.

Farther up the road we came upon the explanation of the explosion. In a broad valley north of Tremestieri we were confronted by a great gap, where the bridge had been broken off jaggedly. Our column halted, for the drop to the stream bed was too abrupt to be negotiated. Sappers went to work with bulldozers and beehives. The colonel looked impatiently at his watch. It was about eight-fifteen now and every moment was precious to him. He was anxious that his troops should arrive in Messina before the Americans. "Going to do a bit of reconnaissance," he said. I asked if I might go with him, and he answered, "Jump aboard."

I had not been prepared for the adventure which we now undertook. Goaded by the colonel, Trooper Bill Holmes, the driver, guided our jeep through a diversion and onto the road beyond. We passed the point of our column, creeping cautiously along the wall of buildings, keeping a sharp lookout for enemy snipers. The colonel urged Trooper Holmes to drive faster and faster toward the city. "If we get there quickly enough, we can round up that mayor chap," he said, enthusiastically. "Be nice if we could sort of capture the city." I ventured that it might be wise to stop and see if there were any snipers and mines about. The colonel didn't seem particularly disturbed. He merely told the driver to slow down a little and then picked up a submachine gun which had been lying on the floor.

I noticed a great Scotch sword and bagpipes in the rear of the jeep. The colonel told me, laughingly, that he always took them into battle, and that Brig. Currie was similarly equipped. If the Fourth Armored Brigade should be the first outfit into Messina, then we might expect to hear the skirling of the pipes.

I watched the road carefully, hoping I might be able to spot a mine before we ran over it. I was reassured when the colonel put on his helmet; that indicated that perhaps he was growing a little more cautious. I continued to feel very conspicuous, sitting up in the high rear seat, unarmed, and looking into the empty windows of the myriad houses, each window seeming black and mysterious, like the eyesocket of a skull.

Suddenly we heard the popping of rifle fire from the city to the north. We slowed, and the colonel lifted his tommygun into the ready position. I expected that at this moment, German snipers would open up on us, and I had visions of a squad of Nazi infantry, running from a side street, surrounding and capturing us.

Miraculously, when we reached the last bridge before Messina and looked into the windows of the buildings on the far side and studied the pavement for signs of mines, no one shot at us and the bridge did not explode underneath our wheels. We had reached our objective!

We crossed the bridge. My heart suddenly stopped and fell away when I saw something moving in the wreckage of a house. A human form stirred in the darkness and, fascinated, I watched. Suddenly the face of a mad old hag appeared, the gums bared in a snarl. It might have been a smile, but there was no mirth in it. Only strange animal sounds, which could not have been words in any language, came from the toothless mouth. The old woman, the first human being we had seen in this deserted city, had been shellshocked into insanity.

We quickly recovered from the sight. We had to be very much on the alert for German snipers and machine gunners. One grenade tossed from a house could kill all of us. if we failed to see the enemy in time. We drove into the shattered town.

We saw two civilians and they ran from us. Three men, in peasant clothing, wandered through the rubble of the street, and we shouted at them and motioned to them to come over. They came, nervous and shifty-eyed, and I asked them in pidgin Italian, *"Dove Tedeschi?"* (Where are the Germans?) I could not understand their answer.

A well-dressed man who actually wore a tie and collar came along and offered to tell us whatever we wanted to know. He said that the Germans had left the city this morning, except for a few snipers. The information did not make us more comfortable. But the colonel's mind was apparently occupied with something of greater importance. Assuming that I knew a little Italian, the colonel said, "Ask the chap if he knows where the mayor is."

The Sicilian answered that, yes, he would be very glad to show us where the mayor was; in fact, he was a personal friend of the mayor. The gentleman appeared to be respectable, and insisted that he was a well-known physician. We asked him to sit on the hood of the jeep and guide us to the mayor. He accepted with alacrity—he had been eyeing the colonel's tommygun with awe—and we started through the battered main street of Messina. We drove through a park, where several old German field pieces had been abandoned, and a few wrecked cars lay. We were going to ask about the *"Americani,"* when suddenly we saw an American soldier in the street. "Sure, we been in here two hours," said the soldier, who wore a sergeant's stripes and whose name was Pete Sumers—of Sturgis, S. D. "The general took the mayor and the police chief back to headquarters."

There was some solace for energetic Col. Churchill, however, in the bit of information passed on by the Italian doctor: about 500 Germans had been evacuated from the southern beaches of the city—where we had entered—only an hour before we got there.

The colonel, with his force of one driver and one correspondent, could not have arrived much sooner without being blown up or captured.

We dropped the doctor, and drove through the streets, looking for more Americans. Near the park, I found them. A command car drove up, carrying a general and Mike Chinigo, INS correspondent who had been covering the American 3rd Division. Chinigo told me that he had come in with the first patrol, and assisted in negotiations for the surrender of the city.

Then we heard the clattering and roaring of tanks, and saw Brig. Currie's Sherman, flying its little pennant from the aerial, rolling down the main street. The other five tanks of the 4th Armored Brigade force came up behind. Commandos, smiling and shouting, sprawled over the exteriors of the tanks, and the little parade was made festive with many-colored flowers thrown by Sicilians. Some of the dirty-faced soldiers clutched huge bunches of grapes.

Brig. Currie dismounted from his tank and, at about the same time, an American command car bearing the three silver stars of a lieutenant general rolled up. Gen. Patton, dazzling in his smart gabardines, stepped out and shook hands with the tall, lean brigadier.

"We got in about ten," said Currie. "It was a jolly good race. I congratulate you."

We wandered about the town looking at the broken buildings and the handful of lean and dirty Sicilians in the streets. About five-sixths of the population had left the city when the bombings began.

As we walked, we heard the booming of our own artillery firing from some place in Messina. From the water front, when we looked out over the wrecks of boats and across the blue Straits of Messina, we saw the spouts of shellfire leaping from the water and into the sand on the shore of Italy. Some of the shells were falling into the buildings of the mainland. We had reached the gateway to the European continent.

From Italian territory came the sounds of fast-paced antiaircraft fire. Black bursts smeared the sky and, in the bright sunshine, swift-moving dots, that were Allied aircraft, were getting into position to drop their bombs on Italy. The tempo of the firing increased, and then we heard the distant thudding of bombs, saw the clouds of smoke rising from Reggio. More of our guns were firing from Sicily.

Enemy land batteries were returning the fire. Lost in my meditation about the closeness of Europe, I had forgotten how dangerous that closeness could be. The first shell shrieked. I saw it blast against the concrete retaining wall on which I was standing. A split second later, two more shells landed, then burst less than 100 yards away. I ran back from the water front between two houses. The next shell smashed into one of the structures. I headed for a British scout car which looked familiar. The driver was frantically trying to start the engine, to get away from the shells. "Wait for me!" I shouted, and jumped on the running board. As the car got under way and two more shells exploded on the water front, I realized that I had seen the vehicle before. It was the RAF liaison car, and inside were my friends, Adlington, Fincham and Bowles.

August 20

Well, Sicily is finished. Today Gen. Alexander, commander in chief of British Forces in Sicily, gave us a résumé of the campaign. At Cassibili, the handsome British leader told us that he had been very much surprised by the rapidity of the Axis defeat. "If you had asked me how long the campaign in Sicily would take, I would have said, 'Anything up to three months.'" I recalled what Gen. Eisenhower had said.

The dapper man—with a dark mustache, wrinkled brow and sharp nose—looked like a slightly more robust Somerset Maugham. He spoke with the "Eton stutter," which is so characteristic of many British officers.

The general said that the Germans in Sicily had been "getting what we got in France," that the Allied bombing, because of their air superiority, had been "oh, terrific, oh, terrific . . . ask the prisoners about it . . . it's unbearable." Yes, the Germans "put up a wonderful fight without air support . . . It shows they're very brave men."

The German, said Alexander, is a "magnificent fighter . . . and don't you belittle him—it isn't fair to our own splendid troops."

The general credited airborne forces with helping the main American force to get ashore near Gela, with the comment, "We can step up efficiency of airborne operations to eighty percent on the next operation, one hundred percent on the next one beyond." He praised the "American friends of mine" for a "remarkable military engineering accomplishment" in building roads over the roughest country.

But these were routine matters. The reporters' eyes looked up from their notebooks and watched when he began to speak about Italy.

"I think the enemy will reinforce Italy all he can. But can he? What's he got? Can he withdraw forces from Russia? I think not. Can he withdraw them from Northern France or Norway? I think not. The Russians know Germany has been badly broken now. The Russians are not going to give up. The end is not going to come next month, but probably sometime in the next year. As long as the Russians go on fighting the German, we've got him, we've got him, you see."

We wanted some indication of the time when Italy might be invaded and Gen. Alexander implied that it might happen before winter. "Since we have such terrific air supremacy, the weather is bound to affect us, and sure to help the German. Winter is a handicap to us."

"If we can get into Italy, we can make Corsica and Sardinia untenable. We will be in a position to hit France and become a menace to the Balkans."

The Best Laid Plans . . .

WITH ONLY THE STRAITS OF MESSINA SEPARATING OUR forces from the Italian mainland, it was no military secret where the coming amphibious landing would be made. But when? It was easy to guess that it would come before the end of the summer. Now, back in Algiers, we saw signs and portents which indicated that we did not have too much time.

In the sunny sidewalk, café of the Hotel Aletti, I met Lieut. Col. David Laux of the Troop Carrier Command. That outfit—an air transport group—had flown our parachute troops into Sicily. Through the grapevine I had heard that the Command would play an important role in the invasion.

Col. Laux, public relations chief for the Carrier Command, was, of course, noncommittal, but said that he would like to have me come along "in case anything happens."

Tonight, we heard that the quota of correspondents accompanying the expedition would be limited. Maj. Marty Sommers, a former *Saturday Evening Post* editor now with the P.R.O., was very mysterious about the job, very confidential. He hinted I might get an exciting story if I went with the airborne troops.

August 24

This morning, Pete Huss told me, "Well, you've got it. You got the airborne assignment. You're to go in and land with the gliders. Or parachute, if you want."

I canvassed the P.R.O. for a bedding roll, knapsack, messkit, map case—most of which are usually left behind or lost in the last campaign. I searched for an air mattress, that golden prize of every field soldier's possessions.

I also made the usual mental preparations for the ordeal—which are getting to be almost automatic. I found a quiet room where I could sit and look down on the streets of Algiers, and come to an understanding with myself.

Always before a mission I try to calculate the odds. This is a dangerous job, no denying that. Airborne attacks always are.

I figured my chances of getting killed or wounded would be three or four out of ten. I had the customary confidence that the worst could not happen to me; that chance would stay on my side.

All over North Africa and in our Sicilian bases, thousands of men these days must be going through some such meditations. For most of the outfits involved in the invasion have already been alerted.

In my case, there is some solace in sticking my neck out: there might be a good story in it.

August 26

Still there is no word about the exact date of leaving, so comradely Quent Reynolds, who is my roommate in the Aletti, Clark Lee of INS, novelist John Steinbeck, Jack Belden of *Time* and various other unassorted characters retired to the room of a certain "mystery man" this afternoon and discovered some Scotch. Anyone who could produce Scotch in Algiers was rightly named a "mystery man." People gradually accumulated around the oasis. One of them was Bob Hope, who had just come back from a tour of Sicily.

August 27

This morning, at about twelve o'clock, I had word that I was to leave in an hour. So in a great rush, I hurried out to the airfield, and got aboard a DC-3 which was going to Soose, where I was to report. Among the passengers were Cy Korman of the Chicago *Tribune* and George Dorsey of *The Stars and Stripes*, all destined for airborne assignments. We landed near Soose and drove to the headquarters of the 82nd Airborne Division in a steaming-hot desert plain. In the camp, a group of tents and Quonset huts, we talked with Col. George Lynch, Intelligence Officer of the Division. He said he would send us into the next operation in gliders, if we so desired. Korman and I both indicated our assent. It will be the first time that American glider troops go into action.

August 29

This morning Col. Laux told us of the projected operation. The colonel nervously warned us, "It would mean shooting if any of you so much as breathe a word about it."

He shut the window as he laid out large maps of Italy on the floor. He told us that the main amphibious landing was to be south of Naples. He did not say just where, but indicated the Bay of Salerno casually with his index finger. "The object of the main force is to cut off the lower part of Italy and capture Naples. The job of the 82nd Airborne Division and the Troop Carrier Command is this: To make a separate landing to the north, dig in and hold on." Again, he did not mention a specific place but swept one hand across the map of Italy north of Naples. "Our job is to land behind the German lines, disrupt their communications, blow up their bridges and hold certain points at all costs. Maybe we'll be able to pin a large force of Germans between the airborne and the main forces. This is the first real test, the first chance, to prove to the world what airborne troops can really do."

Tonight, in the officers' billet where I am staying at Soose, I chanced upon a startling bit of news. One of the pilots, Capt. Ozzie Warner, breezed in with the latest dope from Palermo, whence he had just come.

"Well, the war's over, fellas," he began. "We won't have to go over now."

He was answered by a chorus of Bronx cheers.

"No foolin'," said Ozzie. "A little Savoia-Marchetti tri-motor, with Italian markings, came in to the field this afternoon. All planes were grounded. That's why I saw it all. There wasn't a single ack-ack gun fired.

"Sure's I'm alive, a tall man in an Italian uniform—Italian green anyhow—got out. And who do you think came out to meet him? Gen. Patton!"

It sounded good. We waited for the rest.

Ozzie described the events of the afternoon with all the excitement of a Bill Corum giving a blow-by-blow report from the ringside. "The plane was all black. It had white circles on the wings, and a broad white stripe on the tail. It looked to me like they had covered over the insignia. It was a little tri-motor, a Savoia-Marchetti. It had the big tail and the three fans, overlapping. It was all shiny, just like new. The engines must have been new, or shined up.

"The field was closed between three and five. That's why I saw it all. I couldn't get out. Just before the plane with three fans came in, a C-47 landed. It was Gen. Patton's. He must have flown in from some other place just to see this guy."

"It sounds like Ozzie's been havin' pipe dreams," one of the officers suggested.

"I'd be as mad as a son of a bitch if those Ginzos quit now," said another.

August 30

Korman and I went for a ride this morning in a "whisper ship," as the glider-borne troops call them. It was just a routine practice flight, but it confirmed some of the stories I had heard about the gliders. For instance, that air sickness was very common among glider troops. "They just sit and puke," an officer once told me. The reason is that all movements are intensified, since the tow rope acts as a pendulum.

Korman and I soon found this out for ourselves. Our pilot, Lieut. Frank Moore, of Queens Village, Long Island, told us, as we prepared for take-off, that we should be sure to fasten our safety belts to avoid being thrown around unduly. The "whisper ship" got into the air, and the horizon began to reel with an incessant bouncing, turning and yawing. We leaned against the vibrating canvas walls—which one might penetrate with a forceful finger—and attempted to gasp fresh air from the tiny vents along the side of the cabin. Moore laughingly pointed to the "acceleration indicator" which shows the severity of the air bumps over which the glider is passing, and said,

"It registers two-and-a-half gees, and three-and-a-half is about all we can take. It's rough all right."

We cut away from the tow plane. We were free. Now we found that glider flying can be pleasant. The raucous noise of the wind, whistling and roaring over our canvas conveyance while we were in tow, diminished to a whisper, and we floated in the sky, turning and diving like a power plane. When we came in for our landing, I realized something else about gliders: that there can be no second approach to a landing. Either the pilot's judgment is correct or he's out of luck. When I asked Moore if our approach did not seem a little high, he answered, "I can always get rid of a little altitude, but if I'm a little low, it'll get rid of me."

We came in to the ground with a great rush—the landing speed of a glider is about ninety miles an hour—while Pilot Officer Sam Burnett pulled the "spoiler" lever, activating wing slots which act as brakes. We were safely on the ground, and I thought, "If it is like this on the actual run, it won't be so bad. But the run is to be made at night into enemy territory. There's no chance of rehearsing, to make sure that we land in the right place."

Back at my billet tonight, I talked to Ozzie Warner, who had been to Palermo again today, and he said that the field had been closed this afternoon while the black "mystery ship" took off. "It flew on a direct bearing for Rome with an escort of six Spitfires."

August 31

Today we learned that the main Allied force will land at the Gulf of Salerno, about twenty miles south of Naples.

An 82nd Airborne officer told me that the parachute and glider troops will drop on the Volturno River, forty miles to the north of the main beachhead.

Our mission, the officer informed us, was to blow up the bridges and hold the river at all costs. Two parachute regiments would jump in, grab the D.Z. (Dropping Zone) and set up radio beacons for the gliders. The main force would join us as soon as they could break through—maybe two, maybe seven days after the landing. We'd hold on. If the Italians would fight as little as they did in Sicily, that'd be all right with us.

September 1

Korman and Paul Green, a *Stars and Stripes* reporter, and I have been assigned to the 504th Parachute Infantry Regiment for the invasion of Italy. We reported to regimental headquarters on the sun-baked, dusty plain near Kairouan. The glider-borne troops with which we will be traveling will be attached to the 504th.

We met Col. Reuben H. Tucker, of Ansonia, Conn., C.O. of the 504th, and listened while the blond, barrel-chested parachutist briefed his officers on the mission to Capua.

The colonel was enthusiastic. "This is a truly airborne operation, one that's never been tried before. We used to think about something like this and dream about it. And it's not goin' to be easy; it's goin' to be rough. We're goin' in there and we're goin' to hold this place and we're goin' to stay there." The deep-voiced colonel was discharging his words like volleys. "We've got a big job on our hands. I hope you all realize it. We're really cookin' with gas."

September 2

Tonight, in the situation hut, details of the mission were discussed, including the disposal of personal effects in case one got killed. Col. Tucker said jokingly, "If I get killed, turn my personal effects over to the vultures." (He meant fellow-officers who would grab his belongings in case he became a casualty.) Maj. Don B. Dunham, of Lemon Cove, Cal., said, "I want you to be damn sure that I'm killed, first." (He was killed at Altavilla in Italy.)

This evening we were introduced to Capt. Nock W. Russell, of Ackerman, Miss., a cheerful and smiling young man who will lead the glider-borne artillery with which we are to land. It was reassuring to meet someone who does not share the average parachutist's skepticism about gliders. "I'm damned if I'd want to go down in one of those chutes," said Russell. "I'll take the safe way, and ride in comfort."

September 3

This morning the Italian radio announced that Allied troops had landed on the southern tip of Italy! A broadcast by B.B.C. said simply that the British had landed in Calabria.

The parachutist officers followed the sparse radio bulletins with tense interest. The soldiers, inured to the incessant alarums and excursions which are the paratrooper's life, were taking it calmly. I spotted a group of men sitting under a dwarf olive tree, playing a unique game with a captured Italian generator. The generator was equipped with foot pedals, like a bicycle, intended for use with a field radio. The game was to see how long one could make the gears spin by giving a single determined whirl to the apparatus.

Tonight Col. Tucker was absent at a meeting of the airborne bigwigs in 82nd Division Headquarters. Coming back late, he summoned his staff. We were not admitted. When we asked him for information, he simply looked mysterious.

September 4

At breakfast the colonel said nothing when we asked if the American plans had been changed. When we pressed him for information after the meal, he seemed to be bursting with some momentous secret. All he would say was that the gliders were not going on this show. "But this story will bust the headlines wide open," he added mysteriously.

Later in the day, a high officer at another place dropped us a very definite hint of the carefully guarded news. "You won't have to go by parachute and you won't have to go by glider," he said. "There'll be another way, maybe a plane landing." We asked him where our objective might be. He said, "I can't tell you, but"—and he looked at us slyly—"I dropped a penny in a fountain in Rome, and you know what that means."

Col. Tucker still would tell us nothing. Even in a pep talk to his troops today, he outlined the previously planned mission to Capua, as if nothing at all had been altered.

We heard by radio this evening that the British 8th Army forces in the tip of Italy are pushing ahead with little resistance.

September 5

We took off this morning for Sicily for the attack on Italy.

Col. Tucker, his staff officers and some of his troops had flown to Sicily in other planes. I joined them at the bomb-wrecked airfield near Headquarters of the 504th. I discovered that even the battalion commanders still have not heard about the attack on Rome—if that's what it's going to be.

September 6

This afternoon I flew with Col. Tucker to Airborne Headquarters. At the Intelligence tent, he was given his envelope of orders. He took the envelope to a deserted corner of the olive grove where the camp was set up. Then he secretly read the final details of a mission which may be the hottest in the history of this war.

Tonight the colonel's room in the barracks was darkened. Flashlights were directed at the door to see if anyone was listening. The colonel was confiding information to his closest intimates. I heard the concluding words, "Now you fellows know, and I know what I'm talkin' about. But if anybody so much as mentions the name of *that town*, so help me, I'll have him court-martialed and shot!"

September 7

From scraps of information which I have been able to pick up, I am now certain that the Italians will co-operate in this mission, to the extent of lighting the airfields near Rome, turning over trucks to the troops for transport, and actively supporting our airborne division with two Italian divisions now bivouacked near Rome.

I heard that the guards in our camp area have been instructed that anyone leaving the camp without permission will be shot. The order gave rise to many wild rumors amongst the men: that we were destined to jump on Genoa or even Berlin.

This morning I hitched an airplane ride to Headquarters. The pilot was none other than Capt. Ozzie Warner, who told me that the mysterious Man in Green had made two more visits to Palermo, and that Gen. Patton had been on hand each time to receive him.

Headquarters of the Troop Carrier Command, in an old schoolhouse, were clogged with busy people. The only calm-looking person I saw in the building was the austere, bald-headed acting head of the T.C.C. The G-3 room, where operations were planned, was full of gesticulating officers.

From a well-informed friend I learned a few facts about the coming landing in Rome: There will be two landings on two different airfields. The first waves will land by parachute to make sure that beacons are lighted for the bulk of the planes which are to follow later. There will probably be a triumphal procession into Rome. Then the Italian divisions in the Rome area will group themselves with the 82nd Airborne for the defense of the city. Other American forces may land from ships on the beaches to the west of Rome.

September 8

Korman, Green and I sat at the foot of an olive tree with Col. Lynch, He told us that, according to latest information, the Italians will light the way into the field for us, turn on beacons which will lead our planes to Rome, and even make a diversion for us with their own planes, shooting down German aircraft which might interfere. There are strong German forces in Italy, including a Nazi mechanized outfit only ten miles away, and two German divisions in the immediate vicinity. But if we move quickly and deploy our forces skillfully, we may be able to influence the fate of the entire Italian campaign. We will even have our own fighter planes installed in the Italian airfields around Rome before nightfall; and the Italian planes will be at our disposal, with their pilots.

Col. Lynch assigned Korman and me to the two leading planes, which will carry Capt. Nock Russell's battery of formerly glider-borne artillery. We stopped at Russell's tent, in one of the many bivouac areas overlooking the airfield, and made arrangements to meet him at about four o'clock at the field.

*

Korman and I reached the long line of transport planes standing in close order like brooding beetles. A crowd of AMG officials were grouped around the leading plane, waiting for final orders to get aboard. Capt. Russell superintended, smiling as usual but rather curt.

It was after five, and we were still waiting for orders. All of us were growing extremely fidgety. Suddenly a jeep dashed up, trailing a great plume of dust. A major and lieutenant in suntans, wearing the Air Corps insignia, jumped out. The major went into a whispered conversation with Russell. The lieutenant confided to me, "There's been a reprieve of twenty-four hours."

Russell, gathering all the passengers of the planes together, told us only, "Stick with the planes, get aboard. They will be dispersed.

Don't leave the planes. Don't talk to anyone. Be ready to leave at any time."

We taxied to a dispersal area across the field, with a sergeant at the controls. A colonel who was to pilot the ship in which I was riding had left. As we reached the dispersal area, Capt. Russell told us he had orders that those who had been briefed should be under guard. We climbed out and stood beside the plane.

Luckily our parking spot happened to be near field headquarters, a first-aid station. We were startled, a few minutes after we dismounted, when two jeeps, arriving amidst clouds of dust, discharged four men wearing stars on their collars. One of them was a handsome, lean man in the dashing jump suit of the paratroops— Gen. Ridgway, leader of the Airborne Division. The other officers with star-studded uniforms were Maj. Gen. Lemnitzer, American officer assigned to Gen. Alexander's staff; Maj. Gen. Cannon, second in command to Gen. Spaatz, Chief of Allied Air Forces in the Mediterranean; and a general of the Troop Carrier Command.

It was quite a galaxy. We watched, fascinated, while this group adjourned to the first-aid tent. We craned our necks to see as much as we could of the developments inside. The officers were conducting an intense conference. The driver of one of the jeeps waved at the Red Cross flag and said, "I guess they're cuttin' up Italy on the operatin' table right now."

The generals hurried to their jeeps. The general of the airborne division turned to us and said, "I advise you fellows to get on a radio. Gen. Eisenhower is going to speak." We rushed to a radio at T.C.C. Headquarters. We listened nervously to the static, which was about all that came over the loudspeaker. Nor were we any more successful in our attempts to hear a speech by Marshal Badoglio, which, we were told, would closely follow Eisenhower's. But Bill Graffis, one of the

P.R.O. officers, came dashing out of the near-by building and told us that Gen. Eisenhower had announced that Italy had surrendered, and that Badoglio, coming on the air directly afterward, had confirmed the news.

By seven o'clock, the word of Italy's capitulation had reached the people who began to celebrate riotously. The war was over for them, and in the evening throngs milled in the streets long after dark. I saw the Sicilian *signorinas* directing soft glances toward American service men.

September 9

This afternoon a B.B.C. radio bulletin reported a speech by President Roosevelt, saying that the Mediterranean fighting was not yet over, that we would have to drive the Germans out of Italy as we drove them out of Sicily. There was an item about the main amphibious force which this morning invaded Italy at 4 A.M. The Allied force had landed south of Naples. There was no statement about the degree of opposition. British forces which had landed in Calabria a few days ago had crossed the toe of Italy. The Germans had already seized Rome, and imprisoned hostages. If we had only carried out our mission, we would be grappling with the Germans now, and Rome might be ours instead of theirs.

We heard that Brig. Gen. Maxwell Taylor and Col. William Tudor Gardiner, who had been in Rome making secret arrangements for the landing, had returned. We succeeded in arranging an interview with Col. Gardiner. The burly colonel, once a famous oarsman and former Governor of Maine, led us to a secluded room on the third floor of the schoolhouse, closed the door, and unfolded scribbled notes on the aborted airborne mission to Rome. He read them in the smooth unruffled voice of the trained speaker. He began:

"We left Palermo at about two o'clock on the morning of September seventh, on a British PT-boat. We cruised during the dark through rough seas, and at daybreak found ourselves off Sicily. At 6:45 we sighted an Italian corvette. We came alongside, but, as the waves were high, stood off and waited for a small boat which came over from the corvette. The captain of the British boat had expected one Italian naval officer for the return trip, but now there appeared, in addition, about ten more Army officers, in the small boat. We boarded it and proceeded to the corvette.

"We were met on board by an admiral. He spoke English and French very well, and seemed very cordial, but he knew no details of our mission. We lunched with him on the lower bridge. He told us that he is a native of Gela, Sicily, that he had been well received on a cruise with the Italian naval forces to the United States Southern and West Coasts.

"We arrived at the Italian port of Gaeta about seventy-five miles south of Rome, at about 5:30 in the afternoon. We went ashore in a closed boat. Our insignia was hidden, and we were instructed by the admiral to look disconsolate, as if we were prisoners. I put on a British cape and carried my officer's blouse. I had removed the Air Medal, the Legion of Honor and the Silver Star, but I had left my wings and the ribbon of the Army of Occupation from the last war on the blouse, and did not want it to be seen.

"We walked immediately from the launch to a naval staff car. Then we went through the town, slowing up to avoid passing two truckloads of German soldiers. On the outskirts of the town, we were transferred to an ambulance. Gen. Taylor, the admiral and I, and another man wearing civilian clothes, hat in the rear of the ambulance. Visibility from the ambulance was poor, but we could see German soldiers on the road as we passed through villages. There were periodic road blockades, merely light stone walls around which a car could drive. Some of them were guarded. Twice we were stopped. The driver showed a paper, and the rear admiral leaned forward and showed his uniform. There was just a little slit in the forward end of the ambulance compartment through which we could be seen. We looked disconsolate again.

"We arrived at the Palazzo Caprara, in Rome, at about 8:30. The building is part of the war office, and we were led to rooms which had been prepared for us, small chambers, each with a bed and a tin wash-stand.

"We were met by Maj. Marchesi, who had been present at the conferences with Gen. Castellano. Castellano had been negotiating the surrender of Italy." [Note: he had been the man in the mysterious black plane which Ozzie Warner had seen at Palermo.] "We were anxious to meet Castellano, but did not see him until the following morning. We also met several staff officers to Gen. Carboni. Carboni is chief of the army corps defending Rome, and, since the eighteenth of August, Chief of Italian Intelligence. One of the officers dined with us, and described Gen. Carboni in very glowing terms, as an anti-Fascist. He suggested that we were tired, that we would be left alone for the night, and that we could see the general in the morning. It appeared to me that they were attempting to stall, and later it was evident that they did not expect us to move so fast: it was stated that they had expected our operation September tenth to fifteenth, but nearer the fifteenth. Now we insisted that we should have a conference that evening, and it was arranged that Gen. Carboni should come in after dinner.

"At about ten-fifteen, Gen. Carboni arrived with a map showing the disposition of his four divisions around Rome. But, the Germans had greatly increased their forces in the vicinity. Formerly there had been 3,000 Germans to the south and 8,000 to the north of Rome. German forces had come in since the change in government, and now there were 12,000 north of Rome with 120 heavy and 150 light tanks; and 24,000 to the south. Besides these, there were about 12,000 more Germans around Rome on both sides of the Tiber, with 100 artillery pieces, mostly 88-mm. That's 48,000. The Germans were well supplied and equipped.

"The Germans were suspicious. They had cut off the Italians' gasoline supply and some of their ammunition. There were only twenty rounds for some of the pieces. When I asked Carboni about getting more ammunition, his only reply was that we had destroyed the largest factory. He said that he had the facilities for only a few hours' fighting; that if he moved his armored units more than thirty miles, they would be immobilized. He said that it was impossible to protect the airfields for us unless we gave him ammunition and gas. He added that our force was too small. His view was that if an armistice were declared, the Germans would at once march on and take Rome and restore a Fascist government. His only solution was for us to make a large landing north of Rome. He said that Salerno was too far south; that the natural line of defense for the Germans was across Italy through Formia or Minterna, near Gaeta. Of course, the Italians were not supposed to know that our landing was going to come off in the Gulf of Salerno.

"We asked him about Gen. Castellano's mission and his solemn promises. He said that Castellano did not have the facts, and thought that the Italians had gas and ammunition—and was unaware of the complete disposition of the Germans as of today. Gen. Taylor then stated that, in view of the serious nature of the change in plans, he must ask that the matter be taken to the head of the government. A meeting was then arranged with Marshal Badoglio. Gen. Carboni finally asked Gen. Taylor to concur in recommending that the airborne mission to Rome should be canceled. But this, Taylor said, could not be done: the Italians must assume responsibility for adopting a position and he would report it. Gen. Taylor handled that very well. The Italians were evidently trying to jockey us into a position where we should make that decision.

"At about midnight, we covered our insignia, and drove to the residence of Marshal Badoglio. We were stopped at the entrance to the Marshal's house, and then allowed to pass. There was quite a sizable garden with trees. It was a modern home with much marble and tile. The household servants were up because an alert had been sounded. Gen. Carboni was closeted with Badoglio for fifteen minutes and then the marshal received us in his study. He is an old man, bald-headed, with a very intelligent face, and the voice of an actor. He looks military, yet rather benevolent.

"Badoglio greeted us very cordially and with much assurance of his desire for co-operation. If he declared an armistice, the Germans would take Rome and put in a government unfriendly to us. He suggested that an attack at Salerno might provide advance bases for a landing to the north. I suggested that while he was planning to save Rome, it might be necessary for us to destroy it. He answered that he hoped we would not bomb our friends; why did we not rather bomb the passes in the mountains to the north and cut the German lines?

"Gen. Taylor repeated the statement that the situation was serious, and commented on the consequences of the Italians' apparent change in attitude. Badoglio said he was helpless in the matter and accepted the suggestion that he write his own message, declaring his decision. This he did in Italian. He asked Gen. Taylor to agree, but Gen. Taylor said he could only transmit the message and that the decision must be made by the Italian government.

"We parted with expressions of regret, respect and friendship. Badoglio and Carboni stood at attention and clicked their heels. We returned the gesture, endeavoring to click our heels as loudly as the Italians. There was quite a contest. Badoglio said in a soft voice that he had been a soldier for fifty years. Messages from Badoglio and Gen. Taylor, to Gen. Eisenhower, were dispatched. Gen. Taylor's message asserted that, due to the failure of the Italians to declare an armistice and to guarantee airdromes, the landing in Rome was impossible, and that we awaited instructions. We left shortly before one o'clock."

We asked Col. Gardiner how he felt about the Italians' backing down at this time, and he replied, "I was a little disturbed." That was certainly from the department of understatement. The colonel continued with his report:

"At about 8:45 this morning Maj. Marchesi appeared. He said that the messages had gone out, and he talked with us for some time and gave us the same reasons for the change in plan. A staff officer arrived and announced messages had been received.

"At twelve o'clock, Gen. Carboni called. He suggested Corsica as a base for landing in the north, saying that an uprising there could be arranged. We had already told him we had decided to return to North Africa, and he agreed to send a deputy chief of staff. We piled into the ambulance and drove to the airfield. We took off in a Savoia-Marchetti tri-motor, and reported to Allied force headquarters that evening."

The truth was all too apparent. Certainly our airborne mission to Rome had gone completely agley.

Action at Altavilla

September 13

FOR FOUR DAYS I HAVE BEEN TRYING TO GET OUT OF SICILY and over to Italy. Elements of the 82nd Airborne Division will go into Italy after all.

The largest part of the 504th Parachute Infantry, under Col, Tucker, will make a jump. But it will be an unopposed drop behind Allied lines in Italy to reinforce a portion of the beachhead which Allied forces have already established in the Bay of Salerno.

The correspondents attached to this Division have decided to travel with another airborne force going into Italy by boat. Our little fleet of LCIs will land at a previously established bridgehead.

This evening, before we sailed, Bill Graffis came down to the boat to give us the latest radio news. He seemed worried.

"It looks tough for the boys at Salerno," he said. "The B.B.C. says the Germans have thrown in tanks. I hope you'll be able to land some place."

September 14

After a day of inching along at low speed across the Mediterranean, we spotted land on our starboard bow. But it was only Palermo! We had not yet left Sicily. Col. Lewis, senior troop officer of our little convoy, went ashore for orders. When he returned to the ship, he told us only that we are proceeding to Italy, and will land some time tomorrow.

September 15

The day dragged. I passed the time listening to paratroop songs and yarns. We were unable to pick up any news bulletins.

It was late in the afternoon when we sighted a dark wall of land rising from the mist of the horizon. It was the towering mountain mass of Italy. From this distance, the wedge of land seemed level-topped, like a plateau. I fancied it looked like the far-spreading curtain of a huge stage. We had arrived.

A destroyer and a corvette emerged from the gloom ahead, then swung around and escorted us. We must be nearing our anchorage. The misty horizon was now marked with dashes of gray, closely spaced. They were the shapes of ships—scores of them.

From the direction of the land, we heard the quick-time drumming of anti-aircraft fire. Col. Lewis busied himself shooting the men below decks. "There's an air-raid condition on," he observed. The drumming increased in tempo and volume, and our own anti-aircraft gunners prepared their weapons. Our fleet churned along at full speed, ready for the expected attack. It seemed a fitting way to reach Italy. Suddenly the quick thudding of the anti-aircraft stopped. The air raid was over.

The dotted gray line of ships in close order in the anchorage emerged as a collection of assorted shapes and sizes in the mist around us. The boat which was to guide us had not shown up. There was nothing to do but wait. We watched the orange flashing of guns several miles away on our left, figuring that they were being fired from ships bombarding German positions farther up on our beachhead.

As night fell, we were lost in the middle of a great throng of ships: depot ships, Liberties, corvettes, PCs, bustling tank lighters and LCIs. Looking for the command ship seemed a hopeless job. Now, with the increasing darkness, it was growing difficult even to distinguish one type of ship from another.

The commodore of our fleet, a British naval lieutenant, was saying in his tired voice through the public-address system to several passing ships, "Can you direct us to the command ship?"

Finally, by pure chance, we nearly collided with the command ship. The commodore's bored voice was amplified by the bullhorn, "Nine British LCIs carrying American airborne troops. Have you any orders?" A voice boomed back from the dark bulk of the ship, telling us to follow the American LCI which would lead us to the beach, two miles to the north.

It was getting darker and darker, with unbelievable rapidity, so that the LCIs which followed us were almost lost from sight. It had become so dark that one felt as if each flash of light from our busy signal lamp would infallibly lead Jerry in to bomb.

The long, low shape of a small ship came sliding directly toward our beam, turned and struck our stern a glancing blow. It was the American LCI which was to guide us to our landing point. The skipper's voice came from the dark, telling us to follow. We swung in a wide circle, blinking toward the other LCIs the information that they should follow along behind us. By this time, however, the LCIs had scattered in an effort to avoid ramming the leader, and they had disappeared into the thickening cold mist.

Maj. Hank Adams, a parachute officer, suggested jokingly, "There'll be LCIs wandering around for days, looking for a beach where they can land. Maybe we'll wind up in Rome or Genoa."

Nevertheless we located a landing spot and shoved in toward the shore. Sticking on a sand bar in ten feet of water, still two hundred yards from land, we backed off and tried again. Then we nosed up onto still another sand bar.

Other LCIs were now coming in. The moon was rising and the rakish shapes of barges could be seen to the left and right of us along the straight line of the beach. Somewhere on land, smoke-laying crews were putting up a screen to protect us from enemy aviation. The smoke added to the shrouding effect of the natural fog on the beach. As we backed off the sand bar, we began to move toward the LCI which had run aground near us. We bumped her hard.

Finally we churned our way into the shoals, dragging our shuddering bottom. The donkey engines began to putter, dropping two ramps, one on each side. Troops filed off the ship, wading through the shallow water toward the beach. The men were pushing carts filled with supplies, grunting and cursing. At last it was our turn. We trudged up the beach.

I lay down on the cool sand, and watched the irregular group of men plodding, silent, patient, like tired beasts of burden, moving mechanically. In the faint moonlight and the clouds of man-made fog that drifted across the beach, they were faceless men, one like the other in an unending procession.

September 16

Shortly after daylight, two jeeploads of officers drove up. They were from the 180th Infantry, part of the 45th American Division, bivouacked near by. One of the officers told me that the 45th, with the 36th, is holding the southern end of the Salerno beachhead. British troops hold the middle of the twenty-mile-long line centering around Salerno itself. American Rangers are dug in on the left flank of the narrow front.

We climbed aboard one of the jeeps and churned down the dusty road to the main highway running inland. I was startled to see four wrecked German Mark IV tanks, which had been hit by artillery and left derelict less than a quarter of a mile from the beach. The Germans had come that close to driving our forces out of Italy.

Farther up the road we passed the dust-covered shapes of P-40 pursuit planes. Just a week after the first landing in the Bay of Salerno, a fighter field was in operation.

Near the airfield stood the massive ruins of the Greek temple of ancient Paestum. Across the road from the temple lay the long, low wall of the old city. We turned into a dusty side road and stopped. Col. Lewis discussed plans for bivouacking his troops in this vicinity.

I jumped off and trekked to the 5th Army C.P., a collection of tents carefully scattered and camouflaged in an olive grove. In a dense brake, we found a large, tidy trailer. It was the headquarters of Lieut. Gen. Mark Wayne Clark, 5th Army Commander. I was taken into the trailer, where the general was giving an interview to Packard of the UP and Shapiro of the Canadian press.

General Clark is a surprisingly young man. I would never have guessed his age at more than thirty-five. Actually he is forty-seven.

The general greeted me cordially, and resumed his interview, saying, "I am a little upset by newspaper reports which have been suggesting that the 5th Army is in desperate straits. . . . Supplies and reinforcements are coming through well. We have our chins up, and we're keeping them up."

After the interview, however, an officer at headquarters told me that, only three days ago, the Germans had almost driven our small force back into the sea. They had attacked with tanks which reached a point only a mile and a half from General Clark's advance headquarters. Our troops had been ordered to hold on as independent units fending for themselves.

At P.R.O. headquarters, in a yellow stucco house, the correspondents were gathered for the morning press conference in the principal room, a bare chamber with a few chairs. Soon a big, flat-nosed chap, introduced as Col. Lazar, hulked into the room. He told us that everything was going well, that the 504th Parachute Infantry had landed from the air behind our lines, that other reinforcements were arriving, and that the British 8th Army would make a juncture within a few hours. They were only a short distance to the south of the Salerno beachhead.

The colonel said that if we wanted to see some excitement this afternoon, we might go to a place called Albanella. The 504th Paratroops were moving up from Albanella to the town of Altavilla. There would probably be quite a fight. The 36th Division had previously been driven out of Altavilla, and it was now in German hands. I started for Albanella with Konnan, Bob Capa of *Life* and Reynolds Packard.

As we rolled through the picturesque mountain valleys, peaceful in the summer sun, I was struck by the fact that Italy seemed a far lovelier land than Sicily. There were tall graceful trees, wooded valleys and hills that reminded me of New England.

On the outskirts of Albanella we spotted Lieut. Forrest Richter, adjutant of the 504th Parachute Infantry, who said, "We jumped behind our lines night before last. No action yet. The rest of the outfit is coming up now."

And soon, bull-chested Col. Tucker strode up. He pointed out our objective, Altavilla, high on a ridge to the northeast. It was a collection of light-colored houses etched on the top of a mountain. Puffs of shellfire were spurting from the pattern of the streets and houses. The Germans were in there, and our artillery was attempting to soften up the town.

Col. Tucker told us how the attack would be made by his troops. "We're going to go way around"—he indicated a wide circle to the right— "and then come up on that ridge overlooking the town."

The calmness of the afternoon was almost startling. While we talked, a line of white ME-109s came over and passed far to the right, curving to dive swiftly into a valley, bombing. "Nasty little fellas, aren't they?" said the colonel.

The afternoon wore on. All the troops had not arrived yet, so we wandered through the little town of Albanella. Except for three or four smashed buildings which had been hit by shells, everything seemed normal. The peasants told us that the Germans had pulled out that morning, blowing up a couple of houses to block the road. Still, the war seemed very unreal.

Korman and I reached the 504th C.P., on the hillside at Albanella, at about seven o'clock, in the dusk. Major Julian Cook, who was temporarily in charge, said that the colonel and a couple of battalions had gone ahead, and should be in the valley beyond. Cook was distressed because he had no telephone or radio contact with Col. Tucker. We asked how we could find him. Cook shrugged his shoulders and pointed down toward the valley. "That's the way," he said.

Darkness had come, and we stumbled down the steep hillside through a rocky orchard. After pumping our weary muscles over the rough ground for a half hour, we had seen no sign of a paratrooper. The darkness was growing quite complete, and we began to wonder if we had gone astray.

Finally we saw a farmhouse, and decided to seek directions. We asked the farmer, "*Dove Americani?*" and "*Dove Tedeschi?*" the customary questions. We gathered that the Americans were only a few hundred yards away and that the Germans had passed through here yesterday.

Then we were stumbling down the valley again. We spread out in a single file, listening intently, for the dangers of running into a German patrol, or being shot at by accident, were considerable. Finally we were challenged, but it was an American voice asking for an American countersign. "Red River," said the voice in the dark, and we answered, with a great deal of relief, "Valley."

The sentry led us to a little group of men, hunched up at a corner in a dirt road, under the lee of a steep bank. The lieutenant in charge told us that the Germans had been putting interdicting artillery fire into the valley. We heard the booming of the battery, then the singing sound as the shells came. We clutched the side of the bank as they burst in a string of explosions. I estimated that they were falling less than 200 yards away.

We decided to go ahead in search of Col. Tucker, halting when we heard the shells coming. We came out of the valley to a fairly level place, and found the colonel's headquarters company in a drainage ditch.

Through the trees the colonel pointed out two high hills, or ridges, with a saddle between. "That hill on the left looks right down on Altavilla," he explained. "That's the main objective. Once we get on to it, it's gonna be hard for the Kraut-heads to stay in Altavilla. That other hill on the right should be in our hands by now."

A clear moon had now risen, and a German artillery observer must have spotted us in the moonlight, for many guns, probably a battalion, began to "zero in" on us. We saw the white flashes from behind the silhouettes of the hills ahead, and in a few seconds, the booming of the guns, the whistling of the shells and the jaw-clenching impact of the explosions, to our left and ahead. Then there were other flashes, from another part of the black cardboard mountains, and these shells screeched over us and blasted into the ground behind, some distance away. We lay as low as we could, for the first battery of German artillery was flashing again—closer. The clamor of the shells was louder, and fragments whistled through the air. I found myself curling up my legs, so that I would be a smaller target. The Germans were really getting our range.

Another pause. We had a few seconds to say nervously that the shells were getting too damned close, and then the guns flashed and boomed and screeched, and this time came close enough to shake the ground under us. Fragments buzzed like bees around us, and I heard a loud, clear gong sound in my ears, like a bell. I felt an impact on top of my helmet. I touched my tin hat with my hand; the fragment had not broken through the metal. I was lucky.

More flashes on the horizon told us that more shells were on the way. Again the booming, and we ducked lower. This time the stick of shells smacked down behind us. We were bracketed. Fragments whizzed through the treetops and we could hear the clipped branches rustling as they hit the ground. Now the other German guns flashed, and we knew these were coming close. The concussion seemed to surround us and crush into our heads, and dirt and heavy limbs of trees came smashing down into our trench in torrents.

"We better get outta here," said the colonel, "They're gettin' the range. Let's go." We shoved off the heavy boughs that were lying in a tangle on top of us. I was surprised at their weight.

We jumped up the bank and sprinted across the field and up a hillside. With the motion of our running we saw a farmhouse jouncing in the moonlight; that would be our immediate objective. We saw another ditch as the bouncing image of the farmhouse grew larger. We scrambled into the ditch, panting. We were just in time. The shells came again and exploded between this trench and the ditch we had just left.

The firing lulled, and in the few seconds when thought comes back again, and motion, when the concussion has done its work and gone, Lieut. Col. Freeman (Leslie G. Freeman, of Cortland, N. Y.), the regimental executive, and Major Dunham, came clumping over the no-man's land between the two ditches. They had stayed behind to care for Capt. Tom Wight, who had been hit by the last shell. He was beyond care. A fragment had struck him squarely in the back.

We worked our way forward, out of the trench and over the open country. We ran by fits and starts, halting to look ahead, moving fast and stopping dead along the hedgerows, stumbling across uneven furrows of plowed fields.

As we moved, the contours of the hills and mountains around us seemed to be changing. I could not be sure that we were heading in the right direction. Other hills and crannies which I had not been able to see from our vantage point back in the valley rose under our eyes and our hurrying feet. Once, when we walked through a dark grove on a hillside, Col. Freeman, beside me, reached over to pick up a black wire shining in the moonlight. That would be a telephone line to a German forward artillery observer's position, perhaps the one who had given our location to the batteries when we were in the ditch back there. Col. Freeman said, as primly as if he had been correcting an erring student's paper (he had been a schoolteacher back in New York), "We'll cut that."

As we marched down the far side of the ridge, and across the valley, we saw the steepest hill of all. Col. Tucker pointed to it as the first of our two objectives. We walked cautiously as we reached the lower slopes, talking only in the softest whispers, careful to watch for cover. We were in dangerous territory.

Artillery fired from *behind* us, German artillery, shooting into our lines.

The hill rose very steeply, but we slogged along. I went up with the point. As we passed through the regularly spaced trees of an olive grove, half way up the slope, I heard the soft challenge, "Red River," and the equally soft response, "Valley" from one of our men. American paratroopers slipped from the black and silver mosaic of moonlight and shadows. They were an advance patrol.

The non-com in charge reported to Col. Tucker. The bulk of their conversation was not audible, but we could hear the colonel's basso booming in something like consternation. Apparently the expected troops had not reached this hill yet. Rube Tucker said to me, "We are the point." He meant that his small headquarters company were apparently the only paratroopers at this sector of the front line. We had reached our first objective, but had less than 150 men with which to hold it and our goal, the hill commanding Altavilla.

But the colonel was determined to "seize and hold," according to the motto of the paratroopers. We dragged leaden-heavy legs to the top of the hill. As I walked across the carpet of moonlight I heard a tense voice snap the silence behind me:

"Keep your hands up—high!"

Turning fast, I saw Major Dunham at a nervous crouch, leveling his .45 at three Germans, who had their hands up. They had thrown their guns on the ground. I helped to frisk them. They were sturdy, muscular men, wearing the usual square-visored khaki caps of the German infantryman.

The prisoners were taken over to the center of the open spot atop the hill, and told to sit down on the ground.

The colonel was setting up outposts around the crown of this hill, when one of the Germans said to me, "Madame, photograph madame." He waved at the foxhole, and repeated, "Madame." But I still did not understand. Then he said, "My wife."

I gathered that he wanted to go to the foxhole to get a picture which he had left behind. A guard stood by with a tommygun. I did not believe that the German would attempt to make a break for it, but I watched him. He picked up a leather case, and showed us a photograph of a *Frau* with a baby. He seemed to deliberate for a moment. Then, suddenly, he jumped across the foxhole and dashed for the thicket. In the long seconds while the German was running for his life, the man with the tommygun hesitated. Someone shouted, "Don't shoot!" and, in the confusion, the German hopped into the thicker brush, and was gone.

There was a great palaver amongst the paratroopers, and we sought to find out which of the soldiers had cried, "Don't shoot!" Obviously, that order had been given out of a desire to conceal our position—for shooting would have given us away. But a moment's thought would have reminded this person that, in any case, the escaping German would tell his buddies where we were. The offender could not be found; he kept his mouth shut.

Tempers were snapping. The two Germans, who were still sitting helplessly on the ground, felt the current of anger, and cringed away from us, saying, "No, no." Probably they thought we were going to kill them. One said in fragmentary English, almost tearfully, "I don't know. He shouldn't." He clucked his tongue regretfully. "He will tell them. It is lost"—obviously meaning that the escaping prisoner would tell his buddies they were overwhelmed, which seemed unlikely.

Recriminations were no use at this point. We must go on, across the low saddle from this hill to our final objective. We walked carefully through the narrow path in the moonlight, and reached the last knoll, which was almost bare on top, though edged with thick trees. Here some of us lay down for a minute, exhausted.

Major Dunham dispatched outposts to guard the perimeter of the hill. Because we had to divide our forces between our two objectives, there were probably no more than seventy men deployed on this, the final hill. Unless reinforcements came up, we might have difficulty holding the prize in the face of German assaults. For the Germans, too, must realize that the hill commands Altavilla. If they have the strength, they will surely strike back.

September 17

Temporary headquarters were set up in the fringe of trees just off the crown of the hill. I was wondering whether there were any Germans in the valley just below us, when suddenly we saw tracers flashing in the dark woods and heard the crackle of rifle fire and a few bursts of machine gunning.

Don Dunham sent a patrol of two men, all he could spare, down into the valley. He told them to try to get through to our front lines and pass the word that we needed reinforcements. We never heard from them.

From the opposite side of the hill, behind us, we heard the rapid "Brrdddt-t-t-t, brrdddt-t-t-t, brrdddt-t-t-t" of a German Schmeisser machine-pistol, firing in short bursts. Lines of white tracers blinked across the sky. Then we heard the heavier-toned, slower-paced firing of our own automatic weapons, and a few rifle shots.

Dunham, dragging his tommygun, crawled up the slope to the bare crown of the hill. He kept low, for somewhere on the other side of the hill, very close, according to the sound, snipers were lurking. Don was looking for human game, and he moved like a practiced hunter. I watched his feet, and the one knee bending and unbending like the rocker arm of an old side-wheeler, disappear over the crown of the slope.

A trooper crawled back, and reported "Freeman and Richter got hit." But they had not been badly wounded. It had begun to look as if we were cut off on three sides. There certainly were Germans in the valley to the east of the ridge, where Richter and Freeman had been hit; and probably in the valley to the west, where we had seen the firing and sent the three scouts; and, finally, we could be certain that they would be in Altavilla, beyond the nose of the ridge.

An amber flare glowed in the valley to the west, and, after it, a green flare. The Germans were signaling. It did not take long to discover the meaning of that signal. The white flashes of artillery blinked from two points in the black mountain masses around us. We heard the screeching of shells and the loud crashing of explosions as the projectiles landed with dazzling flashes on the hill we had left behind, our first objective. Our outposts were still there, and that was apparently our only line of communication with the rear—if that still existed. The German batteries were giving us hell.

Shells were falling, and the peril of our situation seemed to be steadily increasing. Korman and I stretched out side by side, while the shells were still sighing and screeching. The rough, stony and sloping ground seemed a luxurious couch. Dunham had not yet returned.

It was about three o'clock when I awakened. I was conscious that artillery was still firing, that Dunham had come back, and I heard the crack of two or three rifles from the other side of the hill. "I couldn't get the sniper," said Dunham. And he added, "Things are not so good. No support has come up. Somebody's got to get through and ask for help."

Dunham decided to try, where other men had failed. He ordered his sergeant to get ready to go. Dunham was tight-lipped, as usual, but his grim face seemed almost relaxed as he gave his map case and pistol to Korman, for safekeeping, and picked up his tommygun and two extra clips. He shook hands with me, and said simply, "Goodbye," as if he didn't expect to get back. He and the sergeant were gone down the wooded slope and into the valley.

A few minutes later we heard bursts of machine-pistol fire, saw the sharp darting lights of tracer bullets amongst the black of the trees down there. Answering fire came from our weapons. We wondered if Don Dunham had got through.

The artillery fire banged on: the flashes, the haughty voices of the guns, the singing shells, the earth-shaking crashing where the shells hit on the first objective. Fortunately none of the shells had landed on us. We surmised that the Germans around us had not yet been able to inform their batteries of our precise position.

I began to dig a foxhole on the bald crown of the hill, under the purely psychological shelter of a dwarf tree. Private Bob Rowan, who had dug a foxhole nearby, helped me to make my excavation. We were working by turns, hacking at the tree roots with shovel and ax, when the sergeant who had gone with Dunham came out of the dark. His eyes had the haunted, hunted look of a man who has been in mortal danger. "I think Major Dunham is dead," he said. "I heard him death-rattlin' in his throat. I couldn't get to him. We couldn't get through. I had to come back."

Freeman, Richter and Dunham were now out of the picture. There was only one officer, Col. Tucker, still in action with our little group on the hill near Altavilla.

After about an hour of sweating labor with shovel and ax, I had finished a presentable foxhole. I was dozing on its clay floor, when the sergeant who had gone out with Don Dunham appeared again in the faint moonlight. He said from hollow cheeks, "The major's dead, all right. We went out and found him. He's hit in the head, the neck and the chest." The first-aid man who had gone out with the sergeant grimly nodded confirmation.

At about seven o'clock in the morning I was snapped awake by the blasting of a volley of shellfire landing on the lower slopes of our hill. A wonderful reveille, I thought, and hugged the ground, and heard the fragments whiz. One came into my foxhole with the usual long-continued buzzing sound of spent shrapnel. I poked my head out as the firing lulled, and Ray Justice, a sergeant who had the foxhole next to mine, said, "That's nothing, they're just getting the range."

Then came another volley, and another, and the shells of the last concentration fell farther away, on the next hill, I was beginning to feel more secure, when "Brrdddt-t-t-t, brrdddt-t-t-t"—a German Schmeisser rattled loudly a few yards away. Our own machine guns chattered back. "Brrdddt-t-t-t. Brrapp!" said the Schmeissers. "Bap-bap-bap-bap-bap," responded the American guns. And the sharp monosyllables of rifle fire sustained the conversation.

The guns continued to chatter and burp. The Germans, I knew, must be charging up our hill. Somewhere very close, from their places of concealment, American paratroopers were taking care of the counter-attack. One could only hope, and wait. Then the action lulled again, and we lay in our foxholes, waiting for the next development.

Planes came over, a swarm of them, and around us antiaircraft guns thudded away at them. When I looked up at the planes with my field glasses I saw the two engines and twin tail booms which identified them as American P-38s. The antiaircraft popped away at them, but the planes swooped into a valley, and out again, and we heard the crump-crump-crump of the bombs.

The Germans were still shelling, and burp guns (Schmeissers) fired occasionally, as our rifles and machine guns responded. The Nazis were probably trying to charge up the eastern slope of our hill—for the sound of the firing always seemed to come from that direction. The noise was close, and one could not lift his head from a foxhole on the plateau atop the hill without great risk. Each time the burp guns fired, bullets grazed over the plateau. But no Germans were visible. Sgt. Justice, the top kick of the paratroopers in this little group, shouted instructions. When the German Schmeisserman who had been firing from somewhere very close to us opened up again, Justice shouted, "Somebody better get that son of a bitch, and pretty quick!"

I watched Justice stand up and dash across the crown of the hill, heading for a foxhole on the other side of the clearing. He ran fast, and bent at the waist, but he was none too swift. A German burp gunner opened up, somewhere beyond the rim of the hill. I ducked, and the bullets whizzed over my head and struck the tree standing near Justice's vacated foxhole, clipping off leaves which seesawed down through the air. But Justice had left the vicinity and reached the other foxhole. He had gone over to "visit" a friend who had spotted some Germans.

A few minutes later, Justice dashed back, breathless, and flopped into his foxhole, just as another burst of Schmeisser fire followed. Again I heard the bullets zing overhead, and Justice said, "My God, he's really got a bead on me! Those were right in front of my hole."

The rapid fire of the Schmeisser, countered by our automatic weapons and Garand rifles, blazed along the perimeter of our defenses on the hill. Our outposts were doing the fighting. Lying in the cool clay at the bottom of the foxhole, I thought about the possibility of being captured, if our outpost line should crumble. I wondered what I would do with my notes. Occasionally, I lifted my head above the level of the ground, but because the men were all "dug in," the plateau on the hilltop appeared to be deserted. There were only the piles of brush which marked the camouflaged foxholes of Rowan and Justice, and the more inexpertly concealed excavation which was Konnan's slit trench.

The small-arms fire had died down, although the heavier stuff was continuing. We ducked into our holes when we heard a salvo coming. Somewhere to our rear, that small, perky gun which was firing on Objective Number One continued to bark. By this time I had figured, from the sound, that it must be less than a mile away. Probably it was a self-propelled gun, like our tank destroyer, or else a tank. It would be like the Germans to move such vehicles into position behind us, so as to cut off our rear, and then attempt to close in and finish us off.

I dug my foxhole a few inches deeper. There was no shooting now. The Germans, who had charged so close to the top of our hill, had evidently retired. But they would be back.

Just as I had finished work on my foxhole; I noticed that Justice had climbed out of his refuge and was moving away. "We're all getting out of here," he said, I scrambled out of my shelter and joined the thin column of men which had begun to move. It was not clear just what the strategy might be, but we were retiring, at least temporarily.

I saw the chesty little Col. Tucker striding along the path. "We're moving over to another ridge," he said. "The first battalion should be there."

Freeman and Richter hobbled along with the column. It was the first time I had seen them since they were winged last night. Both were well plastered with dried blood, and, under their ripped shirts, bandages showed. Their faces were drawn, but quite cheerful.

Richter told me, "We were coming across the saddle last night when two Krauts jumped up. They got off the first shots." Richter's arm seemed quite stiff; a bullet had pierced the rear part of the shoulder. Col. Freeman carried his arm in a sling, and his face was gray. But he did not complain.

As we started down the slope of our hill, I felt better as I saw two Germans, in their camouflage suits, lying dead on the edge of our plateau. These two must have charged right up to our perimeter defenses, for they were only a few feet away from our outermost foxholes. There must be others scattered around amongst the trees, for it was from this direction that they had made their most determined attack.

We picked our way along the saddle and continued south. I felt reasonably safe. Little Oscar, the self-propelled gun which had been whanging away at the first objective, was still firing, but we were well beyond the danger zone.

We passed over one ridge and down into a valley through a wood. Then we scrambled up another steep slope which seemed quiet as a picnic ground. Here we met other paratroopers, a much larger force than ours, dug into foxholes in the glade. They were the first battalion. It was reassuring to see Americans in such relatively large numbers. Col. Tucker strode up the hill looking for the commanding officer. He and Freeman and Richter, and several other paratroopers, settled down to a council of war.

A captain, near a field telephone, cautioned me, "There are some snipers—and some mortars. We had some casualties from mortar fire this morning."

I went back to the little council of war on the hillside. Col. Tucker, after talking the matter over with the others, had decided to go back to the objective, and hold on. Now that he had established telephone contact with the rear and could be sure of reinforcements, he would lead his men back onto the hill and dig in.

The walking wounded—including Freeman and Richter—would try to go back through the valley, to be hospitalized, and carry back word that we needed reinforcements—and most of all, food and water.

Korman and I decided to go back with the walking wounded to write our stories of the night's battle.

Near the top of the ridge, Col. Freeman, Richter, Korman and I stopped at the first-aid station. There, wearing the Red-Cross brassards of the Medical Corps, doctors were working over fresh casualties. Stretchers with their loads of wounded humanity lay on the sloping hillside, near a ditch. Some figures of men, bandaged, sat forlornly on the ground. Medical corps-men moved about, helping to administer morphine and apply bandages.

The walking wounded were rounded up—a sad group, ragged and blood-stained and bandaged. One, with a smashed nose, complained that his girl would never look at him again. We assured him that he would be fixed up. Some of the group did not seem to be bona-fide walking wounded, for they had risen from stretchers and could barely hobble. But they insisted they could move under their own power. Trying that long walk through a gauntlet of Germans would be preferable to lying there on the hillside, in the open, with only the ditch for shelter, while the enemy began another artillery concentration, and Schmeissers began to fire as the German infantrymen moved into an attack.

Somewhere near us, the unseen Germans were moving into new positions. At a greater distance, German artillery crews were readying their instruments of war.

We had just gathered our little group of walking wounded together, when shells cr-rasshed!—into the valley below our ridge, close; and we heard stuttering Schmeisser fire.

"Brr-rappp! Brr-rappp!" The Schmeissers were close, just across the side of the hill, in the underbrush. Another Schmeisser spoke, close by; we hit the ground. The bullets zinged past us. I got behind a tree, looked around, and heard the close cracking of the Schmeisser again. The enemy soldier had a bead on us. He was firing over the group of men who were the wounded; over the ditch where they and the doctors took cover.

"Brrdddt-t-t-t . . . brr-rapp!" the Schmeissers snapped, and this time the sound of the bullets was too close. They squeaked loudly, offensively, past my face, and stung my auditory nerves to anger. I moved back a few yards, to the ditch, and the Schmeisser fired again. Too close. One inch, and—zing!—a bullet clipped the tree which I had just left, spattering bark.

Our own riflemen, somewhere across the slope of the hill, were cracking away at the Schmeisser operators. Then the firing halted for a moment. I lifted my head. But shells were coming. We heard them, and we fell flat on the ground again. "Sheeeee—cr-rassh! Sheee—cr-rassh!" The shells were bumping the ground and the air around us, against our bodies and our nerves, while our inner beings seemed to withdraw to the core of our nervous systems. The unannounced explosion would suddenly gash our layers of tissue and leave bubbling, pulsating wounds.

The shells were falling, one at a time, over the whole lower slope of the hill. There were two down there— "Sheee-crrrassh! Shcee-crrash!"—tossing towers of smoke dirty with dust, and the concussions, less severe because they were farther away; and then one crying louder and longer, crescendoing, closer, *closer*, "ShhweeeeeeeeEEEE!"—and that inner being was falling all over itself trying to get indoors, trying to get away from the lightning stroke— "EEEE-CRR-RASSH!" The air penetrated into one's senses, seemed to crush one's head. Eyes against the ground recorded nothing but the darkening of the daylight—smoke and dirt projected over the screen of vision; and there was a distant impression of objects stirred up in the air; a cloud of something—debris, fragments, stray fragments of steel. And consciousness, when the commotion gradually diminished, began to probe itself cautiously to see if it was all right. That one was over.

The next ones were farther away, farther down the hill—where we would have to pass to get out of this inferno. They screeched and crashed, and we ducked—for at the beginning of the scream one cannot be sure which way they are headed—and then we looked up and watched the dark-brown clouds of the explosions. Tentatively, we waited, realizing that a lull had arrived, for what it was worth. It was precious time, for with each delaying instant, the threat of the next salvo increased. We waited a moment, then dared to talk. The lull continued for a little time, perhaps while the enemy was correcting his range.

"Let's go," said Freeman. Richter and he led the pitiful column of the walking wounded. The two officers held their .45s in their good hands, and somewhere along the little column two other men had automatics. This was the armed strength of our expedition— and we might have to run a gauntlet of German infantrymen, armed with Schmeissers and rifles, on the way to the rear. If we ran into a German patrol they could make short work of us.

We jumped to our feet in the lull and started down the slope, heading west toward the valley which would take us out of this mess—if we could make it. As we began to move, the shells screeched again, but we stayed on our feet, hurrying as much as the sad column of limping men could hurry.

Across the field, we could see a concrete Italian farmhouse. If we could get to that house, we would have cover. Meantime, we would have to run for it, across the open space.

Our hearts pounding like our feet, our vision jiggled with our running, but we could see the house ahead of us. We were straining to get there, hoping. . . .

"ShweeeeeeEEE-CRASH!" A cloud of smoke precipitated itself out of the ground, a few yards away, and the force of the explosion rocked us as we ran. Another one was coming, "ShweeeeeeEEE—CRRASH!" And there were more, a cluster of dirt-geysers closer and ahead of us, and we ran through the smoke of their explosions, miraculously untouched.

We dashed through the courtyard of the house, and between the house and a shed, then paused. Two more shells whirred and fell into the field, but the house now gave us some protection.

We grabbed breath, then set out at a run, into the vineyard behind the house. Two more shells smashed into the field which we had crossed, and then one landed with a rumpus of breaking masonry in the courtyard. Whoever our unseen assailant might be, he appeared to be following us closely. But we successfully crossed the vineyard and then moved into a relatively dense woods, and along the side of a valley.

We came through devious courses; we passed to the south of the valley where we had been so heavily shelled last night. We could hear the muffled banging of shelling back in the direction of the ridge which we had left. The Germans were "pouring it on."

We moved cautiously through the wooded paths, watching the trees and the bushes while our nerves waited for a quick signal to jump. There were no Germans visible, until Richter, who was leading the column, halted us. We looked ahead, and saw the figure of a man lying by the side of the trail.

Pistols cocked and ready, we approached the prostrate figure cautiously. It was a German, wounded in the leg. He sat up, miserable and bloody, and he asked for help, said he had been lying there since last night. But what could we do with him? We couldn't carry him. We told him we would send someone back, later. He looked at us as if he had been through enough desolate waiting and pain. Somehow, just as our little crew of wounded had been able to sprint when their lives depended on it, he dragged himself to his feet, swayed, and followed our column of lame and halt.

An hour later, we saw an American soldier and were challenged. We were getting close to our lines; and shortly afterward we reached a field dressing station under the grape arbor of a farmhouse. We were only a couple of miles from Albanella. We could see it, high up on the top of a hill, across a valley. There was phone communication with the rear from this station. There were stretchers and morphine for the men who had hobbled so courageously through the long distance, and fresh bandages for those who had been bleeding heavily. Now the boy with the smashed face was getting the preliminaries to the treatment which would make him presentable once again to his girl.

September 18

This afternoon, I heard at 5th Army Headquarters that Col. Tucker and his men had regained their position on the heights commanding Altavilla; that the fall of the town seemed imminent; that there had been heavy enemy attacks; and that we had sustained some losses.

That is the traditional verbiage which is supposed to tell all about a battle, and actually conveys nothing. But I know what those words mean, in terms of blood and courage and the will to win. This—a battle for a nameless hill which commanded the small town of Altavilla—is the war we are fighting; and the total of all the courage and suffering, the total of the nameless hills and the small towns we are fighting to conquer, one by one, is the war in Italy and the war against Germany.

In the Shadow of Vesuvius

September 19

THE LEFT FLANK OF THE ALLIED BEACHHEAD, NORTH OF Salerno, is virtually unknown to news correspondents. There, a few battalions of American Rangers, shock troops much like the British Commandos, are holding vital mountain positions overlooking the Naples plain.

A *Stars and Stripes* correspondent, Lieut. Kearney, last night told us wild and woolly stories of the fighting in this sector. Particularly graphic was his report of the struggle for a precipitous mountain pass which commands the Naples plain—a pass which the Nazis are struggling feverishly to recover.

"The line on the beachhead is stretched pretty thin north of Salerno," said Kearney. "There's one point, at Vietri, where the coast road is under German mortar fire, even machine-gun fire."

Kearney was planning to return to the Ranger territory this morning. Bob Capa and I decided to go along with him, to have a look.

"We might also take in Capri," suggested Capa, "while we're about it."

The pleasures of the Isle of Capri, now occupied by American and British naval forces, were legendary.

We started out with Pvt. Jack Brown, a former racing driver, at the wheel of the jeep, and followed the highway along the flat coastal plain from Paestum toward Salerno, about twenty miles to the north.

After a long stretch of driving, we began to see British soldiers. Then the military police were no longer Americans, but red-capped Tommies. Artillery banged in the distance, and Kearney told us that the Germans shelled intermittently in the area through which we were passing.

It was late in the afternoon when we reached Salerno, a small city lying in the curve of the blue sea at the foot of the mountains. In peacetime, this would be the beginning of the glorious "Sorrento Drive" along the side of the towering mountain mass which juts from the sea between Salerno and the Naples plain.

At Salerno we had to drive around broken boards and masonry where houses had been knocked out. War had smashed its way through the resort town. Hopeless tangles of electric wire, ripped loose by shells, trailed along the sidewalks. Heavy shells had blasted into the buildings, both from the sea and from the landward side.

At the next town beyond Salerno, Vietri, we stopped our jeep under the lee of a protecting bank and looked down on the deserted Vietri bridge, the narrowest part of the entire Allied beachhead. Here in the shelter of a steep crag, we were completely safe, but once our tires touched the bridge we would be within an enemy field of fire.

We started off with a roaring engine. I could hear Jack talking to his car, crouching over the wheel, "Don't you turn over, baby." And we whizzed across the straightaway, tipping slightly as we reached the curve. There was no sound except the shouting of the motor.

We were nearly across the bridge, when we suddenly realized that there was a fork in the road at the other side. Kearney was not sure which turn we should follow. We would have to stop, with our backs to the enemy machine guns, to get our directions. If we should trust to chance, and make the wrong turn, then we would have to backtrack and come through this dangerous corner again. Brown stopped his jeep. But the enemy did not fire. During our halt of about one second, while we spotted a sign marked "Maiori," a whole hour of time seemed to go by.

And so we followed the coast road, looking down at the breathtaking steepness of the cliff, and the jewel-like brilliance of the blue Gulf of Salerno. We rounded Cape d'Orso and reached the little town of Maiori, headquarters of the American Ranger force. In a ramshackle Victorian structure, we discovered Lieut. Col. William D. Darby, of Fort Smith, Ark., commanding officer of American forces in this area. I had heard much about the heroic deeds of Col. Darby in the initial stage of the Sicilian campaign.

The colonel was a broad-shouldered, thick-chested man; he moved quickly and he spoke with decision. He wore the black and red insignia of the Rangers on one sleeve, and the cut-down leggings which are a distinguishing feature of the Ranger uniform.

He was working with his executive officer over maps spread on the table. He summarized the day's fighting, "We went down and roughed up some Heinies, found out what a few roads are like, and pushed 'em off a few hills."

He outlined the campaign to date in this sector:

"We got up here on these mountains much easier than we expected, on D-day, September 9th. There was no opposition on the beach. We ran into a German engineer battalion about two miles inland—knocked them off—took the hill. Now we're holding on, and the Germans are counter-attacking—trying to get back the heights they very foolishly left to us. So far we've been able to kick them out on their behinds."

That was all. The colonel had covered the situation, and he went back to his maps. "I want to give this a hell of a pasting. I want to start out with the mortars again tonight. I want to blast the crap out of this hill, and the living daylights out of that hill. The chemical mortars will cover that one with W.P." (white phosphorus).

Kearney led us to a church which served as a hospital, and introduced us to the tireless medicos in charge. They provided us with dinner. Lieut. Arnold Block, of Chicago, told us this was merely a clearing station, but, he added, "a busy one." In the nave of the white church, there were lines of beds on both sides, most of them merely stretchers set on blocks, or bare canvas cots without mattresses. From many of them, human limbs in heavy casts protruded in grotesque positions.

It was still light when we started up the winding mountain road leading to Chiunzi Pass, the shell-torn position which commands the entire Naples plain and is, accordingly, the target of concentrated German fire.

Steep pinnacles of dark rock, shrouded by mist, rose on all sides. Where the heights near Paestum in Italy, like Altavilla, had been hills, these were mountains. "This is the place for fighting," asserted Capa authoritatively. "It reminds me of Spain."

It was nearly dark when we had climbed the hill and reached the large house, nestling in the steep side of the cut which was the pass. Parking the jeep well behind the pass, we walked cautiously to the top of the incline, and looked down on the Naples plain, still held by the Germans. Now, as we watched, we saw a fire burning somewhere far out in the plain. It was an unspectacular little bonfire, the "fiery beacon of Vesuvius," which was supposed, in the more poetical accounts of the war, to lead us to Naples.

We went back to the house, a sturdy structure with three-foot walls—it was for these walls that it had been chosen as a headquarters—and found a group of officers studying maps behind the heavy front door. They were the staff of a battalion of the 143rd Infantry, one of the many outfits which were being moved into position to reinforce the Ranger battalions. The Rangers had originally seized the beachhead, but would need considerable support before they could overflow from the high mountains on the northern coast of the Gulf of Salerno onto the Naples plain.

The commanding officer of the 143rd Infantry, Lieut Col. Fred L. Walker, of Metuchen, N. J., told us that they had just moved into position to relieve the Rangers. This house had been used as a first-aid station. Dr. Emil Schuster, of Oakland, Cal., medical officer of a Ranger battalion, had done such good work here, under heavy fire, that the house had come to be known as "Fort Schuster." On the outside, in large letters, one of those enameled Italian road signs announced the name "Tramonte." On the map it appeared as "Chiunzi Pass." You could take your choice.

Col. Walker and his executive officer, Maj. James L. Lamb, of Chester, S. C., were discussing the arrangement of their troops, the probable position of the enemy. Maj. Max Schneider, of Shenandoah, Iowa, of a Ranger battalion, had come up to the house to give the officers of the new regiment "the dope."

Later in the evening we went up to the top of the hill and watched an American barrage. The mortars fired behind us, close to the house. We saw the showers of white phosphorus rising like luminous fountains from a spur on the slope which led down to the plain of

Naples. The big W.P. shells lit up the area like photographers' bulbs flashing in the dark.

But the enemy had guns, too. Just as our observation had spotted a German concentration on the spur of land which we targeted, enemy observers must have noticed activity in Chiunzi Pass. They returned the fire of our mortars. We got behind the three-foot walls and bolted the heavy door when we heard the first few shells land and shake the pass. From some mysterious source, Col. Walker had gathered five or six mattresses which were placed on the floor. Now we stretched out and waited for the firing to subside. The building rocked with the force of the explosions in the pass and along the surrounding high ground. But somehow the house made us feel secure. American guns fired back at the Germans. The Nazis fired some more, and the shells landed close in the street outside, battering the heavy door. The firing lulled, and we heard wounded men crying in the pass. We went out and carried them to the building. A doctor dressed gaping shell-fragment wounds bubbling with blood.

September 20

This morning, cautiously working our way along the sides of the pass, so that we could see the Naples plain again, we had another look at Vesuvius. Viewed from this direction, the daytime volcano was as disappointing as it had been at night. A thin wisp of white smoke drooled from the crater. More interesting, perhaps, were the little caves carved by our troops in the sides of the pass. They had dug themselves in like cliff swallows. Each small shelter, barely large enough to permit a man to lie down, had a roughly circular entrance. As a matter of fact, the little caves were probably fairly warm and dry, and certainly they provided considerable protection against the shell fragments flying around the road.

Lieut. Kearney had told us about a dashing artillery officer, one Capt. Chuck Shunstrom, who commands the mobile artillery of the Ranger battalions. We listened to hair-raising tales of the way Shunstrom darted his half-tracks into the pass in full view of the German batteries and withdrew just in time to escape counter-fire.

This evening I had a chance to watch one of Captain Shunstrom's half-tracks in action. I heard the rattling and roaring of the vehicle as it moved into position in the pass, shortly after dark, and began firing. From the front door of Fort Schuster, I could see the flashes of orange flame just beyond the cleft of the pass. Each blast of the big gun illuminated not only the vehicle itself, but the open mountainside around. Anyone on the far-stretching Naples plain below could have seen that blast. The crew knew they were inviting counter-fire. But only by pushing their half-track smack into the open could they train their gun on the nose of rock below, where there was supposed to be a concentration of German troops.

For a long time, the crew worked feverishly by the light of the blinding cannon flashes, firing as rapidly as they could; they were working against time. Sure enough—but not until many telling rounds had been fired—the German batteries began to boom, and shells whistled our way. The half-track rattled and clattered through the pass in reverse, like a boxer side-stepping a counter-blow.

September 21

I was awakened at about 3:15 A.M. by shells banging close. There was a terrific crash and clap which seemed to come from above us, and the house shook violently. From upstairs we heard the rattling of broken glass and rending timbers. After the second's pause following the explosion, wounded men cried and moaned somewhere near us. A shell must have hit directly into our house. The colonel said, "All right, we've got some wounded. Everybody up."

We opened the door to venture out, for the men were crying, in the street, but the shells were still coming, close. "SheeeeeeEEE-CRASH! SheeeeeeEEE-CRASH!" the concussion forced an abrupt current of air through the door with each explosion, and the night grew light momentarily with the flash of each shell burst. The wounded were brought in.

There were two men. They had been lying under the halftrack, hit by shell fragments. One of them was shivering, as if in a condition of shock, and a jagged fragment had excavated the flesh of one shoulder. The other man was bleeding from the legs, where he had been struck in several places. The medical officer, Capt. James Graham, of Dallas, went calmly about his work with a forceps and knife, probing for fragments. A group of men stood around in a circle watching the wounded, and one of them said, "We'll just have to go down into that valley and get those bastards out."

The man who had been wounded in the legs said through clenched teeth, "Save me a place."

The enemy high explosive was falling all around us. Twice, the house must have been hit, for it shook violently under our feet. The colonel called Headquarters, back at Maiori, and said, "Unusually heavy shelling now. It might be preparation for an attempt to take the pass." And he asked for a plane to drop flares on a certain enemy position. "It might quiet 'em down."

Later in the morning, I started down the hill to visit a Ranger battalion headquarters. I found Majors Max Schneider and Roy A. Murray talking with two ragged Italians. The American majors had spread out maps on the ground and were apparently trying to learn from the bewildered natives about the disposition of German forces. The Italians had recently come from enemy territory. One of the two Eyeties spoke English, with an unmistakable Brooklyn accent. He was a dried-up little man with a blue-and-green striped shirt, open halfway down the chest, and a spotty brown vest. His cheek was covered with a gray stubble of beard. "There's what yuh call like three, four acres of land there. Water runs in one side, on the outskoits. There's Germans in there."

While the Italian was talking, Schneider handed me a paper, which, he explained, had been brought in by the Italians from Angri, a town on the Naples plain.

"Don't let anyone tell you that our artillery isn't O.K.," said Max.

I read the text, written in English, which was headed, "Commune di Angri, Salerno Province" and signed by the mayor or *podesta*:

"To the English Commander: Excuse me if I communicate to you that is many days that your batteries let come on our city a shower of projectiles that make a great destructions of houses and men, women, children and so on.

"All the population of the city, more than 20,000 inhabitants, are sudden fear for the men wounded and death.

"Will you please change the position of your cannons and do not shot on our city. This is the appeal that all the population of Angri does to you.

"Commander, save our children, save our old men, save our women, save this population, please God bless you."

Maj. Murray wrote out an answer which he gave to the English-speaking Italian, and told me that he would check to see whether there were any Germans in the town or not. The message read:

"We will try to respect your wishes, as we certainly do not intend to harm the Italian population."

I went back to the hospital to spend the night, and found a fresh influx of casualties. The Germans had been shelling all along the line today, and on the right flank, enemy infantry had made several counter-attacks.

I saw a young lieutenant, from the 143rd Infantry, whom I had met at shell-battered Fort Schuster. I noticed almost immediately that he was a case of battle fatigue. He looked lost. His eyes were sunken; his chin and neck jerked nervously in spasms, like a turtle's head poking out of its shell. But he recognized me, and confided, "It's the God-damnedest feeling. I can't sleep, and I can't rest. I can't stop the jitters."

I looked at one boy who had a slight swelling at the neck, a swelling which seemed like a rather innocent-looking wound. A bullet had gone through his throat. Plasma was being administered, and two enlisted men brought up an oxygen mask and tube.

The boy was snorting and blowing now, and rattling a little in his throat. Two men rigged up the rubber bag of the oxygen inhalator, placed the mask on his face, over his open mouth. The bag, index of breathing, inflated once, then remained slack. The Catholic chaplain halted to watch the last signs of life fading, and gave unction. Lieut. Block lifted the eyelid several times, and the last time, I saw that the eyes had grown glassy, fixed. The doctor turned away. "Well, that's the way it is," he said. The man's chest heaved twice more and then the body was still.

On a near-by stretcher lay another boy hit through the stomach. He was getting plasma, groaning. Block said that the man had probably suffered a ruptured spleen, that they would have to operate in the hospital's crude, but adequate, surgical department.

A transfusion was being prepared for the man with the ruptured spleen. The soldier who was giving the blood talked as the vermilion liquid filled the glass tube: "You know, a year ago if somebody told me I'd be doin' one-thoid of the things I'm doin' I'd tell 'em they're crazy." The soldier told me his name was Isadore Berger, that he came from 777 Fox Street, in the Bronx, and that he had been manager of a drug store before the war.

The man with the ruptured spleen was placed on the crude wooden scaffold in the operating room. The surgeon, a British major named Arthur Bullock, stripped down to shorts, and pulled on low white boots still slightly stained with blood. He was sun browned, and said that he came from four months in Tripoli.

I looked at the tag which had originally been attached to the wounded man's body, scribbled in pencil by some busy first-aid man on the battlefield. The legend said, "Shrapnel cuts on the hand and body." The major commented, "Understatement." I asked the major about the locale at which the man had been wounded, pointing out that in the blank space after the printed caption, "Place where injured," the first-aid man had written simply, "Hill." And the doctor smiled and said, "That's what they always say."

September 22

This morning I walked over to see the boy who had lost his spleen last night. He was being fed intravenously from a bottle of liquid on a stand, connecting through a rubber tube to his arm. He was able to speak now, and he said to me, "I feel much better." Lieut. Block said quietly, "He'll be all right if he doesn't catch pneumonia. That sometimes happens."

September 24

During the days with the Rangers I had been isolated from 5th Army Headquarters. I journeyed back to Paestum today and caught up with the current news about the whole 5th Army effort.

At the morning briefing, Col. Lazar was talking about the difficulties of the advance against the Germans in the Italian mountains.

"Jerry has pockets of resistance—but not strong—in the hill mass. Wherever there's a gorge, it's easy to put a machine gun or mortar or a little artillery in it. Then they can hold us up for a while. But we're happy about everything, in general. Benevento" (thirty miles to the northeast of Naples, in the mountains) "is probably our next main objective. When we get that road net, he'll have to retire. But the big objectives are to get Foggia" (near the east coast of Italy) "for airfields, and Naples, for a port. So far, everything for our 200,000 men is moving across two small beaches, south of Salerno. The dust on the beach is about two or three feet deep. And if we get caught by the rains without a port, we're going to be in a bad way."

But the securing of Naples as a seaport was still a minor matter in comparison with Foggia, said Lazar. The high command admitted that the principal reason for invading Italy was to get air bases for the assault on Germany. Rome itself was principally of sentimental value—although we would get it too.

September 25

Several of the correspondents had decided that the war was going to be relatively stable for some days, and had made plans to go to

Capri. I joined the party and we climbed aboard a swift aircraft-rescue boat at Paestum. The Isle of Capri, near German-held Sorrento, had been seized by the Allies and is now being used as a PT-boat base. I had wanted to see this famed resort, especially after Red Knickerbocker's description.

Knickerbocker had visited the island a few days ago, and had gone into raptures about it. The place had been untouched by the war, and was as lovely as ever. "Island of romance!" said Knick. "Even the bricks made love in Capri."

Knick had rhapsodized over the Blue Grotto, the stunning local countesses, Luigi's Bar and the Morgano Hotel. But aboard the aircraft-rescue boat I heard sophisticated comments by the members of the crew. The delights of Capri were apparently old stuff to the American Navy men based there. Ensign Bob Taft, of Minneapolis, skipper of our ARB, opined, "Capri's romantic for about two days, then it wears off. Everybody's a little bit blasé about it now. Too many souvenirs, and that sort of thing."

Coxswain Manuel Aguirre, of Wichita, Kans., standing next to the skipper on the bridge, agreed. "And that Blue Grotto—it's just a big hole in the wall. It's blue all right."

As we saw the steep-sided jewel of an island rising from the sea, and slipped into the curved harbor and rode up the picturesque little funicular, I was inclined to disagree with the jaundiced members of the ARB. The Morgano Hotel seemed like something transplanted from the United States, especially to us who had been sleeping on floors or on the ground, and had not seen a modem bathroom since Algiers.

There was a streamlined bar in the hotel, and a bartender who actually served cocktails! I beheld two countesses, and both were sleek and attractive. The Italian nobility had chosen Capri as a refuge from the hurly-burly of the mainland. We shopped for souvenirs—

mostly coral or tortoise-shell jewelry, and inlaid boxes—and walked through the little square, which looked exactly like a Hollywood setting for a European spy melodrama. Finally, we had dinner at a restaurant, where we enjoyed octopus, lobster, fresh vegetables, fruit and wine.

September 26

This morning I heard more enthusiastic comments about Capri. Up at Anacapri, a little town at the highest part of the island, Sgt. Anthony Sinkiewicz, of South Boston, bubbled "I'll stay here for the duration, plus, if they'll let me." And his buddy, Sgt. John E. Graf, of St. Albans, Long Island, "You could live here for a quarter a week."

As we talked, three pretty girls walked by arm in arm. Yes, Capri had its charms. It is too bad that all of the Allied armies cannot vacation here occasionally.

I dropped in at the PT squadron headquarters, aboard the Italian excursion boat which used to run between Capri, Sorrento and Naples, and I heard some harrowing tales of the work they were doing. For instance, the job of dashing in to within two miles of the enemy batteries along the shore of the Gulf of Naples, and deliberately drawing fire so that they could chart the location of the enemy guns.

Walking along the dock, I could see a huge fire towering over the distant Bay of Naples. The trunk of smoke, like a great tree, mushroomed into a cloud as massive as a thunderhead. Other, smaller fires were spaced at nearly equal intervals. To the south the beehive-shaped cone of Vesuvius still trickled its persistent wisp of smoke.

I asked a sailor what he thought the fires on the shore might be, and he said, "Oh, that's Naples. The Heinies have been burning up the city for a long time."

I sought out Lieut. Arthur H. Bryant, of Alexandria, Va., the skipper of the ARB squadron, and asked if there were any patrol trips going into the Bay of Naples tonight.

"We might be able to fix you up," he said. "Why don't you come around about supper time?"

At about eight o'clock, Bryant and I went down to the harbor and boarded an ARB. The destination would be the island of Ischia, a few miles off Naples. The boat was loaded with soldiers wearing British uniforms. I stood up on the bridge with Bryant as we slipped out of the harbor and were confronted by the glow of the great fire which was still burning in Naples. Three other fires, merely streamers of smoke by comparison, ranged along the bay, from a point north of Pozzuoli to a position near Castellammare, twenty-five miles to the south. The great beacon of the central fire, apparently in Naples itself, reflected a pale-gold light against the entire sky. Bryant said that he believed the blaze must be originating from the docks, where the Germans had been making extensive demolitions. The blaze of Castellammare might be anything, but more likely would be the water-front installations. The conflagration to the north, near Pozzuoli, would probably be the great Italian torpedo works.

The evening was cool and refreshing, but the chill of the air made one feel that a storm was impending. Our little craft rocked slightly as we speeded through the black water. White flashes lit the sky suddenly from the direction of the mainland, and I asked Bryant if these might be guns firing. All of them might have been lightning. We heard thunder, but that might have been the sound of gunfire. The magnificent night sunset of the fire over Naples seemed overpoweringly brilliant by comparison to the feeble but everlasting glow of Vesuvius.

This Is Naples

September 27

I RETURNED TO PAESTUM THIS AFTERNOON AND FOUND that the P.R.O. and 6th Corps Headquarters had been moved farther up toward the front. The place was deserted. The few soldiers who remained told us that the Jerries were retiring. We drove to Pontecagnano, near Salerno to the north, where the P.R.O. had set up in a storehouse.

September 28

Maj. Phillips, substituting for Col. Lazar, was full of cheer at the morning press conference. "The British have driven through the Cava area on the road to Pompeii and the Naples plain. They're pushing an armored division up and may break through very soon. American troops are approaching Avellino."

Phillips sketched the general Allied plan of assault on Naples. British units near Salerno would force their way through the mountains overlooking the Naples plain, while the bulk of American troops would swing far inland along the flank. Then the Germans would be forced to retire from their defensive line across Italy. The

Rangers, on the extreme left flank of the Salerno beachhead, would hold their position until the British had made a breakthrough.

Noel Monks of the *Daily Mail*, Reynolds Packard and I started out for the British sector of the 5th Army front and worked our way up the highway running north of Salerno. German 88s, 15- and 17-cm. guns had inflicted havoc on the little villages. When we reached San Severino, ten miles due north of Salerno, we talked to Italians in the town. They told us that just two hours ago, heavy German 17-cm. batteries had been firing from this area. The enemy withdrawal must have been precipitous, for it is unusual that such big guns should be so close to the front line.

Back at Pontecagnano we discovered that other correspondents, following another road, which we had believed impassable, had gone through Vietri, Cava and far beyond with a rapidly advancing prong of British armored forces, and on down to the Naples plain. The British had actually penetrated Scafati, the town adjoining Pompeii. The correspondents had been with them, probably a little too close, for three newspapermen had been instantly killed in a shell burst from a German tank. They were A. B. Austin, Stewart G. Sale and William Munday of the British press.

September 29

All through the night, I had heard traffic moving up on the road outside the P.R.O.—occasionally, the heavy clattering of tank treads and bogies and the roar of their engines. This morning, as Monks, Packard and I started out in our jeep, the highway was glutted with traffic. The solid column of vehicles—tanks, trucks, armored cars and jeeps—strung bumper to bumper for miles, was evidence of the strength of our forces, and incidentally of the fact that we have complete air supremacy. Otherwise, we would not dare to expose ourselves in this way in broad daylight.

Somehow, we got through the traffic, through Salerno, and onto the less congested highway beyond. We passed through Cava, where shells had smashed many houses. A charred Sherman tank, with the turret blown off, lay beside the road. There were wrecks of trucks and a burned Bren carrier or two.

And then at last we descended onto the Naples plain. From the town of Angri, I looked up at the mountain bastion which the Ranger force had seized and held so gallantly. In a sharp-cornered valley in the mountains I could discern Fort Schuster, in Chiunzi Pass, the castle whose stout walls had protected us from such heavy artillery fire. From where I stood now, I could see how the Germans had been able to shell the pass so accurately.

Beyond Scafati we saw a sign painted on the wall of a house: "Pompeii." Many of the windows of the tourist shops and hotels in the historic town had been blown out by the new, man-made earthquake. Some of the houses were shattered by direct shell or bomb hits.

We halted our car at a neat brick toll gate, marked "Scavi di Pompeii," the entrance to the ruins of the ancient city. Beyond the gate, I could see the weather-beaten brown remains of the two-thousand-year-old amphitheater, and a line of broken columns. Along the semi-circular driveway, British trucks and armored cars were ranged.

A tall British lieutenant summed up the tactical situation. "Jerry's got a few armored cars, a few machine guns in the vicinity. Those shells you hear falling on the right are our own—a few of our self-propelled guns. The Jerry doesn't seem to have any artillery left." The lieutenant showed us a map and indicated a line marked in red. "A few of the enemy along this line. The armored cars are covering the bridges. A good many demolitions. A very slow business."

Monks, Packard and I wandered into the ruins of old Pompeii watching carefully for mines. We found an Italian near the toll gate. With much gesticulation, he told us that he had been a guide before the war. The amphitheater, he said, was intact, although a bomb had landed in the open space at the center. The forum had been damaged; the museum had been struck squarely; and some of the most recent excavations had been hit. The House of the Vetii, the best-preserved building of the ancient city, had been struck by a 500-pound bomb.

As we talked, a group of American soldiers, who had come down from the Fort Schuster vicinity, walked from the ruins. They were not impressed. "Just a lot of old junk," said Pfc. Jim McNamara, of Clinton, Mass. He waved at the amphitheater. "This is a pretty good thing right here, this stadium." Lieut. Harold M. Gutterman, of Elkhart, Indiana, searched for something complimentary to say. "They certainly make 'em to last," he offered. Pfc. James Vigilis, of Jackson Heights, N.Y., said, "The Heinies must have been bivouacked in that stadium. There's a lot of straw laid out on the ground. And somebody dropped a bomb right around second base."

September 30

We went ahead into Torre Annunziata on the Gulf of Naples, occupied by the British this morning. The town, famous for the production of spaghetti, had not been too heavily damaged. The people were out in force to welcome us.

At the town assembly hall, where the Fascist deputies had formerly convened, a sort of provisional congress had elected a new mayor. The self-constituted electoral body had fashioned a Union Jack from an old Communist flag, adding strips of cardboard to simulate the British banner. I joined Packard and Monks on the second story, where Packard had just delivered a speech, in Italian. They insisted, said Packard.

We all laughed as Pack told us about the little Communist who made a long speech about the British radio because it told the truth. Then, said Packard, the Italian suddenly realized that he was talking to Americans, and hastily added that he also tuned in regularly on the American radio. "I listen to Mayor LaGuardia every day," he said.

We went on through the town to a northern suburb, Sacrosata, on the road to Naples. Here vehicles were parked in the shelter of buildings. A few soldiers lounged about in the bright sun, but there was no other evidence that this was the front line. "The curve of the road ahead is the front," a British officer explained. "About 200 yards up there." A few seconds after he spoke, we had auditory proof. From somewhere around the bend came the liquid chatter of a German machine gun. "The Germans are in a house around the corner," said the officer calmly. "They also seem to have small anti-tank guns a bit farther up the road. But there's no evidence that they have any artillery. Apparently just a delaying party."

At Pontecagnano tonight we heard Gen. Clark's announcement that Avellino, in the mountains inland, had been captured by American forces. But those in the know at Headquarters say that, despite the fall of Avellino and the rapid progress of Allied units on the Naples plain, the city is not likely to fall immediately.

October 1

We started early from Pontecagnano, breezed through Salerno and Pompeii, through Torre Annunziata, and then began to be alarmed at the prospect that we might have missed the entry into Naples. By the time we got to Sacrosata we were really worried, for traffic was passing through the curve of the road where the Allied front line had been held up yesterday. We told our driver, Private Delmar Richardson, of Fort Wayne, Ind., to hurry. Delmar, a former dirt-track racer, needed no urging. We whipped into Torre del Greco, next town north of Torre Annunziata, and dashed past the slow-moving column of British vehicles.

We had to slow down a little because of the throngs of hand-clapping, cheering peasants who crowded into the street. The walls of shouting faces leaned out at us, and arms pelted us with grapes and chrysanthemums. "*Viva, viva!*" screamed the voices. "*Viva Ingleterra!*" Some of the eyes focused on our American helmets, and the voices cried, "*Viva America!*"

Then we were through the crowd and passing along the cobblestone street, where occasionally we had to steer around masonry knocked to the pavement by stray shells. Delmar, expertly maneuvering the jeep, whisked us through the narrow street. By the time we reached Portici, the traffic had thinned out, and we were one of the few vehicles on the road. And, judging from the vehemence of the welcome, we were among the first to reach the city. The crowds were pelting us with purple and yellow flowers, and there was the same tapioca pudding of moving faces on both sides of the road. There were more flowers and more grapes, and this time we were actually showered with very scarce candy! They were sweetened fruits of some sort, wrapped in transparent yellow paper.

We ducked to avoid the flowery and fruity missiles, except poor Delmar, who had to watch the road to avoid running over stray Italians. Bunches of grapes bounced off Delmar's helmet, and flowers and fruit littered the jeep. Suddenly Monks let out an oath. He had been hit in the eye by a package of figs.

We stopped for a moment to ask directions, and a crowd charged up to shout at us, "Viva! Viva!" A young girl seized my arm and said fervently, "Grazie."

As we shoved along, we saw nothing of Allied vehicles or soldiers. The crowds grew thinner, until there were only a few people moving in the street. Then we passed through the tall gates of the town of Portici, entrance to Naples.

Abruptly the street was deserted. On both sides ran continuous red walls, and the ground was covered with rubble flung from the buildings. Bombs had struck into the rows of tenements, warehouses and factories. On the right we saw one of those neat, enameled signs which announce the name of each town. This one said "Napoli."

We did not know how far we could safely penetrate the city, for the bombed-out buildings were strangely quiet and gave no clue to any human habitation. The Germans might be lurking here, somewhere in the irregular line of broken masonry, in the caverns carved by bombs.

The stretch of gray beyond the mass of windowless, battered buildings was Naples harbor. The wreckage of broken cranes angled against the sky like awkward elbows, towering above remnants of sheds and storage houses. The once splendid water front had been blasted into a snarled mass of blackened girders.

We had no way of knowing whether the road was mined. I watched for irregular spots in the pavement which might mark a buried *Teller*. We had only our senses to guide us, for we had not seen a single soldier, or any other person. We skirted tangled electric wires and circumvented the deep pits which bombs had blasted in the street. We kept to the main road, passed several more shattered factories and tenements, a sad old prison building, which bombing had left even more decrepit, and came eventually to a broad square where we were confronted by a massive building with an elaborate portico. It was the railroad station. In the street across the square we could see a barricade of bricks and cobblestones, thrown up for street fighting. We slowed our jeep. When we spotted a group of ragged civilians, hovering in the distance, we halted. The civilians peered at us, then came running.

We had intended to ask them about the Germans and whether the Allied troops had arrived in the city, but before they reached us, we realized we were going to have trouble. Anything we might have said was lost in the blast of shouting which enveloped us. Men swarmed over our jeep, tried to grasp us hysterically in their arms, tried to kiss our cheeks, and, when that failed, kissed our clothes. I tried to push off three or four people who clawed at my shirt, and one man wanted to kiss my hand. Someone breathed a strong odor of garlic on the back of my neck. *"Viva! Viva!"* *"Viva America!"* shouted the men. *"Grazie! Grazie!"* *"Americani!"* They were so frantic that some of the words they were uttering fell over each other in a torrent of sound. Some of the Eyeties were weeping hysterically.

Delmar flipped into gear and we began to move, while the Italians clung to the moving jeep. We shouted to them to get off, and they protested. Then we began to shove their bodies away, loosening the stubborn grips of their hands, pushing their arms and legs. Delmar was hard put to it to rid himself of three Italians, one holding onto the windshield, the others attaching themselves to him and to the jeep from the rear. Every Italian insisted that he had a special reason for going along with us. Each wanted to ride triumphantly with the leading car of our procession, for it now became evident that we *were* the leading car.

We swung up one of the main streets, glad to be rid of the mauling mob, but not knowing which way to turn, wondering whether there were Germans still in the town. Rifle shots cracked somewhere in the city, to the north. Barricades of paving stones were heaped in the littered streets.

In the Piazza Garibaldi we slowed again in indecision. We saw a few men in a crowd, and stopped, thinking they were alone. But they ran to us, and from many directions, like ants, swarmed toward and over us. There must have been two or three hundred people—all men, for the women had not come out yet—and we were the target of their attention and affection.

Before we could move, the Italians were again scrambling over the jeep. The men tried to pull us into position to kiss our cheeks, to grasp our faces between their hands. When we pulled away, they grabbed at our shirts, so that it seemed our clothes would be torn off, bit by bit. They kissed the sleeves of our shirts and the legs of our trousers.

An old man in a white uniform clambered over the chubby, protesting figure of Reynolds Packard. In the back seat I was assaulted from all sides. A sailor in a neat Italian uniform joined the mob. One wild-eyed long-haired youth jumped up on the hood, waving a carbine in one hand and shouting ecstatically. His shirt was open to the navel, and a bandolier of ammunition flopped across his sweating chest. He reminded me of the typical romantic picture of a revolutionary climbing the barricades.

Other youths, sixteen or eighteen years old, swarmed up, brandishing carbines. Somewhere in the square Italians were firing rifles into the air, in sheer exultation.

The jeep sagged under the weight of the swarming mob. There must have been at least thirty of them. Delmar was trying to free himself so that he could start again. Something of the hysterical excitement must have come into our consciousness. I began to worry that the car's springs would give way under the load. The frantic crowd was altogether too close and too numerous and too excited.

Then the car began to move. Delmar had freed himself, and the jeep was pushing ahead while he raced the motor. We shoved the Italians away and loosened their grips. The vehicle staggered from the square, then gained impetus as the load of Italians was lightened, one by one.

We permitted a single Italian to stay with us. He spoke English, seemed relatively calm, and clean. We drove back toward the railroad station, and turned up a deserted street, looking cautiously for Italians, who might mob us, and incidentally for German snipers, who might fire at us from the houses.

When we stopped, our chunky, sad-faced passenger told us that his name was Edward Capitelli, that he had been born in the United States, that he had managed a glove factory at Gloversville, N. Y.

"You are the first troops in Naples," he told us. "I heard the rest are still in Portici. They haven't been here yet. Everything is quiet. Most of the Germans left three days ago. We've been waiting for you. We're suffering."

We thanked our Italian friend and told him that we must hurry back to the rear. We headed down the highway, and at the southern end of Naples, just north of the gates of Portici, saw the first vehicles of the British armored column, which roared past at high speed.

They were trying to get through the town, rapidly. The main bulk of British and American forces had swung around, trying to pass the city and seize the heights to the north. Only a skeletal force would stay in Naples, while the rest of the troops sought the enemy in the open country.

Behind the British tanks and armored cars followed some American soldiers, in trucks. They halted. We stopped to get their names—the first American troops to enter Naples.

They were Lieut. Ray Carey of Schuylerville, N. Y.; Pvt. Ralph M. Wise of Chicago; Pvt. Robert Miller of Chicago; Pvt. Jack Sheriff of Detroit.

And behind followed the peripatetic paratroopers. They were Lieut. O'Brien, of Oelwein, Iowa; Pvt. Joseph A. Supinski, of Providence, R. I.; and Pvt. Hayes B. Petty, of Bellville, W. Va.

We whizzed back to Pontecagnano, filed our stories, and then returned to Naples, to spend the night.

We searched for a hotel, but when we talked to pedestrians—they had calmed down considerably since this morning—they said that all the hotels had been blown up by the Germans, except the Parco and the Turistico. We were directed to the Turistico, described as "buono" and modern, in the Via Giuseppe Marconi. The Turistico was a neat, handsome little building.

The assistant manager told us that there had been some fighting between the Germans and Italians in Naples for the last few days. Five days ago, in Vomero, one of the suburbs, the Italians had begun to fire at the Germans with rifles, from the windows and streets. "The Germans have come with the . . ." He paused, made the noise of a machine gun, and we supplied the words.

And in Campo Littorio, north of Naples, the Germans had taken forty-five hostages, women and children, because the Italians had fired at them, he said. The Italians, then, had "come in the night and restored the women and children to liberty, and killed thirty Germans." In Capua the Germans had slain a number of hostages.

Monks, Packard and I decided to take a walk through the devastated water-front area. As we reached the street, we heard sounds of rifle fire from the north. There must still be a few German snipers in town; or perhaps the Fascists and the anti-Fascists were firing.

We walked gingerly along the dock side, looking for possible mines. We were encouraged when we saw that Neapolitans strolled about quite freely in this section.

There were evidences of terrific destruction, caused both by German demolition crews and Allied bombers. The upper portions of three small ships stuck out of the calm waters of the harbor, and a larger craft lay on its side, like a stricken animal, with one of its propellers protruding helplessly from the water. The sheds and houses of the water front had all been smashed. The best pier, the New Maritime Station, had been blown up and burned.

All along the streets which fronted the harbor stood sad remnants of buildings struck by bombs, some of them sliced or crumpled by projectiles. The railroad sidings which ran along the dock front, and some of the railroad cars, had been torn up and broken by bombs. Aerial damage was a little less selective than the demolitionist's art. The Flying Fortress, as Marshal Coningham had said, was "an absolute killer."

We fell into a conversation with two Italian men and their girls, who were strolling along the water front in the still of the evening. One of the men wore the uniform of an Italian sailor, and the other introduced himself as a journalist. They spoke no English, but Packard translated.

We were accompanied to the hotel by our new friends. By candlelight we sat down to eat C-ration. The Italians gobbled our meat and vegetable hash with zest—something startling to see, for we had lost our taste for the dish.

We asked our guests about their political opinions; they were of course anti-Fascist. They volunteered that they did not particularly like the present King, who had played ball with the Fascists. Nevertheless they favored a monarchy. They asked us anxiously how long we thought it would take to drive the Germans out of Italy. Packard made a speech about the fact that it would be "much labor" to drive out the *Tedeschi*. "*Ecco, ecco,*" cried the journalist, and the other three nodded vigorously. "Hear, hear."

After supper, Packard and I stepped outside the door of the Turistico to talk to two shabbily dressed men who spoke English. One of them, with a rough Brooklynese accent and hoarse voice, told us that he had spent two years in the United States. His uncle had managed a restaurant on Broadway. We asked him several questions about the Germans. "The Germans'll walk right up to you in the street. They take a watch right off your wrist; they take any God-damned thing." And he quickly changed the subject to something more profitable—for him. He asked us if we wanted women. We declined, with thanks.

The streets were silent. It was a dark night and occasional drops of rain touched our faces. We walked between tall black walls of buildings, keeping to the middle of the ebony street. The only sound was of raindrops dripping from the eaves intermittently.

Down the Via Giuseppi Marconi moved a pinpoint of light and the purr of a jeep engine: Military Police were on the prowl. The car came close and a light found our faces. The light went out and the purr of the jeep with its pinpoint of blackout bulb faded into the darkness.

We reached a square, stepping from the curb onto an expansive dark pavement. We passed under the lee of a slender column with a statue reaching into the night at its top. White flashes of lightning came in the northern sky. At that moment we heard guns snap a few blocks away. Then the single crack of a rifle. Then the slow crack-crack-crack of a machine gun. My ears and reflexes leaned out for the rapid *brrdt-ttt* of a German burp gun; but it failed to come. The sounds we had heard were made by single snipers, said my mind, relaxing, or perhaps a trigger-happy sentry.

We picked our way along a narrow street, watching for sentries. Fascists or Germans. But the street, like the other streets of Naples, seemed deserted. Occasionally in the dark wall of houses, however, we saw a chink of light shining through the edge of a blackout blind. And from several houses we caught the mutter of voices. At one dark comer we heard a piano playing, somewhere on the third floor, and the sound of men and women singing. Suddenly a glass object, probably a bottle, clunked into the street. We moved on a few yards and saw an open door with a dim light behind it. A man and several women moved in the shadow, and the man quietly bid us good evening. He said that if we wanted to we could come in and see the women. We told him that we were just out for a walk.

In the canyon of the dark street near the water front a light glowed dimly from a public building. Two American helmets stood in the shadows. A bodiless voice spoke from the darkness: "Halt!" A man's figure took definite shape and we saw the white letters M.P. on the sleeve. The soldier relaxed in a minute into the American boy. "Pretty dark, isn't it? We got twenty-two snipers in here tonight—some Italians, some Germans. Yeah, some of the Germans got killed, about three or four, I think." The American voice was comforting. "Some pretty good dames around here. Did yuh see 'em?"

October 2

It had been pleasant to sleep on a mattress with sheets. This morning, Signore Fantocci, the proprietor, told us that the Germans had piled up all the mattresses in one room and set fire to them, hoping to burn down the hotel. But he had gone in and put out the fire. He said the Germans had been living in the hotel until very recently, and in some of the rooms, we found Nazi pamphlets and postcards, and some empty cans bearing American labels.

We walked along the Corso Umberto past the modernistic Fascist buildings miraculously untouched: the Questura, or police station, the Naples Province headquarters, the post-office building.

We marveled at the perfectly normal appearance of the stores in the Via Roma, which is the main shopping street. The shops were closed, but one could see food, neckties, men's shirts, women's purses and hats. I wondered if the Germans had actually looted everything in the town, as the Italians insisted. However, the radio shop on the Via Roma presented a barren appearance, as did the Kodak store. The Germans had probably taken the most valuable articles with them. The Singer Sewing Machine showroom had been smashed, by bombs or looters.

Packard wanted to look at the Royal Palace, seat of the Prince of Naples, and long a government headquarters for Southern Italy. We turned into the street on which the barn-like red building stood, and observed that the visible damage was slight. In several places, stray bombs had penetrated the roof and a few corners had been broken off, but the general shape was unchanged and the row of colossal statues fronting on the Piazza Plebiscito undamaged. Nor had the Naples Cathedral, the Greco-Roman structure across the square from the Royal Palace, been touched.

We were anxious to see "Hotel Row," the harbor-front area where the finest Neapolitan hotels were ranged. Saddest of all was the Hotel Excelsior, on the point of land overlooking old Castel del'Ovo, and the sweep of the Bay of Naples, with Vesuvius on the left. The Excelsior might have been described by a GI as a "sad sack." The once-luxurious hotel sat, bare and disconsolate—now a mere shell. Besides blasting some of the walls with dynamite, the Germans had burned out all the rooms. Next to the Excelsior lay the wreck of the Santa Lucia. From the street one could look through at the back wall of the room which had been the lounge. The other hotels of the area had suffered systematic destruction: the Continentale, the Vesuvius, the Reale.

October 3

The American military-government officials—formerly known as AMGOT, but now calling themselves AMG (Allied Military Government)—had set up headquarters in the Municipio, the former City Hall of Naples. Col. Edgar E. Hume, of Frankfort, Ky., AMG governor of the Naples region, had come into the city on the morning of October 1, the day on which the Allied troops reached Naples.

Col. Hume, a tall, broad-shouldered man, wore many rows of ribbons indicating distinguished service in the armed forces. Some of them were Italian ribbons. "I was here in 1913 in charge of the

Relief Expedition after the Italian earthquake," he said to me. "I put the decorations on to make the Italians feel at home."

Hume had an impressive background in military government. He had been Military Administrator in Serbia from 1919 to 1921. In 1918 he had gone into Trieste with occupying troops.

All the other AMG functionaries in the Naples area had either been government officials in the States, or excelled in the specialties for which they were being employed in Italy, the colonel said. The head of police forces in Naples was Maj. Ross McDonald, former Deputy Chief of Police in Los Angeles. The fire chief was Capt. Glenn Griswold, also of Los Angeles, the inventor of the fog nozzle. Maj. Park Gardiner, curator of the Kansas City museum, was to be custodian of "Ruins, Works of Art and Museums." A former vice-president of the Chase National Bank, Lieut. Col. David Nielson, had been chosen as finance officer for the Province of Naples. The regional finance officer had been an executive of the Guarantee Trust Company; he was Lieut. Col. Tupper Barrett.

The "Mayor of the City of Naples," Lieut. Col. Carl C Kraage, had been an engineer in private life and owner of a telephone company covering three counties in Kansas. He said that in general the situation of the city was "not too bad." The food shortage was "very tough, but a solution will be found. A few mills are already working, and the population is being given 150 grams of bread daily, 50 per cent more than allowed by the Germans." And, said Col. Kraage, six food ships, bringing flour and condensed milk and powdered soup would be in "any day now." The Germans had blown up the water main running from the principal reservoir. And the hydroelectric plant which supplied current not only for illumination, but for the heating of houses, had been completely knocked out. But the engineers were working; there would be at least a partial restoration within two or three weeks.

"Sickness has been far less than we expected," continued the colonel. "Instead of 40,000 bodies, as they said in the wild stories about Naples, we found only about 200 in the hospitals and homes. There were about fifty Germans and about fifty Italians dead in the streets of the northern part of the city. There isn't any typhus epidemic yet, and the number of cases is no more than two or three per cent higher than it was last year."

The colonel said that the buildings of Naples were "about three-quarters undamaged, although the docks and railroad station are good examples of hundred-percent bombing." The big problem was not housing at all, but the shortage of food, water and electric power. The Germans had taken away "about half of the food and burned the rest." Without power, even large supplies of wheat would be no good since the *pasta* (spaghetti) and flour mills of the city depended on electric power. Fortunately, however, the Germans had overlooked a small reservoir, so that some water was available to the Italians. And American tank trucks would reinforce the supply. Except for these fortunate chances, the Germans would have succeeded in leaving the Italians, their former allies, on the verge of death by thirst.

I asked Col. Hume how bread would be given out to the populace, and he replied, "We'll use the same system as in Serbia. We'll give the flour to a commissioner who will in turn sell it to the bakeries. It will then be sold through the individual shops on a ration-card basis. In this way we will be able to give out dole. We'll dispense money through regular Italian relief channels, and the needy ones can do their own buying."

During the afternoon, we heard many sharp blasts, like distant bombs. The Germans had set heavy charges of TNT by fuses and booby traps in many parts of the city. Most of the explosions were caused by American engineer crews setting off the charges, and Col. Kraage told us that about twenty mines had been found and discharged by Navy engineers in Naples harbor. The Parco Hotel, one of the two which had been left apparently untouched, had been mined, it was found. Engineers had discovered twelve cases of explosives.

October 5

Gen. Clark arrived with Gen. Alexander in Naples today. They were met by Gen. Ridgway, Military Commander of the Naples area. We saw the cavalcade of eight armor-plated jeeps, equipped with machine guns, rolling through the main street. It was not an official visit, and there were no crowds watching as the columns swiftly passed through the Via Roma, viewed the ruins of the docks and railroad station, the oil-storage area where fires were still smoldering, and also blasted Capodochino, the Naples airport.

Now the sidewalks are crowded with Italians, and shops are opening up again. More soldiers, British and American, are finding their way into town in search of souvenirs. Shelves are well filled. Canny Neapolitan shopkeepers must have buried or hidden most of their choice items. The lira has been set at one cent, where before the war it was worth four cents. But already prices are zooming.

The barber shops are open. Many offer an amazing variety of goods rare in England or North Africa: safety razors and blades, unrationed; well-made scissors, liquid shampoo.

Sidewalk sweetshops display synthetic chocolate and candied fruit bars of Italian make. Cafés, which also sell bottle goods, have wine, cognac and champagne. You can buy good Capri wine for about fifty cents a bottle, and the best cognac for three and four dollars. And the champagne comes at two to three dollars, while it lasts.

The clothing stores appear to be well stocked. Attractive, full-bosomed Neapolitan girls, who have become affluent with mysterious suddenness, are thronging the streets, proudly exhibiting new sheer black silk stockings. And in the women's stores one can buy, besides stockings, gloves, hats, dresses and underwear—and even girdles.

Naples is coming to life again.

"The Volturno Is Quite an Obstacle"

October 6

THE JERRIES ARE WITHDRAWING NORTHWARD SO RAPIDLY that the P.R.O. has moved forward again, from Pontecagnano to Naples. The vanguard of the advancing Allied forces is already twenty miles north of Naples, along the line of the Voltumo River.

The new P.R.O. headquarters are palatial: a handsome apartment building overlooking the harbor and Mount Vesuvius. The bathrooms, done in colored tile, are ultramodern—but, unfortunately, there is no water.

October 7

Gen. Clark greeted us as pleasantly as ever and gave us a short interview this morning. He was almost buoyant. "This is my official or formal visit to Naples. I've stayed away from here until now, except for flying trips, because I wanted to capture Naples rather than have Naples capture me."

When we asked how the campaign was going in Italy, he said, "Fine." Was he optimistic about the early capture of Rome? "You bet your life," he said, "and I hope it will be soon."

Later in the afternoon, I started out in a jeep, hoping that I could see something of the fighting along the Volturno front. Surprisingly, there were no demolitions on the highway through Aversa and farther north toward Capua. Wrecks of several trucks, however, lay sadly in the rain at the side of the road; they had probably been knocked out by artillery or planes. After driving about fifteen miles, we stopped at a line of British lorries pulled over on the shoulder of the highway.

"You can go only a little distance beyond," cautioned a Tommy. "Perhaps a mile. Then you'd better leave your jeep. Bit of mortaring up there."

We drove until we reached a point where one jeep, with British markings, had been pulled off the road. We stopped and went forward on foot. Everything was quiet: no sounds of machine-gun fire, no crashing of artillery shells. Perhaps a half mile ahead, the severe square mass of a modernistic Fascist factory was now a haunted house, marked by broken windows and sagging sashes. It was desolate under a mother-of-pearl sky. Beside the factory, the road climbed and terminated abruptly. The Nazis had blown up the bridge across the Volturno into Capua.

I walked on toward the bridge, keeping a wary eye on the ditch along the side of the road, planning on diving in if anything came my way. Before I could go up the grade, a mysterious lone Italian wandered up and warned, "Mina! Mina!" He gesticulated toward the pavement. He pointed at the brown path cutting across the meadow to the river, an alternate route to Capua, and he said, again, "Mina!"

I worked my way cautiously across the fields, looking not only for mines but for British Tommies. As good troops should, they had faded into the ditched meadows—lost themselves somewhere amongst the trees and scattered houses of this outlying district of Capua. If one looked closely, one could see a few brown blobs against the wall of a house—Britishers in their long overcoats. As I followed my curving route toward the river, I reached a meadow spotted with brown gouges in the earth: soldiers in their foxholes. It had begun to rain, and the dark figures crouched dismally in their excavations.

A sergeant told me in sing-song Cockney, "Things are a bit quiet, you know. Last night a patrol ran into Jerry in the town. Jerry 'ad ruddy machine-pistols and mortars on the other side of town. A bloody nuisance."

In this sector, at least, Allied forces had halted to gather their strength for another push. Perhaps the crossing of the Volturno would require considerable strength.

As I started out in the drizzle, the Jerry mortar crews made their presence known. "Thwung!"—I heard the mortar from somewhere on the other side of the river. And then the "carrrumph" as the shell crashed into the ground near the bridge.

I walked briskly along the road toward the rear, not crouching, not stopping—because the explosions were more than two hundred yards away, in the trees along the river. Suddenly, three mortar shells crashed into the ground about a hundred yards behind me, and I heard a loud strange screech. Automatically I dived into the ditch. The undulating screech grew louder. Something struck a tree across the road, and whammed into the ground. I saw curds of brown mud flying, heard the hollow plopping sound. But there was no explosion. The shell had landed about twenty feet away. It was a dud.

An American parachute infantry outfit had been holding a closely contested sector to the west. I decided to get to that area if possible. I jumped into our jeep and we drove down the road to Aversa, and then turned westward toward Villa Literno. We stopped at a battered house in the flat swamp-like plain. It was Headquarters of the and Battalion, under Lieut. Col. Mark Alexander, of Lawrence, Kans. He said proudly, "We had been running into delaying parties of enemy, but nothing serious, until we got to Villa Literno, five miles south of the Volturno River. Patrols of F and G Companies occupied the town, but the Germans opened up from the housetops with machine pistols. We killed six or eight of them, and the rest were driven out. We sent three platoons into Arnone and Cancello, right on the Volturno River. The Jerries caught one platoon in Arnone and put in one of the heaviest artillery concentrations I've ever seen. After they came across the river, we withdrew. Now we're holding a line north of the canal, but Cancello and Amone are a sort of no-man's land."

Col. Alexander cautioned us against moving too far forward along the road running across the swampland. We drove northward watching carefully for distant puffs of shellfire which might indicate the beginning of an enemy concentration. We went on to a point near the canal, where, along a sort of dike, we found paratroopers ranged in a skirmish line which extended for perhaps a half mile.

In the mud of the ditch, I talked with Capt. Neal McRoberts, of New Orleans, who led the company which went into Arnone yesterday. He pointed out the town, visible from the ditch, distinguished by a tower rising above the mass of buildings. It was not more than two miles away. McRoberts told his story; it was typical of the small "feeler" actions going on along the Volturno front: attack and counter-attack, with the opponents testing each other's strength.

"I started with ninety-four men," said McRoberts. "There were about twenty casualties. The Heinies came in with an artillery barrage that was really rough. We could take the shellfire. But when they came around our rear, that was too much."

We drove back to the P.R.O. Ned Buddy, the newsreel photographer, was wearing a large patch on his forehead. He and Neal Sullivan, another photographer, had been wounded by flying fragments of masonry when a great mine blew up under the Naples post office. Noel Monks kept repeating, "It was awful. It was awful." He estimated that more than 100 people, including Italian civilians—men, women and children—were killed. Other estimates were lower, but all agreed that the first-aid crews were hauling many bodies from the debris. The worst part of the news was that several American Army engineers had been killed. They had taken up quarters in one corner of the handsome post-office building.

October 8

The Army is issuing C-rations to the Italians. Civilians line up at certain stores where the bread units—crackers and candy—are being sold. This morning I talked to Maj. Frank Toscani, formerly an employee of the New York City Sanitation Department and now Civilian Supply Officer for the region of Naples. He spoke about the food ship which is expected daily in Naples harbor. He said, "It's a small coastal lugger, the *Bruce Mike*. It should be coming in today or tomorrow. I've got a liaison officer on the dock waiting for the ship, and another one on the ship itself."

Maj. Ridgeway Knight, Col. Hume's Executive Officer, said that the water situation is improving. The Army engineers are patching up a ninety-foot break in the main aqueduct. The water supply should be restored within three to five days. The sewage system has been repaired and is functioning in parts of the city. Col. Kraage,

AMG mayor of Naples, reported that engineers have been working on an auxiliary plant which might restore sixty per cent of the city's power. The hydro lines will be running in about six days.

The number of people killed in yesterday's explosion—rescue crews are still working to remove bodies—is twenty-three: seventeen soldiers and six civilians, and "several hundred" wounded. Engineer crews are still searching the principal buildings of the city for mines.

*

Maj. Gen. Alfred M. Gruenther, Chief of Staff to Gen. Clark, briefed the correspondents this evening. He indicated there will be a crossing of the Volturno in strength within a few days. "Our first-phase line will be the high ground north of the river. The problem is to get ground forces across so that small-arms fire will not hamper them. This will be the first major river crossing in Italy."

October 9

This evening we were briefed again by Gen. Gruenther on the preparations for the Volturno crossing. He told how five divisions, two English and three American, would make the push along the Volturno.

Said the pale, quiet-spoken Chief of Staff, "The weather is bothering us considerably. We must have good weather to get our bridges across. It is my personal opinion that the Germans will defend every inch of the way—that they're going to take a stand between here and Rome. It wouldn't surprise me if they'd shove some more divisions down.

"There are about six German divisions against us now, but they are not full strength. The one division we met landing was probably the only full-strength outfit, the 16th Panzer. And the only reason we got ashore at all was that they were spread thin."

Gruenther explained that the reason the Germans don't bring more troops to Southern Italy is that they would then risk an end run by an Allied amphibious landing behind their lines.

"But there must be a spring to the German withdrawal," the general continued. "You push the accordion a certain distance and it'll spring back and smack you in the puss. The Germans are building up a lot of spring. Resistance will get tougher." He indicated on the map a line running across Italy from Terracina. "They could defend along this line." (Note: Terracina is the pivot of the German defense line now running through Cassino.)

I ventured to ask the general how soon we might expect the amphibious landing by Allied forces, the "end run" of which he had spoken. He hesitated and then said with a smile, "Right now we have quite a close maintenance problem."

October 10

German mines are still exploding in Naples. This morning we heard a thud, like the concussion of a bomb in the distance, and our windows rattled. A charge of TNT had gone off in one corner of a barracks tenanted by American engineers. The building had been searched, but the mine had been buried deep in the cellar. The last count of those killed is twenty-three, and about twenty-five injured. The rescue crews are still clearing the wreckage.

October 11

Ships are coming in to Naples in large numbers now. Hardworking crews of Army railroad engineers have reopened the rail line in the Naples area as far as Caserta. Dock sidings have been restored, and this morning we watched an Italian locomotive, run by an American crew, shunting cars into position along the water front. It carried the name "General Grunther" (misspelled) in large letters.

The lights of Naples harbor are on again. They burn all night while stevedore crews busy themselves unloading vital supplies. Power is being furnished by two Italian submarines which ingenious American engineers have hooked up to the electric-light system.

October 12

This morning, 5th Army Operations Chief, Gen. Brant, briefed us. "You all know what's planned for tonight," he began. "We're going to cross the Volturno.

"Now the Volturno is quite an obstacle. It's got the damnedest banks you ever saw, at some places as steep as forty-five degrees. Those banks are mined.

"The Germans have studied all this, and they know darn well where we're going to cross. There's no doubt about it.

"The British 56th Division will have the toughest job: the banks are steepest at Capua.

"The American troops, of the 3rd and 34th Divisions, will cross farther on the right flank, near Limatola. The American 45th Division will be on the extreme right.

"What we're up against is to get the infantry across and far enough in, so that the bridges can be put across. The 3rd Division will make the leading attack.

"Three German divisions are facing us, so we can't be too optimistic about it. It's going to be a tough scrap. One of the handicaps is that we can't use air support because of the weather.

"The 3rd and 34th will wade the river with assault boats, life rafts and heavy life preservers. The critical thing is that you go across with light formations, without any anti-tank guns. The Germans know that and they're ready to counter-attack.

"A heavy artillery barrage, with more than 100 guns altogether and 160 pieces supporting the 56th Division alone, has been laid on. Our only advantage lies in our tremendous artillery superiority, about six or seven of our guns to one of theirs."

Col. "Lazy" Lazar, our briefing officer, tipped me off that the best place to see the show would be a certain O.P. looking down on the Volturno plain from the mountains of the 3rd Division sector near Caserta. He said that Gen. Clark had enthused about the view from that place. He had called it, "A $5.50 seat."

At eight-thirty this evening we started for the 3rd Division sector of the Volturno front, near Caserta, to see the kick-off. As we drove up the magnificent road, the guns had already begun to fire from the Capua sector.

Reaching Caserta, where the C.P. of the 3rd Division was set up in the palace grounds, I left the jeep and went up to the O.P. with some artillery officers. It was a long hike up the steep, stony trail in the dark. We climbed to the top of an old three-story house which dominated the hill and the Volturno valley below.

In the gentle moonlight the Volturno was a winding dark path against the lighter plain. Across the valley rose the German-held peaks, black and hulking. There the enemy must be sitting in O.P.S like ours, trying to spot the flashes of our batteries. The big show, the barrage which would precede the crossing of the Volturno at this sector, would begin about one o'clock.

October 13

I tried to snatch a few hours' sleep before the beginning of the big show. I woke up at about twelve-thirty and stumbled through the dark corridors of the house to the quiet little room which was the O.P. Two men, who occasionally peeked through a spotting scope, talked in hushed voices about the imminent offensive. Down in the valley below us, where the road curved along the side of the mountain, we could hear the sputtering of engines. Tanks and trucks were moving into position for the push.

From behind us occasional field pieces cracked, and we heard the shells whistle just over our heads, and watched the dots of white light against the black mountains beyond. There were long periods of silence while we listened to the sound of the night wind blowing around the corners of our house and the undertones of the movement of our vehicles along the roads leading to the river. The river itself, and the surrounding valley, showed no signs of life in the now bright moonlight.

I trained the spotting scope on a U-shaped bend in the weaving line of trees which outlined the river. Where the Volturno meandered sharply in a hairpin turn, I could make out the sloping bank on the far side. Beyond that bank, the Jerries were waiting. Our crossing would be somewhere in that vicinity.

The time was now one o'clock, and the blasting of the guns began in haughty chorus behind us. One proud voice overlapped the next, and the deep notes ran into an uneven beating sound, as if drums of many timbres were booming simultaneously. The shells sighed over us in a ceiling of sounds. The irregular hills across the river erupted hundreds of flashlights as the shells landed. The Jerries did not fire in return. We waited, expecting the shriek of an enemy shell, the smashing sound of the explosion, the beginning of counter-battery fire.

But none came, except ten or twelve rounds which cracked in the air far off to the left. They were time bursts, pricking the sky with orange flashes; possibly the Germans had spotted movement of troops and vehicles along the road on the ridge next to ours.

We watched as our barrage swept across the valley and the highlands beyond, stabbing the ground with short-lived diamonds of light. An artillery spotter, Capt. Alvin Netterblad, of Miami, Ariz., had come up to report on the firing. In the dark we heard the cranking of a field telephone, and the voice of Capt. Netterbladf, reporting: "Only sporadic firing from the enemy—no counter-battery, yet."

Our barrage continued, undiminished. The shells were like plucking hands; it seemed that they must be pulling the enemy hills to pieces. And then, suddenly, I saw a white line of tracer bullets darting across the valley, from the German side of the river.

"Brapp! Brapp!" A few seconds later, the sound of the firing came to us. Then from our right, on a slope leading down to the river, answering fire. The American tracers were red, and brighter colored than the German. The distinct, dashed line sloped across the valley, up-angled sharply as it ricocheted from the ground. The faint white streaks of German tracers came back. We heard the sound of American machine guns, slowed by a distance of about two miles: "Pap-pap-pap-pap-pap." The Americans must be getting their assault boats into position; the Germans had spotted them and opened fire.

It was two o'clock, zero hour. Our infantry must be moving across the river down there, in the sharp U below our O.P. We knew this because the machine-gun firing grew heavy, with German tracers darting from several positions, the fine lines of light sometimes crossing near the bend in the river. Heavy streaks of red tracer zipped from our covering machine guns, and the chatter of the two types of voices continued: the rapid, yet confident, German gun contending with the more deliberate, yet equally assertive, American tone. And while our artillery barrage went on, new points of light were breaking on our side of the Volturno. Were they enemy mortars? We learned the answer from the sound of the bursts. "Car-rummp, car-rummp."

Somewhere in the din of the firing below, American soldiers were moving assault boats into position and preparing to wade the river. From this vantage point, high up on the mountain looking down on the battle, I was conscious of a strange detachment. As I watched the struggle with a sort of Olympian perspective, conscious that men were dying and being wounded, I was also aware of the astronomic beauty of the shellfire and the tracers.

Bright flares arched into the sky, hovered and disappeared. Our infantry were signaling. And the artillery complied. Smoke shells, brilliant fountains of fire which projected huge silvery clouds, struck into the valley. Evidently the infantry needed protection from the severe German fire. They got it. A smoke screen soon shrouded the irregular line of the river.

The sounds of small-arms firing, of rifles and machine guns, continued in the smoke-covered valley. By two-thirty, the screen was dissipating in the high cold wind. Again, we could see the occasional dashed lines of tracers, crisscrossing the valley, and the pinpricks of light, which we had spotted on the American side of the river, were now appearing on the German bank. Had the Americans successfully crossed? Were the Germans now mortaring them on the far side of the bank? Or were mines being exploded by American soldiers? There was no way to tell, from our observation point. Capt. Netterblad cranked his phone again and reported, "German machine-gun fire is not heavy, but it is well distributed."

I asked Netterblad, "Do you think we've got across the river yet?" And he answered, grimly, "You bet we have, if I know those troops."

At the moment, there was no way to find out whether the crossing had been successfully made. But we were sure that our own artillery fire was lifting, stretching out farther into German territory, probably to allow room for the advance of our infantry. The flashes of explosions along the far bank of the Volturno—caused by enemy mortar fire or mines—indicated that at least some of our troops had made the crossing. I went back to the C.P. of the 3rd Division, and got positive information.

When I woke up from a short sleep, I went forward along the same ridge from which the American machine guns had been firing at the time of the crossing this morning. There was a fine O.P. within a quarter of a mile of the river. I had to move cautiously, because this hillside had been under sporadic enemy fire. The view was magnificent. To the left, one could see the U-shaped bend where the German machine guns had been firing early this morning. Plainly visible were life rafts, small square objects abandoned at the river edge, and one bright-red life preserver on the bank to the right. The panorama of the fertile Volturno valley stretched in front of me. I located the small conical hill, rising in the valley, which had been the first objective of our troops crossing at this sector. Figures of men, barely discernible dots, moved over the hill.

But there were no signs that any great battle was being fought. Puffs of smoke rose in clusters at different parts of the plain where our shells were landing. The rest of the countryside seemed as peaceful as it had been for centuries. There were no shell bursts on our side of the river, no evidence that Jerry was doing any artillery firing.

Now our troops were pushing across the plain, and were apparently encountering only light enemy resistance. We heard the chatter of a burp gun from our right, and the answering fire of American rifles and machine guns.

American artillery behind us stepped up their firing, and we saw a cluster of black bursts puffing from the ground near an isolated white farmhouse two or three miles north of the river. More shells came, thirty or forty more, and we watched them strike near the house, setting fire to a hay rick. Abruptly, a little "cub" aircraft appeared and sailed back and forth over the house, giving corrections by radio to the batteries which were firing behind us. Later I found out that there had been two German tanks hiding in the vicinity of the house.

I worked farther forward on the ridge so that my position was now more than halfway down the slope on the side facing the Germans. And still, because of the cragginess of the mountain, I was unable to see the engineers who were building a pontoon bridge across the Volturno. Farther up the river, I saw dark spots at intervals moving slowly across the coffee-colored band of water. They were our troops. Only those who were actually crossing the river were visible. Those who reached the other side quickly faded into the foliage. Like other landscapes where battles are being fought by experienced troops, this one was characteristically empty, seemingly peopled only by a few soldiers, and by the groups of shell bursts which wandered here and there across the countryside.

At the P.R.O. this evening Lazy Lazar pronounced the crossing of the river a success, particularly in the American sectors. He commended the 3rd and 34th Divisions for doing their job on schedule. The British had a little trouble at one time with Jerry counter-attacks.

"But," the colonel said finally, "everything is under control. Our troops are pushing well beyond the river. The battle for the Volturno is practically over."

Politics in the Wake of War

October 14

I TRIED TO GET ACROSS THE VOLTURNO TODAY IN THE 3RD DI vision sector. The narrow, muddy road and one-way pontoon bridge were jammed with military traffic: tanks, trucks and self-propelled artillery moving up in an endless column. The Germans are falling back toward Cassino.

October 15

At the briefing, Col. Lazar was buoyant, "The news today is all good. Jerry is definitely on the run. We're connecting with everything—the left hook, the right hook, the center. He's been over with air for the first time, trying to slow us up. There were four enemy sorties with twelve to forty planes over the Volturno. They blew out two bridges, but they were repaired in an hour and we're moving over them now."

Col. Lazar also told us that the advancing divisions had encountered a new type of mine, made of concrete or wood, which was virtually undetectable. The "Hoover" mine sweeps are insensitive to the new device.

October 16

This multiple war has become a political as well as a military assignment. The military front is now widely separated in geography from the political front in Naples. It requires at least five hours to drive to the battle zone and back to Naples—and all the time one must worry about developments in the political scramble. There are persistently irksome rumors that the Italian big shots—the King, Badoglio, Count Sforza, Benedetto Croce—are due in the city. One must also cover the restoration of civilian life under AMG auspices.

October 17

The headquarters of the various command groups are moving forward swiftly on the heels of the German withdrawal. The American 3rd and 34th Division CPs are now located well to the north of the Volturno. The Germans, however, are resisting our advance while they fall back to their next defense line.

An Intelligence Officer put it this way: "The Germans are trying to effect a maximum delay for a minimum exchange of ground. They're defending high terrain and blowing every bridge. They don't have to leave much of a screen in these mountains—just a few self-propelled mounts, machine guns and mortars."

We crossed the pontoon bridge over the Volturno near Limatola. A long train of trucks crawled over the bridge. The rubber pontoons had been hitched to the charred pilings of the original bridge. On the far bank lay the engine of a truck which had been blown clear of the body. Across the side of the smashed driver's compartment, painted in neat yellow letters, was the name, "Aliquippa, Pa."

Our car threaded its way through the continuous line of military traffic, passed the zone of clattering American artillery pieces, swerved off the road to avoid the wreckage of blown-out bridges, and came at last to the front line.

At this time our forward elements were out of contact with the enemy. On the way back, we could study the features of the troops moving up with the tide of the Allied advance. They were tired, their faces expressionless.

October 19

Prince Umberto, eldest son of King Victor Emmanuel, has come to town. He drove through Naples in an open car, stopping whenever he saw a crowd. He was listening for political reverberations; it was a sounding expedition, although he insisted his visit was only a family affair.

At the Villa Santa Maria, the tall Prince told us, "I have come to see this poor city that has been so terribly smashed. I have been to visit my aunt, Duchess of Aosta." And he added ruefully, "My big house has been completely squashed."

October 20

This morning, the Secretary of the Treasury, Henry Morgenthau, landed secretly in Naples. Sammy Schulman, INP photographer, who accompanied the Morgenthau party on a tour of the front, told a story about the visit.

"When we went through the wreckage of the railroad station at Caserta, Mr. Morgenthau held us up to look at the bomb damage.

I asked him what he was going to do about all this destruction. He gave me one of those sour looks and said: 'I suppose we'll have to fix it all up.'"

Later in the day the Secretary issued this statement: "We haven't really begun to make any sacrifices in the United States as yet. In contrast to what I have seen today, our little annoyances and sacrifices seem small indeed. . . . All day I've been impressed with the ruthlessness of the German Army—their murder of innocent civilians, the peaceful farm buildings and crops they have destroyed and the homes they have ruined. The people at home should see these things."

October 21

At the briefing today, Col. Lazar said that the Nazis were still falling back, but that "a first line of defense appears to be the high ground just north of Mondragone, on the left, swinging in an arc to the north through Acernia and Cassino."

The colonel gave total casualty figures, to date, for American and British forces in Italy. For the Americans: 925 killed, 3,091 wounded, 3,852 missing. Thus far, our losses have been no heavier than those suffered in Sicily or on Guadalcanal. The British casualties have been slightly heavier than ours, yet no greater than in Sicily. The British figures were: 1,134 killed, 4,778 wounded, and 2,408 missing. This totals 7,868 for the Americans, and 8,320 for the British. Allied casualties in Sicily had been 19,235.

Gen. Eisenhower flew into Naples today, and tonight, at about six-forty, the city had its first air raid. The ack-ack began to clatter, and the big gun in the lot next to us made the windows of the P.R.O.

shiver. We went up to the second story to watch the fireworks which now trellised the sky. The dashed lines of tracer crisscrossed, some red, some white, and all over the pattern twinkled the temporary stars of exploding shells. Far out over the harbor a line of brilliant flares hovered, shimmering like moonlight on still water. When we saw that, we knew that this was a real raid, and that the bombs would be coming soon.

The yammering of the automatic weapons—the 40-mm. Bofors and the more rapid-paced 50-caliber machine gun—mounted into a monkey chorus. The more phlegmatic, more deliberate voices of the bigger guns thudded and crashed.

The original line of flares was sinking toward the harbor, and two more rows appeared over different parts of the sky. Then, at about seven o'clock, we heard the noise of the first zooming plane engine, and another after it, and amidst the flashes of anti-aircraft guns from the harbor—for the ships out there were firing with everything they had—we saw the slow-settling light of a bomb explosion rise and fade. Then something smashed very near us with a blinding glare and a heavy concussion. With it came the sound of glass showering into the room, the thumping and banging of furniture close to us.

I realized at once that the window at the left side of the room had been blown in, and with it the door frame, shutters and other appurtenances which had fallen in great disorder over the furniture. The floor glittered with hundreds of pieces of broken glass. I touched my face and felt no blood. But from another part of the house came the sounds of excited voices. Several of the P.R.O. enlisted men had been cut by flying glass, and their wounds were being dressed; they were not badly hurt.

A shaken British officer staggered in and told us that his gun crew had been hit by a bomb. Twelve or fifteen, maybe more, were killed. He needed help to carry the wounded. Could he get an ambulance?

When the raid was over, we had time to appraise the damage. The bomb which had come so close to our house, not more than 150 yards away, had landed squarely on an anti-aircraft gun. Fifteen men, East Indian artillerymen under the British officer, had been killed, and four more wounded. The gun itself had been blown out of the emplacement and thrown onto an embankment, as if it were a child's toy. The aim of the German dive bomber had been precise—or lucky.

In my debris-strewn bedroom I pushed away the broken glass and examined the precious air mattress which was the only bed I had. It was still inflated.

October 22

At the briefing today, Col. Lazar gave us the results of last night's air raid: About twenty-five to thirty planes had attacked Naples. Twenty flares had been dropped, ten or more bombs, and seventy-five to a hundred Allied soldiers killed. One of the bombs had hit a QM company on the water front, and that was where most of the soldiers had been killed or injured. One bomb had struck a hospital, killing eight patients. But there had been no damage to any of the ships in the harbor. At least three Jerry planes had been shot down.

October 26

We stopped in at the Psychological Warfare Branch headquarters and tried to find out when Badoglio is due in Naples. We were able to get no information about the Italian Premier, but did discover that Benedetto Croce, the famous Italian philosopher and liberal, is in Sorrento. Homer Bigart and I made arrangements for an interview tomorrow.

Meanwhile we drove up to Pietramelara, the latest town conquered by the 3rd Division in their push to the north. It is an insignificant village which has the misfortune to be situated on a main road.

This morning our advance patrols, driving toward Teano, had passed through Pietramelara. When we arrived, there remained only a few GIs and the crew of a bulldozer struggling to push away one of the piles of debris which clogged the streets. Beyond the town, our advanced patrols were working forward. The American guns were banging away behind us, and the shells were cutting into the terrain beyond Pietramelara. The war had moved on beyond the town itself, leaving the streets clogged with wreckage.

We stopped to ask directions of a group of shell-shocked peasants, clad in rags, some of them wearing hunks of cloth wrapped around their feet in place of shoes. Their eyes had the dull color of earth. Plainly, they did not understand why the Germans should blast their houses into the street or why our artillery should spatter the town with a steady rain of terrifying shell explosions, and why, finally, the Germans, who they had been told were allies, should take all their food and ruthlessly destroy their property.

While we waited for the bulldozer crew to push the rubble of one road block aside, we were startled by the screech of a shell coming our way. It exploded near the town. We heard the sound of airplanes. The people in the streets began to gabble frantically, and then, as the next German shell smashed into the town, ran off like rabbits into the ruins of their houses.

From one of the broken buildings, we heard the voice of a woman, screaming and wailing. An American engineer sat on the curb of the street, calmly eating the cheese unit of a K-ration. He looked up and explained, "She's been yelling like that all day."

The German gun spoke again and the shell sang into the town and landed "burr-ramm!" in the street, closer than the last. Suddenly, a tall, emaciated girl in dragging black stockings and a torn black dress, rushed out of one of the buildings and ran down the street, screaming hysterically: "How long will it go on! How long will it go on!" The engineer put down his cheese ration and thoughtfully watched the girl's thin figure running toward the open country, while another shell screeched into the town and exploded. He said, without excitement, "Sometimes I feel kinda sorry for these poor bastards."

October 27

We rolled down along the edge of the blue Bay of Naples, past Vesuvius trailing its everlasting plume, and came to the peaceful little resort town of Sorrento. Off the track of the war, it had suffered very little damage.

The Croce villa is on a cliff overlooking the Bay of Naples. Benedetto Croce is a surprisingly old man. He is stooped, and his skin is a gray color, and wrinkled. The effort of walking seems to tire him, but there is a twinkle in the slightly cast eyes behind steel spectacles. He speaks briskly.

The old man said that he had just finished a three-hour conference with the heads of the Committee of National Liberation—composed of representatives of all the political parties in Italy. They had come to ask his advice and to discuss their views. "I have not yet formulated my own beliefs on the political situation," he explained. "But when Count Sforza arrives, I may be able to reach more definite opinions."

We asked whether or not he believed a new cabinet would be formed under Badoglio, to unify Italian sentiment. He replied, "Such a cabinet will be formed, but the names of the men who will be chosen should be discussed with Count Sforza and Marshal Badoglio."

We had not mentioned the possible abdication of the King or the liquidation of the monarchy, but Croce volunteered, significantly, "You know I am in the Liberal Party still, and Liberals preserve open minds on political subjects. They can accept any change, even the most radical, if it is achieved by the processes of liberty—by discussion. I will consider anything and make suggestions about any issue. Whatever may happen, I am a philosopher, and my primary interest will continue to be scholarship."

October 28

Large numbers of Italian officers, in their sharp gray uniforms and shiny boots, can be seen in the Piazza Plebiscito today. They came ashore with the troops of the Montova Division, assigned to the job of garrisoning the city of Naples, thus freeing a large number of American troops for combat service.

It was the first indication that the Italians have become co-belligerents in the Allied camp.

October 29

Badoglio failed to come in today. He had been scheduled to fly over from Bari, the provisional seat of the Italian Government.

The Allied advance is progressing so rapidly that the drive by jeep from Naples and back occupies almost all of the day. Our 34th Division has crossed the Volturno again (the river turns sharply east of the original crossing and runs directly north). There has been some severe fighting in Ailano, near the second Volturno crossing. Because of the distance to the front, the P.R.O. is moving to Caserta.

October 30

Marshal Badoglio arrived this morning. Wearing a heavy blue military overcoat, and still shivering slightly from the cold—for he had made the flight at high altitude—he joked good-naturedly with the reporters and indicated his willingness to talk to the members of the press at length.

Whatever his past record in the Ethiopian campaign, Badoglio's manner and appearance were those of a benevolent old man, with a ready smile and humorous puckers at the edges of his blue eyes. The complete baldness of the crown of his head, the horizontal lines across his forehead, accentuated the impression of age.

At the Parco Hotel he sat down with newspapermen at a large table. An aide, Dr. Franco Montanari, did the translating as Badoglio answered our questions candidly.

He said, "I have come here to see Italian political leaders, in order to find a broader basis for the Italian Government. They are Senator Croce, Count Sforza, Dr. Rodino, and any others they may suggest."

Badoglio definitely promised to give up his post as premier as soon as the Germans are driven out of Italy.

Questions centered around the maintenance of the monarchy, and the marshal said, "The chief aim now is to keep the country peaceful and united; to keep it that way until the Germans are driven out. Anything as important as the abolition of the monarchy would create friction and disturbance."

Someone asked the marshal if he "owes his loyalty to the monarchy." And he replied, "Completely."

Would Count Sforza have an active part in the new Government?

"Yes, if he is willing," answered the Italian leader. "First, because he is a friend; and second, because he is a strong personality and would be an important addition to the Government."

Did the King agree to this? And the marshal replied, "Yes, he agrees perfectly with this Government. Naturally, any decision has to be laid before the King because he is the ruler of the country."

Now that our questions were being answered so directly, someone asked whether the marshal felt that the armistice between Italy and the Allies was premature. "We thought it would be about the twelfth," he replied. "It was the eighth. That surprised me. But it was quite natural that there should be some misunderstanding in such matters. Of course, we had some rather hard moments. As I left Rome on the ninth I passed a German Panzer division going in the opposite direction. I was riding in my usual car, but they did not recognize me."

Will the war continue after the Germans are driven from Italy, with Italy fighting on our side? "Yes," said Badoglio.

What form of government do the people want? "The chief aim is to drive out the Germans. The people don't think so much about the actual form of government."

If a constitutional republic were indicated by a plebiscite, and the people did not want a monarchy, what would be the result? The marshal answered, wrinkling his brow, "If they choose a republic, they will choose a republic; we must follow their wishes."

October 31

Count Sforza is the latest arrival in the procession of Italian notables. A troop of newspapermen trekked up to his apartment for an interview. We were interested to see whether the Count, long a foe of Nazism and Fascism, could be won over to the extent of taking a cabinet post under King Victor Emmanuel. He gave the answer in his interview.

Sforza is an impressive man, erect of posture, straight in his thinking and his talking. He gave the impression of great sincerity.

He began: "There are periods when nothing happens for two months, and then history makes itself in ten days." He was referring obliquely to Badoglio's attempt to form a coalition government.

"Do you foresee the success of Gen. Badoglio's mission?" someone asked.

The Count, who incidentally speaks perfect English, answered that he was ready to give the Badoglio Government his "parallel collaboration, for the only thing which matters—driving the Germans out of Italy." But, he added, it would be difficult to unite Italy in allegiance to the present monarchy. He phrased it this way: "It will be difficult to revive the unanimous fighting spirit of the Italians if we do not give them some striking manifestations that all links are broken with the Fascism which brought upon Italy the most terrible visitation of our history. All Italians know that Badoglio has always been in his heart of hearts against the Germans. But I do not think that we will have the unanimous wave of enthusiasm which may save Italy, if proclamations are signed by the same names which announced a few weeks ago that the future of Italy depended on the most loyal allegiance to Nazi Germany."

Benedetto Croce had come in and sat silently, nodding in agreement, as Sforza talked. One of the correspondents asked the Count about the question of a regency, for it has been suggested that the seven-year-old Prince of Naples should inherit the throne, and the King renounce it. Sforza answered that some "legislative spirits" opposed a regency, presumably under Badoglio, as unconstitutional. If the "legislative spirits" should succeed in invoking the constitution in this way, then "the Italian flag would not be the banner under which a million men have died during our loss of independence, but it would be the red-and-white standard of a dynasty" (the flag of the House of Savoy).

The Count went on to say that he and Senator Croce "see eye to eye" on the matter of the monarchy. And then he closed the interview with a tribute to the patriotism of many thousands of Italians who want to fight against Germany, "but they want to die for Italy, not for tricks and compromises. . . . There must be a great wind of enthusiasm, and you will see a beautiful Italy if this happens."

November 1

Barry Faris, Editor-in-Chief of INS, had come in from the United States via Africa for a short visit with the P.R.O. He was eager to see the front.

If he was looking for a sample of action in Italy, then we certainly got to the right places today. First, the town of Prata, another village even more viciously scarred by artillery fire and ruptured by German demolitionist crews who had blown whole buildings into the street in the effort to impede our progress. But in this town there was also something new in the German record of crime. In blowing up one of the houses, the enemy engineer crews failed to notify the people who lived in the house. It was early morning and they were still asleep. So eight of them, including two children and an old man and woman, were killed in the blast.

We watched a group of ragged townspeople picking through the hill of wreckage where the house had stood, extricating two bodies. Two other corpses lay on top of the wreckage, covered with sheets. As we had entered the town, we had passed two Italians carrying one of the victims away on an improvised wooden stretcher. From its small size, I judged that the body was one of the children.

We offered Lifesavers, the issue candy, to the hungry-looking Italians who were combing the wreckage. They accepted gratefully. One little man introduced himself as Peter Terreri, aged forty-eight, and told us in broken English—for he had been a shopkeeper in Liverpool—that the Germans had imposed the most severe discipline on the town. "They shoot three persons for having lights," he said. "They robbed everything." And he lapsed into his native tongue as he struggled for words to describe the Nazis. *"Animali, tutti"*— "all animals."

We went on up to the road running northwest from Prata, along the floor of the valley leading toward Venafro. The Germans were shelling occasionally, for Venafro, a key road and railway town, has not yet been captured. We stopped in at the C.P. of the 2nd Battalion of the 168th Infantry, the forward-most regiment of the 34th Division.

At Fontegreca, a little town on the side of the valley, we could look down toward Venafro and see lines of shells bursting across the plain. They would be our own shells, landing in German territory about three miles away. There we found a small German cemetery which gave evidence that the enemy retreat in this sector had been hasty. At one end of a row of barrows—each marked with a wooden cross—gaped a half-dug hole. The German burial detail had not had time to finish the last grave.

This might have been enough excitement for a visiting editor's one-day tour of the front. But there was more to come. We headed back toward the P.R.O. and reached a curve of the road when MPs began to blow their whistles in short, sharp blasts, the signal for an air raid.

We had been moving with a column of empty trucks going south to pick up supplies. It would be a fine target for enemy strafing or bombing. The whole column halted. Men ran from the vehicles.

As the anti-aircraft guns began to clatter all around us, I noticed that a group of German prisoners were being hurried out of one of the trucks. They needed no urging. I focused my field glasses on the bursts of anti-aircraft fire overhead, counted twenty-four silvery single-engined planes high up. I expected to see them peel off and dive at us.

I looked back at the curve of the highway, the line of parked vehicles. Suddenly darts of golden tracer bullets spewed into the road, and a mass of little spurts of earth, like an inverted shower bath of fine dust columns, sprang up. My instantaneous thought was that some of our own anti-aircraft guns were firing far too low. In the din of the anti-aircraft, I heard the concentrated chorus of rattling machine guns and popping cannon, and realized that we were being strafed! A fraction of a second later the white shape of a plane whizzed by, less than fifty feet away from the protecting slope on which I was lying. The plane was small; it had a blunt nose; probably a Focke-Wulf. Then the wings showed white as it climbed sharply, bobbing and weaving in evasive tactics, turning as it followed the curving of the valley. Ack-ack tracers streaked the sky, reaching out from all directions for the diminishing target, but in a matter of seconds the plane was gone from sight.

MPs were blowing their whistles as a signal that the air raid was over. The guns had all stopped firing, and the flying flak had settled to the ground without injuring anyone in this locality. Down at the curve of the road, GIs were climbing back into their trucks. Evidently, none of the German bullets had struck anything explosive, like gasoline or ammunition. The German prisoners were clambering back onto their truck. I stopped to talk, through an interrogating officer, with a prisoner and asked how he thought being strafed by a German plane compared with an Allied air attack. He said, "Ours are as good as yours, but you have very many more."

Back at the jeep, we found Barry Faris looking a little bedraggled. Faris had taken a dive into a clump of bushes and found a minor cliff on the other side, down which he had plunged. But he only laughed over his mishap.

November 3

The political wiseacres are saying that Count Sforza has definitely declined a job in the Cabinet under Badoglio, as long as the King retains his position. The selection of a cabinet is going ahead nevertheless.

King Victor Emmanuel drove into town today. I did not see the monarch arrive in the city, but I talked to the King's aide-de-camp, a magnificently uniformed colonel, in AMG headquarters, and this was his story: "In Avellino, as we drove in, the welcome accorded the King was just marvelous, even though we were traveling in a closed car. Reaching Naples, we changed to an open car, and in the Via Roma and the Vomero there was great adulation. At the Piazza de Martiri, His Highness halted, for the traffic was held up, and a crowd gathered and applauded. The King stood up and saluted the crowd, and the throng shouted 'Viva il Re!' "

There were, however, conflicting reports about the monarch's reception. Some of the correspondents maintained that, in the outlying districts of the city, the King had been virtually ignored.

November 4

Since this is the anniversary of Italy's armistice with Germany at the end of the First World War, there were patriotic speeches in Naples, including one by Count Sforza. This morning, in the Piazza de Martiri (Square of Martyrs), a little guard of about twelve Italian soldiers paraded in their mismatched uniforms. They stood at attention while wreaths were placed on the war monument. The crowd cheered. "Long live Italy! Long live the United Nations! Long live Liberty!"

At the University of Naples a large assemblage stood on the steps, listening to loudspeakers—provided, I was told on good authority, by the PWB—which carried the voice of Count Sforza, speaking from inside the building. The throng shouted approval as Sforza made a plea for a new government, and demanded the abdication of the King.

"If we can prove we are mature for democracy, we will have all necessary help from the United States and Britain. In a few years our cities will be built up again. Our sufferings will not have been in vain. . . . All those who have taken the responsibility of defending our political liberties, and have not defended them, must disappear from Italy." And the mob shouted, "Out with the King!" *"Via il Re! Via il Re!"*

When the speech was over, the Count was nearly mobbed. The Italians pushed each other violently as they tried to embrace the Great Man. They shouted, *"Viva Sforza!" "Viva Republica!"*

As yet, however, the Count has made no public announcement of his role in any new government. It is clear that he will decline an appointment to the Cabinet unless the King abdicates.

November 8

Just a year ago today American forces landed in North Africa. We started out for the 3rd Division sector of the front, since this Division, which had been doing a large share of the fighting in Italy, had also landed in North Africa on November 8, 1942.

On the road north of Capua a column of jeeps, one of them bearing a tall radio antenna, passed us. We spotted the red license plate, bearing three silver stars, of Gen. Clark's vehicle, and we followed.

Our jeep skidded from side to side as we bumped over the rutted roads and detours. We arrived at 3rd Division Headquarters, about five miles southeast of Mignano. The camp was only a collection of sodden tents, clustered on a hillside in a grove of trees. Shabby camouflage nets covered some of the tents; strewn branches somewhat disguised the roofs of others. The Nazis' renewed aerial activity makes camouflage and dispersal desirable. Yesterday the Germans had strafed and bombed roads in this sector.

Gen. Clark unwound his lanky form, climbed out of the jeep, and shook hands with stubborn-jawed Maj. Gen. Lucien Truscott. They sloshed through the ankle-deep mud with some British officers who had come up for consultation.

When Gen. Clark finished his conference with Gen. Truscott and the other officers, he gave us an interview outside the Intelligence tent. "Just asked Truscott," he began, "if he remembers where he was a year ago; and he couldn't place it. Since then we've made a lot of progress. It shows in the way the troops have been handling themselves in difficult terrain and after a long time in the line." He turned to Truscott again, "How long have you been in?"

"Fifty-two days," said Gen. Truscott.

"I'll say that's a long time. We couldn't have done that a year ago," said Gen. Clark.

We asked the general how soon he thought we would be getting to Rome. "I can't prognosticate. But I get mad every time I look at those signs along the road, saying so-and-so many miles to Rome. But we'll get there."

We asked the tall 5th Army commander what he thought of the current military situation, and he answered, "We're meeting pretty tough opposition here. We're taking terrain that the enemy wants and we want just as badly."

Tonight, at the briefing, Lazy Lazar told us that the Germans are strengthening the forces opposing us, and apparently preparing to stand and fight after many weeks of methodical retreat before the steady pressure of our forces. "In the Venafro and Mount Lungo areas, along a line running back into Cassino, Jerry is well fortified. There are pillboxes, barbed wire, holes dug in the rocks. The entrenchments go right back to the Cassino area. There is no doubt that this is going to be his winter line. He's going to fight here."

There were movies tonight in a little theater near our camp. The film kept breaking, but despite this constant vexation, the audience had a good time. During periods of darkness, the crowd turned their flashlights on the screen, while the spots of light, deftly maneuvered, chased each other like pollywogs in a fishbowl. I had seen the same game played in the South Pacific. And, this time, there was another game to be played with flashlights: turning the beam on the nurses sitting in the balcony with their escorts. They, in turn, tried to spot the culprits below. And when the possibilities of these sports were exhausted, someone began to sing, and soon everyone joined in "The Old Mill Stream," "I'm a Member of the Souse Family" and "Home on the Range." There was nothing wrong with the morale of these soldiers.

November 11

The P.R.O. told us there would be an Armistice Day ceremony at Avellino, where a military cemetery is being opened, with an address by Gen. Clark.

The cemetery was a peaceful square of graves, the white crosses ranged in precise rows in a former potato patch. Some of the graves carried, instead of crosses, the six-pointed Star of David. The 5th Army graves-registration officer, Lieut. Col. Arthur L. Warren, of Berkeley, Cal., told us that sixty-one Germans were buried in the cemetery, "with no difference as to identification or treatment."

On three sides of the cemetery stood even rows of infantrymen. On the fourth side, a row of colonels were ranged, near the staff where our flag flew at half mast. As Gen. Clark arrived, all stood at attention. Then the 5th Army chaplain, white-haired Lieut. Col. Patrick J. Ryan, read the prayer.

While the band, with a proud blare of brass, played "The Star-Spangled Banner," a sergeant tugged at the shroud lines, sending the flag slowly from half-mast to the peak. The row of soldiers standing at the far end of the field stood stiffly with presented arms. The salute completed, Gen. Clark, grim and purposeful, strode to the foot of the flagpole and faced the troops.

"Here we are, a quarter of a century later, with the same Allies as before," he said, "fighting the same mad dogs that were loose in 1918.

"It is fitting to assemble in this beautiful cemetery to pay honor to our dead comrades who gave their all in order that the 5th Army should succeed.

"They gave their lives in order that we could make a successful landing at Salerno, take the great city and port of Naples, cross the Volturno River and move along on the road to Rome.

"They gave their lives that the people at home could pursue the life which we have always wanted—a happy life—and that their children could go to the schools and churches they want, and follow the line of work they want. And we are fighting, first, to save our own land from devastation like this in Italy." The general paused as he switched to a subject which had evidently been close to his heart. There has been much talk of sending the veterans of the fighting in Italy—some of them veterans also of the campaigns in Sicily and North Africa-home to the United States. He said, abruptly:

"We must not think about going home. None of us is going home till it's over. None of us wants to go home until it's over.

"It would be foolish to break up the 5th Army after its long experience. We've got men at the front who are masters of the Germans; they're killing the Germans. Every one of us must take a pledge that we will carry on until it's over.

"We've caught the torch that these men have flung us, and we'll carry it to Berlin and to the great victory—a complete victory—which the United Nations deserve."

The speech was over. "The wreath," said the general in a firm voice. It was brought forward to him—a horseshoe of white, purple and green. He placed it at the foot of the flagpole, and stepped back.

"Hen—shun!" cried a sergeant. "Lo—ay!" The rifles up-angled in a row, ready to fire the salute. "Fi—!" The guns cracked sharply, and wads from the blank cartridges fluttered onto the row of graves like a flurry of snow. Twice more commands, crack and snowfall were repeated.

Then the bugler stepped forward and began the faint, very pointed cry of "Taps." It was answered by an echoing "Taps" sounded by a distant bugler from the green arbor behind the cemetery.

There was a slight pause, and Gen. Clark said, relaxing the tension, "That was a good ceremony."

November 13

In the ornate offices he had inherited from an Italian functionary, Col. Hume gave us a mimeographed list of about 450 Italian civil service employees who have been thrown out of their jobs after investigation by AMG. It is the first large-scale purge of pro-Fascists in government positions since the Allied conquest of Southern Italy. About 100 more Italian officials with violent Fascist beliefs have been detained in prison for trial. The rest of the Italian civil servants, about two-thirds of the total in occupied territory, have been allowed to continue at their posts.

Col. Hume explained, "We're not trying to govern Italy; we're trying to get the Italians to run their country so that we can pursue our principal objective, to beat Germany.

"A special effort has been made to find and throw out the 'castor-oil boys,' members of the party since the early days of Fascism, or the 'Squadristi,' the ultra-Fascists. But there are many competent officials who have not been active Fascists—men who wore a party button only because they couldn't get a job otherwise. We don't want to remove a man because he has been practically forced to become a Fascist, if he is a competent man. . . . Leaders are leaders in all countries. In Fascist countries many of the leaders happened to be Fascists.

"As a general rule, the top man in each organization has been thrown out, and the assistants put in charge. The top man had usually been put in because of political influence. But the second or third man made a career of it."

Among the prominent Neapolitans who had been arrested was the *podesta*, the mayor, Soprano, who "signed all the German decrees but stayed on." And Achille Lauro, maritime commissioner, one of the fabulous figures of the Fascist regime, a *"milliardaire"* whose fortune came from many enterprises tied closely to military operations and contracts. He was the owner of scores of ships traveling between Italy and Spain, a bosom friend of Count Ciano, a large stockholder in the Bank of Naples and a controlling stockholder in the Neapolitan newspapers. The arrest of Lauro was described as "one of the healthiest, for it showed the people that the Allies are acting in good faith and are not afraid of international bankers."

November 14

I checked with the highly confidential Counter-intelligence Corps headquarters this morning to see if arrests of Fascists are continuing. Hardboiled Maj. Maxwell J. Papurt, formerly psychologist in the New York Department of Correction and now head of the C.I.C. in Italy, said that the latest Fascists to be taken into custody are the prominent Guggenheim brothers, Renato and Carlo. "They had *pasta* and almond factories with large German military contracts. We have photos of Renato with Col. Sholl, the German commandant in Naples, and the actual pass issued by Sholl—even evidence that he had allowed them to use his car." But the best proof, said bespectacled Maj. Papurt with a smile, was that "The Germans destroyed all the other almond plants in Naples except the Guggenheims', and they even appointed a special squad of engineers to blow up the factory of their principal competitor. That squad came back three times to make sure that the competing factory was properly blown up."

November 15

At the 3rd Division headquarters, we talked to Gen. Truscott on the subject of the German "winter line." "It's by far the strongest area of defense we've run into so far in Italy," he said. "But it is in no sense comparable to the Western front in the last war, because now I could send a small patrol to pierce the defenses at any point; I could take Cassino tomorrow if I wanted to make the expenditure of men. We have learned that the Italians have been working on the German defenses for the last six weeks, and there are some strong positions. They've got the mountaintops fortified with pillboxes blasted out of the rock, and reinforced with concrete. On the lower features, they've got very deep intrenchments—wired in. In a great many places they have machine-gun mounts.

"We're already in advance of the outer line which the Boche hoped to defend. But there is a belt of unconnected strong points hingeing on Cassino."

We asked the "Iron Man" whether he thought that after the Cassino position cracked, we might roll to Rome. "No, this kind of country is too easy to defend," he said, "and the Boche is still a good soldier. We mustn't kid ourselves about the fact that there's still a lot of fight left in the old son of a bitch."

Tonight, Count Sforza returned to Naples and issued a flat demand to King Victor Emmanuel that he should abdicate in favor of a regency, with the young Prince of Naples as monarch. The King gave no sign of complying with this ultimatum.

November 16

At the dingy headquarters of the Committee of National Liberation, in Naples, we found the leaders of the six political parties in excited conclave. Arangio Ruiz, the chairman, was not present, but Claudio Ferri, the local head of the Political Action Party, acting chairman, told us that the Committee had written a message of confidence to Sforza. "We ask the formation right away of a political regency," said the little man. "We are in accord with Count Sforza." We asked precisely what was meant by a "political regency," and he said, "A regency, political, and not dynastic." Which meant that, like Count Sforza, the Committee feels that neither King Victor Emmanuel nor Prince Umberto should have the throne, because of their background of collaboration with the Fascists.

November 18

With both the political and the military fronts at a virtual impasse, I decided to go up to the front, even though it is stable. I first stopped in at the 34th Division C.P., about nine miles south of Venafro. There I talked with Col. Reichman, the Intelligence Officer: the enemy are reinforcing their positions with fresh troops and artillery. "They've brought in two regiments opposite us," he said. "And we've had some heavy artillery recently—fifteen and seventeen cm. Some stuff came over this command post last night that sounded like freight trains.

"The Germans have strewn mines promiscuously. Sometimes, German patrols have been blown up by their own TNT. The terrain is extremely rugged. Some of our companies are up on hills you couldn't possibly get a mule on. We're trying to relieve them every few days, and get 'em back in buildings where they can have a charcoal fire and get dried out."

We drove up to Venafro. The Rangers and the 509th Parachute Infantry have been put into the line to fight as foot troops in this vital sector. At the Ranger C.P., a few soggy tents in an orchard on a stony mountainside, we found Col. Darby talking on the field telephone, energetically inquiring about an officer who had been wounded. "Is he still breathin'?" he asked. "Well, then come off sayin' he's bad hurt. By the time the rumor gets down here, they'll have him killed."

The telephone conversation over, the husky Ranger colonel gave us a quick summary of the current position: the Rangers and the

Parachutes hold the two peaks, Mount Corno and Mount Croce to the west of Venafro, and the long ridge which runs between them. The mountain mass, rising at the peaks of Corno and Croce to a height of more than 3,000 feet, commands the whole Venafro plain and also looks west toward Cassino. The relatively small groups of Parachutes and Rangers have the job of holding this sector in the present static situation. Most of the fighting is patrol activity, as small groups probe enemy lines.

At the C.P. of the Parachutes, I found an old friend, Lieut. Col. Bill Yarborough, C.O. of the outfit, and asked about the "winter line." Yarborough commented, "It looks as if they're really dug in with the expectation of staying all winter. Our men have discovered lots of food—potatoes, bread and corn. The Heinies had a lot of blankets, mattresses, and warm clothing. Some of their dugouts—caves hollowed in the mountains—were as big as twenty or twenty-five feet across and seven feet high."

It was getting dark, and as we would have a rough drive under blackout conditions back to the P.R.O. Yarborough suggested that I spend a night at his C.P. Then we could visit the outposts and have a look at the fighting. I said I'd be back in a few days.

November 19

This afternoon, Maj. Papurt told me that the arrest of Fascists is continuing. Between 4,000 and 5,000 people in the Naples area have been checked by C.I.C. officers. He said, "One of, the biggest pinches is still to be made: Giuseppe Frignani, president of the Bank of Naples. That job should be done tomorrow. Frignani was the pay-off guy for the Party. He used to make big loans, which were not going to be paid back, to Fascists whom Mussolini wanted to reward."

Papurt showed me a copy of a letter sent to Frignani by Mussolini in 1928, when Frignani became president of the bank, which said, "You are well trained for this position as well on the professional as on the Fascist side. My instructions are simple: from the political point of view we must Fascistize this old and famous institution."

It might be interesting to see just how the arrest of a famed Fascist would be made. I asked Papurt for permission to go along with his agents. The request was granted.

November 20

Jack Rice, the photographer, and I followed a group of seven officers from the C.I.C. into the Bank of Naples. It looked like a pinch by G-men hack in the States. Bank employees stared as the group of men, about half of them in plainclothes, came through the glittering modernistic lobby and sought out the office of the president. Curious Italians peeped around the corners and whispered. Possibly they had heard that Frignani was going to "get his."

The leading agent, who wore civilian clothes, made it known only that he wanted to look at certain rooms which were being requisitioned by British and American authorities. Frignani, a thunderously dark man with black eyes, glanced about nervously as he led the squad to the offices. Then he slipped into a small room, where we could see him in heated conversation with two other men. And the poker-faced American agent waited, confidently. I wondered then why he did not worry about the possibility of Frignani's escape. I learned later that guards covered all the exits.

Time dragged. The slight man who had been interpreting for Frignani asked the leading agent nervously, "Excuse me, do you need Mr. Frignani any longer?"

"Yes," said the agent. "We'll go to the office to arrange for requisitioning these rooms."

We were waiting for the keys. There was an awkward pause as we stood in the president's chamber. The little interpreter talked faster, more nervously, as we asked casual questions about the furniture. Jack Rice sought permission to make a picture now. And the poker-faced agent, turning to the interpreter, asked politely, "Would Mr. Frignani like to have his picture taken?" And Frignani, somewhat muddled, not sure whether to protest or assent, finally sat down at his desk, while Rice snapped a flash bulb.

"That's a nice picture," I suggested to the agent.

"If you have to waste film," he said. And then—for the keys had come—he said to the interpreter, "Will you tell Mr. Frignani that we're very sorry but we're taking him into custody for the Allied Governments?"

The interpreter gulped and looked as if the floor had fallen away from under his feet, and he stuttered, "I—I don't follow, sir."

"We're arresting him," said the agent. When the interpreter relayed the message, Frignani's black eyes looked more like thunderclouds than ever.

By the time we had taken him to the file room, and he was being asked about certain letters from Count Ciano, he had regained his composure. He wagged his head negatively, and the interpreter translated, "Mr. Frignani says that in the matter of Count Ciano he has nothing to say." The bank president's intense face seemed more relaxed—possibly because he had discovered that he was not going to be tortured, as he might have expected had this been an Axis arrest. All he wanted to know, said the interpreter, was whether or not he was going to prison. The lean, dark face did not betray a ripple of emotion as the agent said, "Yes, to prison, to be questioned."

The employees were buzzing with excitement as we left the building. Here they had concrete evidence that a new era, for better or worse, was emerging in Italian politics. It might take them some time to learn that they would really have a chance to govern themselves after twenty-two years of Fascism. It might take time to generate "the wind of enthusiasm" which Count Sforza had called for, to shape the "beautiful Italy" he envisioned.

At least, I have been privileged to watch the beginnings of that movement and possibly the regeneration of a "beautiful Italy."

But politics is not my field; I am a war correspondent. Therefore, I am relieved to hear that Mike Chinigo, of INS, has been assigned to cover political developments in Italy. I am free to return to the war—not an unmixed blessing, but a change from the elaborate plot and counterplot stewing in Naples.

Tomorrow I'll be going back to the front lines, to visit the Venafro sector, to go out on a patrol again.

Souvenir

November 21

THE LURE OF THE FRONT IS LIKE AN OPIATE. AFTER abstinence and the tedium of workaday life, its attraction becomes more and more insistent. Perhaps the hazards of battle, perhaps the danger itself, stir the imagination and give transcendent meanings to things ordinarily taken for granted. The basic drama of men locked in a death struggle, with the stakes their own lives, offers a violent contrast to the routine conflicts in Naples.

It was late afternoon when I reached the Venafro plain and almost dark when I arrived at Ranger headquarters. There, the Executive Officer, Maj. Frederick J. Saam, was busy at the telephone. He put his hand on the mouthpiece as he explained to me, "It's Col. Darby. He is up on Mount Corno."

I waited while he resumed his conversation with the colonel. Then he said to me, "It's pretty hot up there. The Krauts have got into a cave near the top of the peak. They're trying to throw us out of our positions. We're holding on, but they're tossing hand grenades and everything."

Saam relayed Col. Darby's instructions to Maj. Bill Hutchinson, C.O. of chemical mortars, the big 4.2-inch sub-artillery which had done such heroic duty back at Chiunzi Pass.

Somewhere near us, our mortars pinged and we could hear the distant crashing of the shells landing somewhere on the other side of the mountain. I looked up the slope leading to the sharp peak of Mount Corno. I saw the sudden flashing of golden tracers from a small rise in the ponderous mountain mass running in a high saddle between Mount Corno, on the left, and Mount Croce, to the right. A few seconds after we saw the tracers, we heard the slow-paced pap-pap-pap-pap-pap of an American machine gun. The tracers lanced through the twilight sky, and I could see that they were disappearing *behind* Mount Corno. That would mean that the firing was being directed at the far slope, that the Germans had not yet reached the peak.

Maj. Saam explained the importance of the ridge of mountain terrain which formed Mount Corno and Mount Croce.

"If the Germans can grab the top of Corno," Saam said, "they'll have wonderful observation of the whole Venafro plain. Then they'll be able to blast hell out of all the artillery we have spread out down there."

As we were talking, we heard a loud screech coming in our direction. I jumped, with a group of shell-weary Rangers, into a ditch near the C.P. tent. The shell burst, a splash of black smoke and debris rising on the middle slope of Mount Corno. We grinned; it had seemed closer than that. The precipitous mountains had amplified the sound.

When two more screamed, we did not duck, but watched the explosions on the trail which led up toward the top of Mount Corno. "See what I mean?" said Saam. "The Jerries haven't got observation. All they can do is fire blind at numbered points on this side of the mountains—just in the hope that some of our people will be there when they shoot. That place up on the trail is one of the spots they can reach with their guns. And they're always putting concentrations down on the turn of the road at Venafro, hoping they'll catch some traffic there."

Col. Bill Yarborough, C.O. of the Parachutes who are working with the Rangers in this sector, dropped into the C.P. just after dark. He said that he would be going up to the top of the Corno-Croce ridge tomorrow with Capt. Tomasik (Edmund J. Tomasik, of New Bedford, Mass.), his Executive Officer, and that if I wanted to, I could go along. I accepted with alacrity.

We went down into Venafro, to Col. Yarborough's headquarters on the bank of the stream which runs through the town. One of the men had set a huge fire in the hearth and the heat was a welcome change from the dank out-of-doors.

We spread our blankets on the floor. We joked about the vermin and the possibilities of being blown up at any minute. We talked about home and other pleasant places. The three enlisted men reminisced about girls they had known during a stay in England. One of them contended that English girls are just as good at jitterbugging as American dames. Then we heard the first shells coming.

In the beginning they whined and crashed some distance away. We listened for the sounds to grow closer and louder. Waiting here on the floor was much more comfortable than lying in a ditch outside—and probably safer.

November 22

This morning we could see how close the shells had landed. One fresh crater, no more than fifty feet away from the house, had come closest. Three others had landed within a radius of 100 feet.

Col. Yarborough, Capt. Tomasik and I started out in a jeep for Ranger headquarters, to check on the latest developments on Mount Corno. Maj. Saam said that the fighting had quieted down after last night's outburst, but that the Germans still held the cave on the far side of Mount Corno near the top.

"It's something to see," he said. "You can watch 'em sticking out their heads and throwing grenades. Our plan for today is to carry up bangalore torpedoes. The boys on Corno will try to lower 'em close to the cave and blow out the Krauts. We've already flopped with dynamite and grenades. This has got to work. There's only a squad of Germans in the cave itself, but on the far slope, two fresh battalions of enemy troops are moving up. If the squad in the cave can hold on long enough, the rest of the Krauts will creep up and grab the ridge."

Tomasik, Yarborough and I started up the steep, craggy slope of Mount Corno in our jeep.

"We might as well go as far as we can by jeep," said Yarborough. "It'll take us long enough to walk up the darn mountain after that."

So we chugged through a stony orchard, bouncing over the outcrops of rock, and came to a virtually insurmountable slope. We left the jeep and began to clamber up the rocks on foot.

Col. Yarborough said, "I know a place where you can watch the fireworks, if you want to. You'd better leave that mackinaw behind." He indicated the heavy coat I was wearing. "We'll work up enough of a sweat if we go in shirtsleeves. It's only a couple of miles, but it'll take a couple of hours."

We were certainly perspiring as we passed beyond the fringe of scrub trees which covers the lower slopes of the mountain. Progress was slow up the stony mule track leading toward the bare summit.

There was no firing now. I kept my eyes on the rocks underfoot—and soon realized that we were following a literal trail of blood! Some of the stones were spattered with dark-red spots. This trail was the only negotiable route up the precipitous slope. Consequently, the wounded were bound to leave marks on the white rocks as they staggered or were carried down the winding path.

The track had a macabre fascination for me. I watched the variations in the trail of red spots; occasionally, the drops covered more rocks in one area, indicating, possibly, that a man had been wounded at that spot, or had stopped for a rest as he struggled to the aid station.

We walked in single file, at wide intervals, so that we would not all be killed or wounded by a single shell. This territory might be under heavy enemy fire at any moment, without warning. We halted several times and sat down in the trail, streaming sweat, but even when we rested, we remained scattered.

After another hour of climbing, we heard the sound of tumbling rocks from somewhere above us. Tomasik whipped out his .45; we halted and listened. "It might be an enemy patrol," Tomasik whispered. The sounds continued: falling stones, large objects brushing through the tall grass on the flank of the hill above.

We waited, frozen, and then saw an American helmet, then another, in the underbrush—one of our own patrols. We breathed more freely.

Farther up the trail, we spotted a single figure of a man, wearing an American uniform. When he came closer, we recognized Col. Darby. The Ranger leader was grimy and disheveled. A great rent had been torn in his trousers, exposing his long woolen underwear. Despite his ragged appearance, he spoke with his usual energy. "Rough up here last night," he said. "The damn Krauts were giving us hell." He pointed out a great knout of rock clinging to the flank of the ridge. At the top of the rock mass, we could see a sharp cleft through which the trail passed. "The sons of bitches were laying 'em right on there. Had to hang on so we wouldn't get blown off."

Yarborough, Tomasik and I stopped at the cleft in the rock, where twenty or thirty bedraggled and dirty Rangers sprawled. They had been up on the white rock at the top of Mount Corno, battling with the Germans who were trying to seize the peak. Other forces had relieved them.

They looked utterly exhausted, all the more unhappy because they reclined amidst a litter of ration cans, pasteboard boxes and empty shell cartons.

Gradually we progressed along the flank of the ridge running between the peaks of Mount Corno and Mount Croce. Near the top of this great massif, I realized, as always in mountainous terrain, the vastness of the hills in which we are fighting, and how puny our destructive efforts have been. We could wipe a town off the map with concentrated shelling, but we could not do more than scratch the hide of the earth. Up here, we were like fleas picking our way across the ribs of a mammoth animal.

We turned off the mule trail and started up the steepest part of the ridge. "You can get a good look at the fighting on Mount Corno from the top of this ridge," Yarborough offered.

He and Tomasik moved along toward Mount Croce, to inspect other positions. I stayed behind. At the top of the ridge, a few hundred yards from the crest of Mount Corno, I found an American observation post. The view of the peak and the large white rock on the German side was magnificent. With binoculars, I could make out occasional helmeted heads of Americans, barely distinguishable round spots, marking positions where Rangers were dug in on the summit of Mount Corno. While I watched, a squirt of black smoke dabbed the skyline. Then another, and another. They were German hand grenades, probably tossed from the base of the great white boulder. Somewhere at the foot of that boulder, I knew, the

Germans were hiding in their cave. Presumably, the American helmets moving across the peak were the squad which had the job of lowering bangalore torpedoes over the rock and down into positions where they might blast the German strong point.

To the west of the peak of Mount Corno, the mountain mass, speckled with small trees, sloped steeply downward. Somewhere on that slope, the Germans were dug in. From the stubble of vegetation, a far-spreading cloud of smoke was rising. Large, rapidly springing bursts leaped from the woods as shells were striking. Our big 4.2-inch mortars were trying to keep back the tide of Germans inching up the grade.

From the ridge top where I was lying, there spread below me to the west the vast panorama of Italy. The brown scattering of roofless buildings in the next valley was the village of Concasale, where the cancerous pittings of shell craters disfigured the green face of the ground. Two ridges beyond, the town of Cassino sprawled up the mountainside. And beyond that, gray in the mist of distance, the mountain ridges were piled up, one on top of the other as far as we could see, like giant stony steps ascending gradually to Rome. Where, I wondered, was the "level, straight route" which is supposed to be ours once we conquer Cassino?

Near me, in a shallow, rocky foxhole, sat Maj. Bill Hutchinson, shouting corrections by phone to his 4.2 mortar batteries near Venafro. He cautioned me sharply against exposing myself in my movements across the ridge.

"We're within machine-gun range of Mount Corno," he said.

One of the group of men scattered over the ridge top was Capt. Shunstrom, the same wild man who had operated the mobile artillery so effectively with the Rangers back at Chiunzi Pass. Now he was fiddling with a 60-mm. mortar tube, preparing to add a few shells to the torrent of explosives falling on the German positions atop Mount Corno. "Here's the way to shoot one of these things," he announced. He braced the base-end of the tube against the ground and gave a demonstration, firing the powerful field weapon as if it were a pistol or rifle.

Usually, the 60-mm. mortar tube, which throws a projectile about two and a half inches in diameter and nearly a foot long, is attached to a heavy base plate when it is set up for firing, with a bipod supporting the tube at the proper angle. A mortar man drops the projectile down the mouth of the barrel and steps back to keep clear of the shell as it speeds from the muzzle. But Shunstrom had his own system. He wrapped the bare tube, without stand or bipod, in an old glove—which would insulate the heat of the barrel—seized the tube with his left hand, aimed it approximately, and dropped the mortar shell down the mouth with his right hand.

His marksmanship was surprisingly accurate. The first burst sprang up less than fifty feet from the top of the white rock at the peak of Mount Corno, and the second blew up on the rock itself. Shunstrom fired ten or eleven shells, three of them landing on the stone, and one close to the cave where the Germans must have been dug in. Shunstrom gave a grunt of satisfaction.

I watched the fireworks: the firing of the heavy mortars which were giving the Germans hell on the far slope of Corno, and had set fire to some of the trees there; Shunstrom's wildcat marksmanship with his mortar; the slender plume of smoke raised by a German hand grenade near the top of Corno. Finally, I saw a great explosion blossoming from the white rock itself—perhaps the detonation of the bangalore torpedoes, or a charge of dynamite. Maj. Hutchinson said, "Great fun, as long as we're dishing it out and not taking it."

Yarborough and Tomasik came back from their inspection tour, and we started down the tedious trail toward home. I felt a healthy fatigue. For the first time in several weeks, I had a bang-up eyewitness story of an action at a crucial sector of the front. But there was an even better story ahead of me.

We reached the cleft rock, the local C.P., and I stopped for a few minutes to talk to some of the Rangers, while Tomasik and Yarborough went on. I would catch up with them later. I got the notes I wanted and hurried after them. Past the curve in the trail where we had listened, tautly, to the approach of a patrol on our way up, I was making my way along the relatively straight stretch where the German mortar shells had been falling on the previous day. Then I got it.

I heard the scream of something coming, and I must have dived to the rocks instinctively. Months of conditioning on many battlefields resolved themselves in that instantaneous, life-saving reflex. Then a smothering explosion descended around me. It seemed to flood over me from above. In a fraction of a second of consciousness, I sensed that I had been hit. A curtain of fire rose, hesitated, hovered for an infinite second. In that measureless interval, an orange mist came up quickly over my horizon, like a tropical sunrise, and set again, leaving me in the dark. Then the curtain descended, gently.

I must have been unconscious for a few seconds. When a rudimentary awareness came back, I knew everything was all wrong. I realized I had been badly hit. I was still stretched on the rocks. A couple of feet from me lay my helmet which had been gashed in at least two places, one hole at the front and another ripping through the side.

Catastrophe had struck me down. My shocked perceptions groped for an understanding of what had happened. It was no use.

There was no pain. Everything seemed finished, quiet, as if time had stopped. I sat up and looked back at the path. Now I saw the motion of figures of men running up the trail at a half crouch, as a man would zigzag through shellfire. There must be danger. I was aware of that at least. I tried to shout at them, but only incoherent sounds tumbled from my mouth, and my voice rattled, as if it were coming from some place far off and beyond my control. It was like a broken, muted phonograph.

My mind formulated frantic questions. What's wrong? Why can't I talk? What am I going to do? And then I felt a slight easing of tension, a slight relaxation. I knew, then, that even though I could not utter the words, I could still think. I had lost my power of speech, not my power to understand or generate thought. It was clear to me what I wanted to say, but I couldn't say it.

By this time the men had gone, and it was evident that they were too concerned with something else to come back and pay attention to me.

A shell was coming. I knew that because I heard the sound of the approaching projectile. But the sound was just a tinny little echo of something which had once been terrifying and all-powerful. And the explosion, while it seemed to rattle my skull, was certainly not terrifying. I couldn't understand the fear written on the face of a soldier who had skidded into the ground near me as he sought to take cover from the bursting of the shell.

I tried, with my distant and almost uncontrollable voice, to talk intelligibly to the frightened soldier during the few seconds he was there. I was trying to say, "Can you help me?" And after a number of unconnected, stumbling syllables, I finally managed two words, "Can help?"

I heard the tinny sound of a little shell, and saw the soldier's face, hollowed by terror. He was saying, "I can't help you, I'm too scared." And then he was gone, running, up the trail.

I have no recollection how soon the first-aid man dropped to the ground beside me and bandaged my head. But it was done, in those few minutes, and I saw the needle of the hypo as he gave me a shot of morphine. I did not feel the prick of the needle. The first-aid man was gone. I was alone on the mountainside.

I knew, then, that if I wanted to get back to the field dressing station, I would have to go under my own power. I would have to get up and walk down the trail in the hope that I might still catch up with Col. Yarborough. Somehow, shock seemed to have allayed any pain I might otherwise have experienced. The quick administration of morphine within a few minutes of the time of injury dulled my concern about my wound.

My glasses were lying on the rocks a few inches away. Miraculously, they had been blown off without being broken. I tried to move my right hand to pick up the spectacles, and realized that the whole arm was as inert as a board. I grabbed the glasses with my left hand and put them on. They were not very secure because my head was bandaged, and they were askew on my nose. I picked up my helmet. It would be a fine souvenir, I thought illogically. That too sat precariously on my bandaged head. I grasped my right arm in my left hand. Touching it was like touching a foreign body, and when I dropped it, it fell limply, beyond control, at my side.

I stood up and started down the trail. My helmet bobbed on the bulky bandages around my head, and finally it slid off and bounced on the ground. Determined to save it at all costs, I picked it up and put it back on my head.

Then a shell came. I heard the same ragged, distant whistling, and the rattling explosion, as I automatically fell to the rocks for protection. I waited for the rest of the group of shells to arrive, and they were close. I looked up and saw tall spouts of smoke and high explosive jumping up all around me—but it was all unreal, like a movie with a feeble sound track. Probably the concussion of the shell burst which had hit me had also deafened me. I was amazed, but not frightened, as one huge shell burst suddenly sprang into being, towered over me like a genie. It was so close that I could have reached out and touched it. Yet none of the flying fragments had brushed me.

When the burst of firing was over, I scrambled to my feet again. Dropping my helmet, I stubbornly picked it up and put it back on my head. My glasses slipped down on my nose again and again. A red drapery of blood ran down over the glasses and blurred my vision. Staggering down the trail, I dropped my helmet again, several times, and doggedly retrieved it. My right arm and hand dangled loosely. I muttered to myself, trying to talk straight, practicing—and still able to mouth only a sort of ape-chatter. If anyone had been there to see me, I would have been a grotesque apparition.

Shells were coming again. This time I headed for a shallow cave carved in the rock at the side of the trail, and took refuge in it. A feeling of simple contentment came over me because the shells were landing harmlessly outside, while I was secure in my hideaway. Here, in a shelter originally dug by a German, I smiled, sat and waited for the spell of firing to cease. I remembered that I must go on as soon as the firing stopped. My mind fixed on the idea that the only way to get out of this was by catching up with Yarborough and Tomasik. If I had to stay up on the mountain overnight, and wait for someone to find me, before I could be carried down, I might not be alive in the morning.

When the firing stopped, I staggered onto the path. I went as fast as I could, dropping my helmet occasionally and picking it up; I was determined to preserve it. I heard the rustle of the shells again, and automatically sprawled on the rocks. The muffled explosions seemed quite a distance away now. I got up. If only I could catch up with Yarborough. Nothing else seemed too important. After all, I had realized the odds and often speculated upon them. Already I had more than used up my chances. If I could get through this thing alive, I thought, I could start on a fresh bunch of chances.

I came around a bend of the trail, and felt a surge of pleasure as I saw Col. Yarborough and Capt. Tomasik, bending over a wounded man. Fortunately for me, they had stayed behind to care for him. Yarborough started to wave to me, then noticed the bandaged head, the bloody glasses and red-stained shirt.

More shells squeaked and rattled into the side of the ridge, and we ducked. When it was over, Bill Yarborough and I started together down the trail. My one usable arm was draped over his shoulder. He provided support for my staggering feet.

Once, we had to stop to shoo from the trail three wild-eyed pack mules, frightened by the shelling and deserted by their keeper. Once, we had to take shelter when the shells came again. Twice or three times, I lost my dubious balance and fell. Yarborough helped me to my feet. The trail seemed endlessly long—actually it was about a mile that we had to travel—and it would have seemed nightmarish had it not been for the shot of morphine, and the great shock of the wound. Still, there was not the faintest trace of pain.

And so we reached a command post, in a peasant house at the fringe of the woods. Two aid men sat me down, looked at my head and expertly slit the sleeve of my shirt to inspect my useless arm. There were no marks on the arm. Then I knew it had been paralyzed in some way. Yarborough gave me five or six sulfa tablets. The dashing parachutist doctor, Capt. Alden, looked at my head, said nothing. I tried to talk. The words were still unintelligible. I lay on the dirt floor and looked up at the line of soldiers staring at me, the Badly Wounded Man. I must have stared just that way at many a wounded man whom I had seen. Now I was on the other side of the picture, for a change.

I had another shot of morphine, and dozed. I remember being sick. Then I was stretched out in the rear of a jeep. I asked again and again whether my notes, and especially my helmet, were aboard. They were. The air felt cool as we began to move down the steep mountain side. A faint light hovered in the sky. It was late afternoon. The time must have been about four-thirty, about two hours after I was hit.

Once we had begun to move, I lost consciousness. We must have stopped somewhere, for I remember being in a tent, and hearing voices that said something about "tetanus shot." I did not see or feel the needle.

Then I became aware that it was dark and cold, and that I was being carried on a stretcher. They put me down inside a tent, where a bright electric light glared. I heard gruff voices. The stretcher bearers picked me up again. We passed into the night, the stretcher bumping with the steps of the aid men. They carried me into another tent, less garishly lighted than the first. It was cold. I lay and shivered.

I was brought to still another tent, which seemed warmer. A voice asked me about my right arm, and, in general, how I felt. I tried to explain these matters, but my words would not come out right.

They were as badly tangled as before. Instead of saying something like "The arm's been like that since I got hit up on the mountain," I said, "The sam—I mean farm—I mean tam—farm, sam—like that since I got bit—rot—rat—hut, on the rountain, I mean fountain— bounty—fountain."

I was feeling warmer. The stretcher bearers came in again and picked me up and carried me to still another tent, which, even in my present drugged condition, I recognized as an X-ray room. I knew that I had been set down on the floor, still on my stretcher, while loud voices could be heard talking. I was sensitive, as I suppose patients in general must be, to the tone of the voices. These were rough and grumbling.

Very different was the next voice I heard talking to me as I was carried back to the tent which I had just left. It was cheerful, very considerate. The man said that he was sorry but that he was going to have to shave my head. He did not want it to hurt.

Another man came in, looked down at me and informed me, "We're going to have to operate on you." This voice was very brusque. I wanted to ask him something. It was the question, "Am I going to die?" After several attempts, I conveyed the intended meaning, but the man, evidently the doctor, wouldn't commit himself.

Then there was another, pleasant man, sitting by my side. I realized that he must be a minister. His voice was very calm and soothing. He was saying a prayer. I thanked him; the mere sound of the words was comforting. Then I had another shot of morphine.

Battle Scarred

November 23—December 10

THE OPERATING TABLE WAS A CRUDE SCAFFOLDING OF. board I was aware of people moving about the head of the improvised surgical platform. From time to time, I heard the efficient voice of the doctor, "If it hurts, we'll give you more medicine." Novocaine had frozen all sensation on the top of my head; cranial operations are usually performed under local anesthesia.

Morphine shots had drugged me into a stupor, but I could distinguish voices occasionally, heard a crunching sound and a snapping of bone as some sort of instrument gouged into my skull.

I was propped up in a semi-sitting position. At the lower end of the operating table, white-masked attendants were fiddling with bottles attached to a metal stand. They were giving me a transfusion of blood and plasma through veins in the foot. As the operation continued (it required four hours, all told) my legs grew stiff and I tried to move them. They were tied down at the ankles. Toward the end of the operation, I was more annoyed about my legs than by the operation on my head. My inability to move them irked and then infuriated me. At first I tried to hold them still, but, after a while, I gave it up. I fidgeted.

Most of the doctor's words seemed blurred, but I could detect, I thought, a note perhaps of irritability, certainly of weariness. He was muttering something that came to me as, "What's the matter with that?" And he said something about "stuffing it back in there." At that moment, I hoped that if he were angry, he wouldn't vent his displeasure on my head. Then it was all over, and I fell into a tortured sleep.

The first few days were an agony of nausea. During the hours of sleep my stomach was constantly on the verge of revolt, and when I woke up, it was always to retch. Subconsciously I had hoped that my speech would improve as a result of the operation, but I was disappointed to find that it came with even less coherence than before. The whole right side of my body was numb. In order to move my right arm, I had to pick it up with my left. My right leg was a foreign body and the right side of my face was as thick and insensible as a layer of felt. My right eye refused to focus.

The doctor who had operated on me came in to see me. He was a young, good-looking man with a smooth face and slick black hair. After many attempts, while he waited patiently for me to shape the words, I managed to convey the idea that I could not put my ideas into words. He smiled and seemed to apprehend my meaning. He explained why I could not speak, why I was paralyzed on the right side. I had been hit in the left side of the brain, in the region which controlled speech in a right-handed person. The fact that I had been struck in the "motor area" had also affected the movement of my right side.

In moments when I was awake, I realized that I was drugged. I was propped up in an Army cot in a damp tent; the ground was its floor. A medical corpsman—the "ward boy" he was called—held the basin. Another patient, on the cot next to mine, had a rubber tube running into his nose. He looked very uncomfortable, but he did not move, and seldom said more than a word or two. He irritated me because he seemed stoical, and I didn't feel that way at all.

The tent was a long, open corridor, with a peaked roof. Rows of cots lined both sides. I was not interested in any of the cases, although I knew when stretcher bearers passed my bed with a new load of humanity, inward bound.

The first or second day, Margaret Bourke-White, the famed *Life* photographer, came in. She took some pictures, using two bright flash bulbs. She wanted me to smile and I tried several times, but the right side of the mouth resisted. Something like a grin resulted, but it felt lopsided, and the eyes were out of control.

After a couple of days of nausea, when innocent liquids like orange juice and even water would not stay down, the doctor arranged to feed me through a vein. A bottle of glucose, a clear liquid, was hung from a stand by the bedside, and a rubber tube ran down from the bottle to the needle which was inserted in my arm. The energy-giving food drained slowly. Within a few hours I began to feel better.

One or another of the nurses gave me pills several times a day; they were sulfadiazine tablets to prevent infection and aspirin to deaden headaches. One of the nurses, who had blonde hair and large blue eyes and a delicate face, like a child's, was on duty during the daylight hours. She had a sweet, piping voice, and smiled quickly. I called her "Goldilocks," when I could get the word out. She asked if I could pronounce her name—Miss McCain.

The ward boy on duty during the day was Bob Trafford. I also learned the name of the doctor. He was a major and his name was Pitts; William Pitts, and he came from Charlotte, N.C. Some of the other doctors visited me. I could register their faces; there were three lieutenant colonels (Sanger, White and Wood). They all came from Charlotte—for this was a Charlotte medical unit, an evacuation hospital. The chaplain (Capt. Kirkpatrick, of Florence, Mass.) brought me a New Testament and several religious pamphlets. He asked what denomination I belonged to and I could not say the word. I knew very well that it was "Presbyterian," but I had not the remotest idea how I could make the sound.

Newspaper friends—Clark Lee, Mike Chinigo, Ernie Pyle, Bill Strand, Red Knickerbocker, John Lardner and others, dropped in and asked how I had been wounded. I stumbled incoherently over my words. All the details of my being wounded were fresh and clear in my memory, but I could not express them. In self-reproach I reviled myself as an imbecile. It was some comfort that at least I had brains enough left to recollect that word.

Sometimes, when there was no one to talk to, I brooded over my bleak future: to be a writer with the self-expressive powers of an idiot, a war correspondent who couldn't talk or use his right arm or hand, or even ask intelligible questions. I thought I would wait until I was homeward bound on the boat. Then I would know whether any of my faculties would come back to me. If I remained, to all intents and purposes, an idiot and a helpless cripple, I could always jump over the side. The prospect was black, but I could hope—and wait and see.

One of the correspondents brought me ten or twelve letters from home—letters always arrive in bunches overseas. I tried to read one of them, but my eyes didn't co-ordinate. I could see the words, and occasionally understand an isolated phrase, but I couldn't put the pieces together. I stowed all the letters away, hoping that someday I would be able to make sense out of them.

Always available was the pastime of listening to the other patients' conversation. It had been an annoyance during the days of nausea; now it was diversion. Sometimes, I also tried to talk, now and then getting out one sentence which was straight; often failing—and sometimes saying, quite unintentionally, things which might have been embarrassing to the nurses.

Dr. Pitts came in one day and tried all my reflexes, using a rubber hammer and a pin. As usual, he preserved professional silence. I watched as he wrote a long report on the chart which was attached to my bed. I signaled for his attention. My words were confused, but determined, as I badgered him for information about my injury. I wanted to know definitely whether I would be able to talk sensibly again, whether I would some day regain the use of my arm and whether I would be able to walk normally.

He told me little: only that I would probably have to recuperate for at least six months; that, later on, a surgeon would have to patch up my skull with a metal plate. The shell fragment had smashed the bone, driving fragments into the brain. These he had removed, and he had covered the hole only temporarily with fascia, or scalp muscle. Recovery, he emphasized, would be a slow process.

As he told me all this, he was still brisk in manner. But later, as I came to know him better, I understood the reason for his briskness. He was working night and day, conscientiously, hard. Some mornings, on his regular visits, he would say, "Well, I had three hours' sleep last night. Feeling healthy today." I found out that he had operated on two other bad head cases the night I had been wounded. It was not until 4 A.M. that he had been ready for me.

There were always new cases coming in to our ward, others being carried out. This was an evacuation hospital, designed to give immediate treatment to badly wounded men near the front; then, as soon as they were well enough, to send them back to general hospitals to the rear.

Each time the stretcher bearers appeared at the tent-flap with a new case, we craned our necks to look at the passing face. Usually the newcomers were unconscious; they were fresh from the operating room. Some of them talked steadily as they were placed on their cots; they were recovering from ether jags. One came in singing a disconnected version of "Pistol Packin' Momma."

It was interesting to see that the new arrivals went through a cycle, being, at first, groggy or sick in their stomachs, totally uninterested in our conversation, or actively annoyed with it; and then they began to feel better and talk about wanting to get out. Those who could walk would eventually be given red corduroy robes, with the letters "M.D., U.S.A." sewn in white on the pocket. Typical of hospital humor was the grim interpretation we attached to those initials: "Many Die, You Shall Also."

I awoke from an afternoon sleep, wondering whether a change had come over my arm. I had fancied in the last moments of sleep that something was crawling over my hand. It was not a dream; the sensation was real. Alarmed, I felt an electric tremor from my elbow to the tips of my fingers. It was as if something were prickling through all of the nerves, and the whole arm began to feel as if it were banging, like a door in the wind. With my left hand I touched the vibrant arm and realized, unbelieving, that it was not jumping at all. It was, in fact, outwardly as still as a statue.

Then the feeling of electric activity crept up into the shoulder, into the neck, and my whole field of vision snapped out of joint. My mouth stretched as if it had been seized by a pair of pliers at one corner and was being twisted across my whole face. There was a dire need for licking my lips—which I did, feverishly—and my mouth was filled with a strong metallic taste. When it was over, I was completely fatigued. My speech thickened noticeably. I called for Miss McCain, and Dr. Pitts hurried in. He asked me many questions while he scribbled a long entry in my report. Again he said nothing. I lay stupefied, waiting for the next manifestation of change. Gradually my alarm subsided and was replaced by unconcern, and, then, with the passing of time, a mounting exaltation. There was more feeling in my arm! I tried a few tentative movements. The hand reacted. My face felt less thick. I could see better.

With an improved right arm—the hand was still numb—I could eat a little more easily. I could also read a few more words of my mail. I opened one letter, tentatively, and found that I could follow at least the general idea. I tore open a few more, and had some success. I saved the rest for later. Still, I could not utter the name of the city where I was born, when Dr. Pitts asked me to read it from an envelope. I knew very well that it was "Elizabeth, N. J." but when I tried, it came out something like "Rooker"—which had no association in either sound or idea with the word on the paper.

Most baffling of all were the cable messages from my friends at INS. One said something about Gen. Eisenhower and, in the same sentence, about me. It mentioned W. R. Hearst and J. V. Connolly, head of King Features Syndicate. I puzzled and puzzled over the message, trying to figure out whether it came from Hearst, Connolly or Gen. Eisenhower. Actually the message read:

FROM J. V. CONNOLLY QUOTE PLEASE BE A LITTLE MORE CAREFUL. KINDLY REPORT THE WAR AND DON'T FIGHT ALL OF IT. GIVE GEN. EISENHOWER A CHANCE TO DO HIS STUFF. W. R. HEARST UNQUOTE.

There was also a note from Gen. Clark. I could not follow it closely, but it was a message of consolation, and said something about my injury. I asked the Red Cross girl to write an answer. I certainly could not write or even dictate.

I learned the name of most of the men in the beds around me. The lieutenant with the tube in his nose, who had been so patient and quiet, was Stewart Walker, of Pennacook, N.H. He was very sick, for he had suffered multiple shell-fragment wounds of leg, arm and body. His ructious stomach demanded frequent attention from the ward boys, but he never complained. Eventually he was transferred to a more isolated corner, where he would not be bothered by the more or less constant conversation of his tent mates.

Another neighbor was a young, black-haired boy whose patient, slightly weary manner made him seem wise and grizzled. He was a Ranger officer; he had been through the Sicilian fighting before he was winged in the Venafro sector. The wound was in the upper back. Casually he showed me the irregular gash in the flesh; not serious. He was an ambulatory case and was listed as Class A, which meant that he would be returned to his unit within a few weeks. Most of the men in this ward were Class B or G—to be assigned, respectively, to limited service or returned to the United States for further treatment.

Our tent, which I learned was designated as Ward 13, was an officers' tent, but it also housed a number of enlisted men, head cases who were under Maj. Pitts' supervision. One of them was a muscular American Indian private who had a penetrating wound similar to mine. He, too, was partially paralyzed, but he had not lost his power of speech, which, however, he employed to a minimum. Maj. Pitts told me that the Indian—Pvt. C.W. Kenjockerty—had uttered only one syllable during three hours on the operating table. It was a grunt, said Dr. Pitts.

One of our best conversationalists was Maj. Bill Hutchinson, commanding officer of the chemical mortar battalion attached to the Rangers. I had last seen him up on Mount Corno. He had been wounded in the foot by a German shell fragment a few days after I was hit. Every day we heard from Bill about the great feats accomplished by the chemical mortars, both in Chiunzi Pass and in the Venafro sector. He had statistics to prove that the 4.2 mortar was one of the most effective weapons in the war. He was loud in praise of his men. He insisted that Purple Hearts were as common as campaign ribbons in the chemical mortar battalion.

Maj. Hutchinson was a staunch advocate of Lehigh University, of which he was an alumnus. When chemical mortars, medals and Lehigh University were temporarily exhausted as subjects for conversation, he would sing. He had a fine tenor voice, and would sometimes harmonize with a tank lieutenant, Paul Stephani, of Ridley Park, Pa. Frequently they would be joined by Lieut. Edgar Forsberg, of Hudson, Ohio, whom we called "Flea Bite." Lieut. Forsberg was being treated for a skin irritation.

Lieut. Stephani had majored in German at college, and Miss McCain used to sit on his cot for a few minutes each day while he taught her conjugations of irregular German verbs. For this reason the rest of us complained loudly in Miss McCain's presence that Stephani was her favorite.

There were several other nurses and perhaps a half-dozen ward boys. One of the night nurses was a black-haired beauty. I was practicing reading poetry in an attempt to bring back my memory of the written word—Maj. Hutchinson had lent me a *Pocket Book of Verse*—and when the nurse with raven tresses would come on duty, I would always attempt Byron's poem, "She walks in beauty, like the night." But I simply could not complete even the first line without faltering. I made a hopeless botch of the difficult second line, "Of cloudless climes and starry skies." But it was good practice.

I came to know Bill Pitts, the surgeon who had operated on me. His brisk manner disappeared when we talked about good old times in the States, before the war. He showed me a folder full of pictures of his pretty wife and little son. That precipitated a general exhibition of photos of patients' wives and sweethearts.

Most of the wounded soon got around to telling us how they had been hit. Within a few days we had heard each story several times. Lieut. Henry A. Pedicone, of Greensburg, Pa., whom we called "Petticoat," had a particularly narrow escape. He had been cut off in his forward artillery observation post when the Germans counter-attacked. Once, the Heinies had passed so close that he heard the sound of their feet, heard their voices. "Petticoat" played possum as a group of Germans watched him from a few yards' distance. One of them deliberately fired at him with a machine-pistol.

"Boy, I've still got the jitters from that one," he related. "I counted the shots—one, two, three, four—up to eight. They must have thought they'd finished me off."

It wasn't clear in my mind whether "Petticoat" had been hit at that time or before. At any rate, he had a machine-pistol wound in his hip.

Two beds removed from me lay a young lieutenant named Kirby, of the 34th Division. He had the same patient, battle-tested manner as the Ranger lieutenant. Kirby had lost one finger of his left hand when a sniper bullet struck him. He was a veteran even though he could not have been more than twenty-two. He told me he had been wounded once before and that his brother had been killed in the same barrage.

Capt. Stewart R. Dobbins, of Akron, Ohio, a 45th Division officer, had also been hit by a sniper bullet, which grazed his chest, making a raw flesh wound. Most of the casualties, however, had been caused by shell fragments.

Because our hospital was less than ten miles from the front line, we could hear artillery booming in the distance. But we were out of the normal gun range for enemy batteries. The night of December 6, the guns blasted away continuously. Next day a couple of correspondents dropped in to tell me that it was the heaviest bombardment so far in Italy. It had been directed against San Pietro, the next town beyond Venafro, on the road to Cassino.

I had fairly regular information from the correspondents about the progress of the fighting. In general, the front seemed to be moving slowly, with the troops inching toward Cassino. The 8th Army drive to force the Nazis out of the Cassino bastion was progressing very slowly. The Italians had moved some troops into the line on Mount Longo, near Cassino. I heard two reports on that. One day, the report was that Italian troops were impressive as they moved into position; the next day they were a fizzle; they had been shot up and driven off the hill. The Germans had sucked them into a trap, then cut them up. The Italians had advanced bravely, if not wisely, up an open slope. When the Germans had them where they wanted them, more than 350 Italians had been killed and wounded in one night's fighting. Now the Italians were being withdrawn from the line.

My right hand was improving steadily. I tried finger exercises, practiced flexing the muscles of the wrist for half-hour periods. Still the hand was numb, and I had a minimum of control of the fingers.

The ability to read was returning quite rapidly. I could now understand all my mail. Only complex sentences thwarted me. But my speech continued to stumble over itself. I practiced reciting lines of poetry, memorizing whole stanzas. I could repeat them mentally, but to put them into spoken words was a different affair. I had pretty well mastered such elementary matters as the identification of myself. I could usually say "Tregaskis" and sometimes even "Presbyterian." However, I had trouble with the elaborate "I want a Flying Fortress with a P-38 escort"—which was the customary way of asking the ward boy for a bed pan and urinal.

I remember distinctly the 8th of December. Then Dr. Pitts told me that I should get ready to leave the following day, or perhaps the day after. I tried not to be too hopeful. I busied myself with collecting full names and addresses of those around me on a piece of V-mail paper which was circulated from hand to hand.

The day passed, uneventfully, and the next morning Maj. Pitts informed me that at last I was to have my trip to the rear. He dressed my head in an exceptionally sturdy casque of gauze and adhesive tape. Later in the day the stretcher bearers came. I checked the belongings in my barracks bag to make sure that my notes, and my broken helmet, were there. Then I was carried down the corridor between the long lines of cots, and out into the sunlight. It was good to be on the move again, especially when I considered that I was going back to the United States.

December 10-22

The General seemed luxurious after Ward 13 of the 38th Evacuation Hospital. The General hospital had been set up in a *building*, north of Naples. There were floors—instead of bare ground—to keep shoes from molding. The rooms were centrally heated, without the bother and the undependability of pot-bellied stoves, which had been the only source of warmth, save blankets, in the tents of the 38th. And there were real iron beds, pretty close to 1,500 of them, each with two white sheets.

The ambulance ride over rough and muddy roads had tired me. When the neurosurgeon, a major named Webster, came to test my reactions, I felt tired and my co-ordination was not too good. I tried to convince him that it was all because I was worn out by the ride. Even though I had just arrived at this relatively luxurious hospital, I was already trying to persuade the doctor that I was fit to be moved farther on the route to the United States. I was naive enough to hope that I might reach home by Christmas, or at least for New Year's.

After the first few days, I was allowed to sit up. I soon learned to operate a wheelchair, although my right hand had very little feeling. I ranged the length of the officers' ward, and discovered some friends from the 38th Evac. One was Capt. Stewart Dobbins; another, a doctor from the 38th, now a patient here, Capt. Bob Miller, who had assisted Maj. Pitts in the operation on my head. Capt. Miller made up a report for my benefit. I learned some startling facts: for instance, the wound had been a "gutter-type" gouge in the skull, about four inches long and an inch wide; some of the bone fragments had penetrated as deep as two inches into my brain.

Maj. Webster used to come in the evening to change my dressings. He tested my reflexes by sticking me with a pin and striking various tendons with a steel hammer which had a wedge-shaped rubber head.

Once he brought along an assistant, Capt. Richard Schneider. They consulted for a moment, and Maj. Webster told me that they would make a "pinch" graft to speed the healing process. The skin would be taken from my thigh and placed on the wound. The following night the job was done.

Dr. Schneider did the slicing, under local anesthetic, and passed the pieces, one by one, to Maj. Webster. Deftly, Dr. Schneider had taken nine circular sections from the leg, and Webster applied the "pinches." When Webster said, "O.K.., one more, please," Schneider replied ruefully, "Oh, hell, you spoiled my design."

As time passed—and it passed slowly because I wanted to get home for Christmas—I came to know my roommates. Most of them were medical cases, suffering from some internal ailment, unlike the occupants of Ward 13 in the 38th Evac. And most of them were "ambulatory"; they could walk to meals and stroll a little in their red corduroy robes.

There were two cases of jaundice. They were slow-spoken, slow-moving Lieut. Morris Knigoff ("Kickoff" to us) of New York City; and blond Capt. Norman C. Linneman, of Hollywood, Cal. Knigoff and Linneman were the "senior members" of the ward, and were, as they freely admitted, a little "stir-crazy." They used to watch their "Icteric index," a medical obscurity, with feverish interest. The rest of us assured them that two years from now, when American tourists would be visiting the battlegrounds of Europe, Knigoff and Linneman would still be in Ward 7.

Lieut. Clyde R. Thorne, a large, beefy man with a deep Arkansas drawl, occupied the bed opposite mine. He was troubled by a "trick knee," a left-over from football days. As an infantry officer, with the 3rd Division, he found it inconvenient that one knee should always be slipping out of joint. We asked him how the Medical Board had overlooked the difficulty. He cogitated. "Why, you know how those old boys do it. A couple of docs stand up there, one over in the front of you, and one behind, and if they can't see through you, well, you're in."

Stew Dobbins and I, having shown each other pictures of our brides, used to dwell nostalgically on the delights of the United States. He had been chosen to go back to America on the "rotation program" which allows a very small number of officers and men to return home after a certain period of duty.

Stew had gone through the Sicilian campaign, and now was recuperating from a bullet wound received near Venafro. We looked forward to double dates with our wives in some café overlooking the bright lights of New York, places like the Rainbow Room and the St. Regis Roof. Somewhere, we found a copy of *Esquire*, and devoured the advertisements for things one could buy, back in the United States—particularly the large full-page advertisements of the liquor companies, which pictured, in full color, bottles of their products. Capt. Gene Salet, a patient in Dobbins' ward, warned us: "You better take it easy with that stuff, you guys. You'll be knocking yourselves out."

Dobbins and I laughed at him. We would have our date in the Rainbow Room before New Year's Day, we wagered. (I did not see Dobbins in the United States. He went back to duty while he was awaiting final orders to go home. He was sent to the Anzio beachhead and killed in action.)

As the days crept by, we came to know the medical personnel better. Cpl. "Frenchy" Brouillard, of Haverhill, Mass., was the ward boy we saw most often. The sergeant of the ward—whom we knew only as "Swede"—ran a close second. The day nurse, whom we called "Sunshine," was Miss Martin. She was small and vigorous, and usually preserved a stony expression. When she came into the room in the morning, we would say, "Here comes the tornado," and warn each other of her approach, for if you interfered with her bed making, you would get yourself knocked down.

There was a night nurse, whom we called "Moonbeam." She was more jovial than Miss Martin, but a stickler for the early blackout. She would hustle in sharply at ten to make sure that the lights were out and the windows open. Once, when some of the nurses brought up a Christmas plum pudding mailed from the United States, "Moonbeam" relaxed and extended our curfew.

Little by little I could read more easily. I could even write with a pencil. The scrawl was practically illegible, and the act of writing was a great travail, but I succeeded in composing a few short notes to my family. My greatest concern was that I had been unable to write to them. I believe that is typical: a wounded man worries not so much about his wound as about the fact that his family may be worrying about *him*.

I also tried to dictate a story about being wounded, but the effort of concentration was so great that, after four attempts, I gave up the idea.

I began to try to walk again: first a few steps, and then I could negotiate the length of the corridor. There remained a trace of paralysis in the right leg. But that diminished, and one day I could even walk downstairs. There I saw some of the other head cases. Then I realized how lucky I had been.

The patients were grouped in a small room. The first case was a private who held his bandaged head rigidly. One eye followed our movements, and the troubled voice talked straight up into the air, as Maj. Webster asked questions. The man could talk, but only a residue of intelligence seemed to remain. The doctor told me that the man had been hit by a shell fragment, on December 8. "It's the brain injury which has affected his eyes. He has only half the normal field of vision." And Maj. Webster explained how, had I been hit a couple of inches farther back in the skull, I would probably have suffered the same fate.

The next case seemed much more troubled and uncomfortable even than the first. His eyes were straight, but glassy, and the left side of his face twitched and jerked continuously, All he would say was "No, no." Maj. Webster told me that the man—he was a sergeant—had undergone two operations, and would have another tomorrow. He had a meningitis infection, and might not live.

The next two brain injuries were not quite so serious. The third man had undergone three operations, and, said the doctor, was better; although a fungus had grown in the wound, and further surgery might be necessary. The last man in the room was the most nearly normal. Although head, shoulders and arms were bandaged, and the right arm ended at the wrist with a great swatch of gauze, he talked rationally. He told us that he had been hit on December 8, by a hand grenade, near San Pietro. He had been on the battlefield for forty-four hours before he could be rescued.

It was a shock to realize how grievous such head injuries seemed to me, now that I was almost an observer, looking into the clouded mirror of the wounded men's faces—and trying to imagine what was going on within. Once, less than a month ago, I had been suffering in that same suspended stage of consciousness. But, now, I must be at least a half world removed.

Dr. Webster reminded me that these were relatively recent injuries. Nature, the recuperative force, would take up where surgery ended, and build the broken skulls and paralyzed bodies back to something approaching normal. A year from now I would not recognize these men; if they lived—and thanks to modern medicine, their chances of living were far better than ever before in history.

*

My own wound was improving day by day; the "pinch" graft had not been wholly successful, but it had closed a part of the unhealed area. Maj. Webster told me that a spot no larger than a quarter remained unprotected. I had to take his word for this; I had never been able to see the wound.

All this was encouraging, for, with the danger of infection diminishing rapidly, I would be free to travel to Africa—and eventually the United States.

On December 22, I actually got into the ambulance and was off for the next clearing point. The hospital to which I was being sent now was the final stop on the route to Africa. I would be transferred from there by hospital plane. I might still be home by New Year's Day.

December 22-26

When I reached the next stop, also a general hospital, I was told at first that I might have to wait one day at least; and then that flight schedules had been postponed indefinitely. One of the doctors advised me to wait and get aboard a hospital ship which was to leave in four days.

There were many consolations in this palatial building; it had been an Italian civilian hospital, one of the most modern and complete in Southern Italy. There were even occasional bathtubs, and, in many of the rooms, washbasins with running warm water! The building was a typical Fascist monument, splendid on first inspection, but actually jerry-built. Phony veneers of plaster and tile had already begun to peel from the walls and floors.

On the day before Christmas, I was told to gather together my belongings and report to the front desk. There a group of about a dozen patients, scheduled for evacuation to Africa, had gathered and were waiting for an ambulance which would take them to the airfield. I still hoped that, with good connections, I might be able to reach America before New Year's Day. But we were told only that the flight had been postponed.

It was a dismal Christmas Eve, although Yuletide decorations had been set up in the corridors. Capt. Ralph Angelucci, the neurosurgeon, showed me the prize ward. Several American-born Japanese soldiers, patients in this room, had set up a Christmas tree, decorated with delicate curlicues of colored paper, and even imitation candles, topped by twirls of cotton simulating flame.

Somehow, the Red Cross workers had acquired Christmas stockings made of net, and were filling each with an orange, a couple of hazel nuts, a small notebook, a child's ocarina and a few pieces of candy. They had set up an extra-large Christmas tree in the mess hall. A party was given for a group of Italian children from the neighborhood. One of the hospital doctors dressed himself up as Santa Claus and distributed gifts.

The doctors who were not on duty gave a party later in the evening. I went with Maj. Henry Carney and Capt. Angelucci. On our way, we stopped at the operating room and peered through the window. All the nurses and doctors were wearing masks, since the operation, Capt. Angelucci informed me, was an amputation of a leg, for gas gangrene. A hospital corpsman told me that the patient, a Jewish boy from Brooklyn, had been pleading with the doctors to save his leg. But it was a case of saving a life; gas gangrene, said Capt. Angelucci, was rare, but it was deadly.

We went on to the party, where the doctors were rejoicing with the aid of a large bottle of cognac, gift of a Catholic monastery. From some place unknown, a trio of soldiers appeared, playing hillbilly instruments. Then the major who had performed the amputation came in. The others only glanced at him, then went back to their merriment. His face was grim and drawn as he grasped a glass of cognac in his shaky hand. It had not been a pleasant Christmas Eve for him.

*

Christmas Day began auspiciously. There was a turkey dinner, with candles on the tables, and nuts and olives and celery and stuffing. But when the long afternoon was over, we came to a crushing disillusionment: cold Spam for supper.

There was many a long face among the wounded who lay on their cots in the corridors, reading the few dog-eared magazines which were available. I sat down with a group of the boys and shared my box of candy. They talked about wounds, and one of them voiced the opinion that when you are once wounded, and go back into action, you have three strikes against you. Most of his friends who had been wounded, and gone back, he said, had "got theirs." And he was convinced that he, too, was going to get it when he returned. But Sgt. Elom Toms, of Bienville, La., who had the patient manner of a veteran, did not agree. When you get hit, he maintained, you have a new start. Your luck actually gets better.

The morning after Christmas, I was instructed to get my belongings together, and this time, keeping our fingers crossed, we got aboard the ambulance and drove out to the airfield. Rain came in gusts as the litter cases were carried to a DC-3. We waited, while other ambulances rolled up and unloaded. The overcast grew thicker, and we wondered if we would have to go back to the hospital. But at last we were taxiing, turning into the wind, and we were winging over Naples and the white-capped Mediterranean.

There were seventeen of us wounded aboard the plane: fourteen litter cases and three ambulatory. Most of the cabin space was filled with stretchers, three-tiered. I looked over the medical records of the patients. They were a weird collection of names: Moroccans—French troops had moved into the line since I was wounded—named "Mohammed" or "Ben"; American-born Japanese, named Mizushima, Ishitani and Taomae; and also Pvt. Elmer Riddlebarker, Lieut. Young, Pvt. Caspar Linehan and Pvt. Floyd Fillmore. There was also a Sgt. Ira Radovsky, who was not, however, a patient. He was a passenger, hitchhiking a ride back to North Africa, where he was an X-ray operator in a hospital. He had been to Naples in an attempt to find his brother, who, he told me, was supposed to be a patient in a Naples hospital.

The ailments of our cargo of patients were as varied as their names: the Moroccans had been struck by shell fragments in various parts of the body, and two of them had suffered amputations; one of the Japanese-Americans had trench feet; Pvt. Riddlebarker had an abscess of the heel; Lieut. Young had been struck in the hand by an enemy bullet.

The trip was rough, and several of the patients grew airsick. A Medical Corps enlisted man passed the bucket between the two principal victims of nausea, a French Moroccan and an American private. About halfway across the Mediterranean, the wind grew less gusty and the sun came out.

December 26-31

I had been afraid that we would end up in a tent, in North Africa. We did. The welcoming gift of doughnuts and hot coffee, administered by a Red Cross girl when we landed, made the transition easier, but it was still a shock to get back to a tent camp, after the relative luxury of the last hospital in Italy. However, the ward to which I was directed was not truly a tent, but a sort of beaverboard and tarpaper structure. Red and green Christmas decorations lent a note of cheer.

After supper on this first evening, I heard that a hospital ship was in a near-by harbor, and that it was being loaded for embarkation to the United States.

I wandered about the camp, looking for the commanding officer of the hospital, hoping that I could arrange a passage back to America. I found Capt. William Weary, one of the neurosurgeons, and asked him about my chances. He said that only about twenty-five patients were being evacuated, and that they were mostly badly paralyzed spinal cases. Besides, there was a long waiting list, and there were few boats going home. Properly subdued, I went back to my ward.

The next day brought even more gloom. I was transferred to another tarpaper shack—and ordered to remain in bed. Lieut. Col. Eldridge Campbell, the chief neurosurgeon, warned me that I must not behave like an ambulatory case, and one of the other doctors told me that my head wound had become slightly infected. The last straw was added when I learned that air evacuation of patients to the United States was a rarity. In any case, said Col. Campbell, I could not leave this hospital until my wound was totally healed. I asked how long that might be, and he said, "Well, perhaps two or three weeks."

There was nothing to do in Ward B-1 except to relax. I resigned myself, after a day or two of fretting, to the stern reality of becoming a resident of North Africa. I found some solace in the fact that I could now read.

I still had my typewriter. By a tedious and clumsy effort, I could now operate the machine with some degree of success. My right hand, still deficient in feeling, was nevertheless improved. I finally managed to write a newspaper story about my being wounded, and I began to make daily notes again.

New Year's Day—January 1, 1944.

Captain William H. DeRouville, of Albany, N.Y., one of the surgeons, told me today that on this morning's tour of the wards, he and Dr. Campbell had been greeted by an amazing sight as they entered the tent reserved for cases of trench feet (a painful disease caused by continued exposure to cold and wet). "When we went into the ward, we found ourselves looking at forty pairs of bare feet propped up for our inspection—each with a red ribbon on the big toe."

Capt. DeRouville said that the most tragic cases he had seen were those who had lost both eyes. Some endured that calamity with more philosophy than others. "One I remember was a very bright fellow. He adjusted quickly. One day I was walking by his bed, when he called me by my name. I asked him how he did it, and he said, 'Oh, that's easy. I've already learned your step.' When this fellow asked me if there was any hope, I told him it was the worst, and he said, 'I suppose it had to happen to someone.'"

Lieut. Dick Stone, a former oil-company salesman, and I had one of our many long conversations. This time it was on the subject of killing Germans. He told me about a B.A.R. (Browning automatic rifle) operator on Hill 759, near San Pietro. When that man caught a bunch of Germans on a slope, and killed about twenty of them, he said, "This is fun; this is like what I dreamed about." Some men, opined Stone, have that killer instinct. "This guy just exulted in shooting the Heinies. I know some other guys like him who get a terrific feeling of power in killing, when they see them fall. But me, I can't look at it like that. The way I feel is that I've got a mission to do, to get the enemy out of the lines. I don't care whether I wound them or kill them, if I get them out of there."

We talked about religion—for there was not much to do except to read and talk. Stone ventured the idea that the experience of escaping death and injury, when others were being killed or wounded, converted many a soldier. Stone told a story about the landing at Paestum, supposedly authentic. A private in the 36th Division—this story came from the private's platoon commander—was notorious for the foul language which discolored his every sentence. But when the 36th hit the beach, and were subjected to shattering artillery bombardment, the profane fellow, lying in a foxhole, began to pray in a loud voice. "Oh, God, please save me," and he continued in this vein. Another private, in a near-by foxhole, recognized the voice, and shouted, "Hey, Joe, why don't you knock off that cryin' for help, and talk to somebody you know?"

Stone asked me the question which has followed me from hospital to hospital. Until I reached Ward B-1, I had not been able to talk well enough to answer it. Now, it was good practice to give my almost standardized speech on the subject: "Are the Japs tougher than the Germans?" Answering that question has helped me formulate my own thoughts on the war against the two Axis powers.

The answer runs something like this: The Germans are a great deal smarter. They have far better equipment. But the Japs are more stubborn—sometimes unbelievably stubborn—and they have plenty of manpower to throw away.

The terrain in the two theaters is so different that you have two distinct kinds of fighting. In Europe the fighting is all in the open. In the jungle the vegetation is like a wall; you have to hack your way through it—and, therefore, tanks and artillery are relatively ineffective.

Because tanks and artillery can be used so extensively in Europe, the fighting is much more dangerous. The Japs, on the other hand, depend mostly on rifles, machine guns and mortars; the Nipponese artillery I have seen is, by our standards, extremely primitive. But the jungle itself is a constant menace.

Generally, the difference between the Japs and the Germans can be measured by comparison of casualty figures. When American soldiers or flyers are thrown against an equal force of Germans, the possibility is that it will cost us dearly; we may lose one American for every German killed. If we are lucky, we may account for two Germans for every American casualty. With the Japs, however, the odds change decidedly in our favor, for the actual figures show that two to five Japs are killed for every loss on our side.

Fortunately, though, neither the Germans nor the Japs have the natural resources available to us. Still, the Japs may be the tougher foe, if only because they have proven to be suicidally persistent, and the Germans, since they are much more intelligent, are less likely to continue the struggle when our strength becomes overwhelming.

Tonight our sewing circle conjured up visions of the things we would do in the United States—a subject of never-failing appeal to servicemen, especially for those of us who were scheduled for an early return to America. Then, in a reminiscent mood we talked about Naples, and, of course, the Neapolitan girls; how much they liked American and British soldiers. One of the officers repeated a remark which is current among veterans of the Italian campaign: "If you put a roof over it, Naples would be the biggest whorehouse in the world."

January 2

This morning I watched the doctor dressing the wounds of Lieut. Nelson, a former bank teller from San Diego, who had lost his right leg in an S-mine explosion near Venafro. Nelson talked quite casually about "my stump." The doctor also bandaged his smashed left leg, where the kneecap had been ripped off by the same explosion. The sight of such mutilation brought a surge of hatred for the Germans. Since I have been in the hospital, my vindictiveness toward the enemy has grown. My conception of war aims has become even more simplified than formerly: to crush the nations responsible for such suffering.

Another leg-amputation case was brought in today. Our conversation stopped while the stretcher bearers lifted the heavy form, clumsy in a cast which extended from the waist down. We waited for the new arrival to make himself known. He turned out to be a sunny-tempered artillery officer, Capt. Herbert Vines, in civilian life a telephone engineer from Birmingham, Ala. He and Nelson almost immediately struck up a conversation about their stumps. Vines suggested to Sitko, the ward boy, that if the two one-legged men could be placed side by side, medicine could be brought for both of them on one trip. "One grain of morphine would take care of the two of us," he proposed.

Capt. Vines related how the Germans had "zeroed in" on his battery, throwing nearly a hundred shells into his position in a few minutes, killing two of his men, knocking out one of his guns, smashing one leg and blowing off his left foot. Lying on the ground, he could see his foot beside him. One of his men came up and asked what he could do to help. And Vines said, "Throw it away. It won't be any good to me now."

January 3

Lieut. Joe Burke, of Chevy Chase, Md., one of our ambulatory cases, started for the officers' store to get some articles of clothing this morning. He was listing our names, and the articles we wanted, when Nelson and Vines began talking about shoes. They discovered that they both wore size ten, and Vines suggested that, since he had lost his left leg and Nelson the right, they could get along with one pair. It would be a good partnership.

This afternoon Nelson and I were talking about the psychological reactions of wounded men.

"As far as I'm concerned, I was pretty much in the dumps at first," he volunteered. "I figured I was all washed up. But then I began to think about it. After all, it wasn't as bad as losing an arm. I still have two hands and can shuffle banknotes. Once I get one of those artificial-leg gadgets, I'll be as good as anybody else."

He glanced over at Capt. Vines across the corridor, and added modestly, "They told me at the bank that I could have my job back after the war."

January 5

Lieut. Bough (the concussion case who brews tea for us each evening) is a dissenting voice amongst the throng of us who would like to get back to the United States as soon as possible. Most of us who will be "Z.I.'d" (sent back to the Zone of the Interior, the United States, for further treatment) would jump at the chance to leave immediately. But not so Bough, the Ranger, who certainly has good reason to feel that he has done his part. Knocked out by shellfire at Chiunzi Pass, he was again prostrated by concussion at San Pietro. Now he is troubled by terrible headaches and dizzy spells. Nevertheless, he feels that he should be returned to duty as soon as possible—and he does not want to go home until the job's done. (In any case, the Medical Board in this theater of war decides whether a case will be Z.I.'d, whether he will be reclassified—put into a sedentary job—or sent back into active service.)

One of the conversational subjects of the wounded men in B-1 is the dread prospect of being sent to a "Repple Depple," a replacement depot. A Repple Depple, I gather, is a sort of clearing station where wounded men who are no longer useful for active duty are sent to new jobs. Many of the patients here have told me that they would desert and go back to their outfits at the front, go "A.W.O. Loose," rather than put up with the delay and inactivity of the Repple Depples.

No matter how much the wounded men's minds dwell on the possibilities of going back to the United States or returning to their outfits, they are always eager for every scrap of news from the front. Each morning there is a scramble for the news bulletins typed up and mimeographed by the hospital staff. We have no radio in our ward.

Most of us discuss at great length the slow-down of the Allied campaign in Italy. We seem to be in agreement that the fundamental cause of our bogging down is that we simply haven't enough strength, of men and material. The Germans have reinforced their lines heavily and we are fighting man for man. In this mountainous terrain we would ordinarily need a superiority of two to one at least to continue our push.

It has begun to look as if we might be stalemated before we get to Rome. The front lines have been moved up only three or four miles beyond Mount Corno and Venafro since November 22, when I was hit. At this rate, it will take us another two months to travel the remaining four or five miles to Cassino.

Some of the boys have heard rumors indicating that there may be an "end run"—another amphibious landing somewhere near Rome. The 3rd Division, the soothsayers allege, is waterproofing all vehicles.

The big news continues to be the Russian advance. The officers in our sewing circle are loud in their praise of the Russians as fighting men. Opinions differ on the matter of the future plans of the U.S.S.R. in Europe. Some say that territorial expansion and the extension of their sphere of influence are the aims of the Kremlin. Others contend that Stalin has no interest in the conquest of Europe. The consensus is that in any case, whether or not the Russians want to dominate Europe, they are welcome to it.

We pass many idle moments speculating upon the future establishment of an international police force. We are in agreement about the necessity for that. Whatever happens, we must keep Germany and Japan impotent, so that they can never again be dangerous to us. That, in the last analysis, is what we are fighting for.

January 8

My wound is healing rapidly. Within a few days I may be able to move. Word has come through from Algiers that the P.R.O. will be able to arrange a flight back to the United States. The news has spread in B-1 that I am going to be Z.I.'d soon. Suddenly I have become the most envied man in the ward.

January 13

This evening I got the news I have been waiting for. Tomorrow is the day. My spirits soared. I was so buoyant that I felt I could take off and fly under my own power.

On this, my last night, Capt. Weary, the neurosurgeon, urged me to see some of the head cases in the other wards. I saw them: the man with the deep hole in the front of the skull, his nose gone, whose mind would eventually come back to normal, whose face would be restored by plastic surgery; the man who could neither talk nor register words, whose brain was now, said Dr. Weary, at the mental level of a rabbit. He, too, with neurological care, would be able to climb back to normal, although he would have to progress through all the steps of biological evolution—from rabbit to horse to dog to ape, and finally man.

There is a parallel to all this in the mass history of our time, I thought, as we left the bleak purgatory of the ward and walked under the starry North African night: time and determination and persistence will perhaps restore this mutilated world to a semblance of order and intelligence once the evil powers which wreaked this horror are crushed. If only we do not forget, when the time comes . . .

Afterword

RT Would Go
A Crusade for Ideals and Survival
Ray E. Boomhower

In the months following the Japanese attack on the U.S. Pacific fleet at Pearl Harbor in the Hawaiian Islands on December 7, 1941, millions of American men pondered what would become of them as their country took its first tentative steps in the worldwide conflict. One of those who wondered what his future might be was a young reporter working on the rewrite desk at the New York office of the International News Service, Richard Tregaskis of Elizabeth, New Jersey.

Tregaskis had suffered several shocking developments since the surprise Japanese raid. He had been rejected for service due to his height (he stood more than six feet, five inches tall) and weak eyesight and had learned he had developed a debilitating chronic illness, diabetes. To get to the fighting, Tregaskis became determined to become a foreign correspondent for the INS, a news agency founded by newspaper magnate William Randolph Hearst. He kept after his boss, Barry Faris, to send him off as to cover the war, believing that the "closer I cam to getting killed in this career, the better my story would be, if I survived."

One rainy March evening Tregaskis learned that Faris wanted to see him the next morning. Tregaskis respected Faris, who, although physically undistinguished, could do any job in the newsroom. He particularly admired the veteran journalist for "his fondness for direct action—the shortest way to a point. This was characteristic of all great newsmen I knew—and it was the quality they had in common with the great military leaders I came to know, the leaders among the brave men."

Faris was polite and to the point, asking Tregaskis if he would rather go to London or Australia. Knowing that Faris did not "brook a 'think it over' kind of answer," Tregaskis seized his chance and made up his mind, picking Australia. Tregaskis was on his way to combat, pleased that "out there in the void of the future was a shape I had dreamed of: men at war in a crusade for ideals, and for survival."

From the Doolittle Raid, the Battle of Midway, and the invasion of Guadalcanal in the Pacific, to the invasions of Sicily and Italy, as well as the drives into France, Belgium, Germany, and back to the Pacific, Tregaskis followed the troops, paying the penalty many others paid in the war, including being gravely wounded by a German shell in Italy. "I gave that effort a lot of my own blood and I didn't hold back when it came to risking my neck to do what I was supposed to do," he recalled.

In doing so, Tregaskis discovered that he possessed an innate affinity for covering combat, writing his sister Madeline shortly after he had finished his Guadalcanal book that it was funny the way "this war business hits you, after you've been meddling around with it for a while. Action, and particularly some new variety of action, gets to be like a drug. You feel let down without it and with it you feel a sort of unhealthy excitement. And frightening—shooting at people and that sort of thing—comes to have a compelling interest, although you're fully aware of the unpleasantness of it." He even began to look forward to the next assignment, hating to miss any upcoming big battle, even if he had an opportunity to return to his family in the United States.

Tregaskis's willingness to go where the action was heaviest impressed me greatly as I researched his career for my book *Richard Tregaskis: Reporting under Fire from Guadalcanal to Vietnam*. The reporter's courage in combat also amazed the soldiers, sailors, airmen, and Marines he covered. One awed soldier told the correspondent, "How you guys go ahead and stick out your necks when you don't have to—well, it just beats hell out of me!" Tregaskis had a simple answer: "But we certainly do have to—that's our job."

Asked by the editors of a national magazine to return to the Pacific late in the war to follow the crew of a B-29 Superfortress as it prepared for bombing missions against Japanese cities, Tregaskis was asked by an editor, "Do you really want to go?" Without hesitating, Tregaskis gave an answer that any reporter who covered World War II would understand: "I don't want to go, but I think I ought to go." He went.

Map and Illustrations

The illustrations in this book are reproduced by courtesy of International News Photo

Photo Essay

Shell-racked Cassino

Italian ships sunk in Naples harbor by Allied air bombs

A charge across a shattered bridge over the Volturno River at Cancello

American troops advance along a Sicilian mountain road.

British Tommies search for snipers in Centuripe, Sicily

Round-up of Nazi prisoners near Salerno

First wave of American troops entering Messina

Full-scale bombardment of Mount Trocchio, near Cassino

An American amphibious jeep rides triumphantly through a Sicilian street

Advance over a railroad cut near Catania, Sicily

An Italian civilian helps American engineers unearth a Teller mine

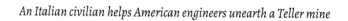

LCTs carry British troops to Calabrian shore

A 155-mm. Long Tom moving into position to shell the Italian mainland

A moment after the explosion of a mine in the post office of Naples

A convoy of LCIs for the invasion of Italy

U. S. Army engineers repair a cliffside road

American truck carrying German prisoners strafed by enemy planes

American soldiers loading 4.2 mortar near Venafro

Americans set up camp near the ruins of ancient Paestum, Italy

Bombardment of shell-pocked Concasale, near Cassino

An American jeep by-passes a British tank crew in Pompeii

Barry Faris and the author interview a native of Pratella amid the ruins of her home

Messina Straits, gateway to the Italian mainland

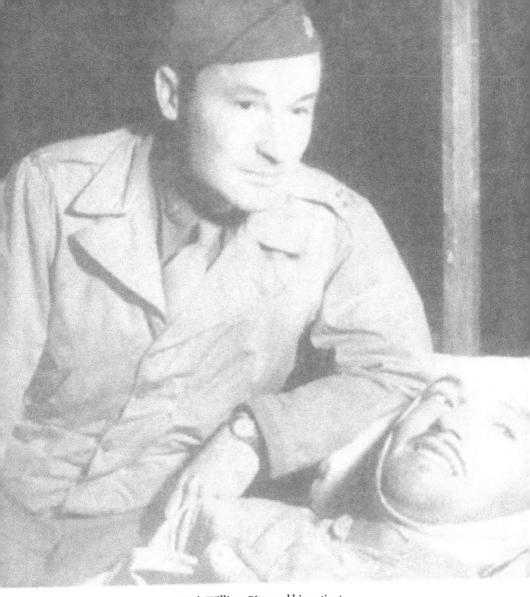

Maj. William Pitts and his patient

WE ARE NOW IN THIS WAR

We are all in it all the way

Every single man, woman and child is a partner in the most tremendous undertaking of our American history. We must share together the bad news and the good news, the defeats and the victories—the changing fortunes of war.

(*President Roosevelt, Address to the Nation, December 9, 1941*)

*World War II poster quoting FDR about every citizen's part in the war. U.S. War Dept. —
Courtesy of Wikimedia Commons*

American WWII propaganda poster by the United States Office of War Information
—Courtesy of Wikimedia Commons

Courtesy of National Archives and Records Administration, cataloged under the National Archives Identifier (NAID) 513519.

ca. 1943 *Office for Emergency Management. Office of War Information. Domestic Operations Branch. News Bureau. Courtesy of National Archives and Records Administration, cataloged under the National Archives Identifier (NAID) 535701.*

Italian World War II poster, "Here are the `liberators`", showing the Statue of Liberty as an angel of death, and the Italian cities in fire after a bombing. They were upset to have their homes and cities destroyed during the fight to secure their freedom. As shown in *Invasion Diary*, every effort was made to only target military targets and not bomb historical sites and personal homes. This picture was issued by the government of the Italian Social Republic, a state now considered as illegal in Italy. —Courtesy of Wikimedia Commons

Index of Names

The index below is taken from the original edition of the book and has been included for reference only

W

Walker, Lieut. Col. Fred L.
Walker, Lieut. Stewart
Warner, Capt. Ozzie
Warren, Lieut. Col. Arthur L.
Weary, Capt. William
Webster, Maj.
Weiherman, Pvt.
Whillock, Chaplain Harold T.
White, Lieut. Col.
Wight, Capt. Tom
Wise, Pvt. Ralph M.
Wood, Lieut. Col.
Wozenski, Capt. Edward
Wymond, Capt. Gilbert O.

Y

Yarborough, Lieut. Col. Bill
Young, Lieut.

Z

Zbylut, Lieut.

Richard Tregaskis Books

SOUTHEAST ASIA: BUILDING THE BASES

THE HISTORY OF CONSTRUCTION IN SOUTHEAST ASIA

CHINA BOMB: A NOVEL

GUADALCANAL DIARY

INVASION DIARY

JOHN F. KENNEDY AND PT-109

LAST PLANE TO SHANGHAI

SEVEN LEAGUES TO PARADISE

STRONGER THAN FEAR

VIETNAM DIARY

THE WARRIOR KING: HAWAI'I'S KAMEHAMEHA THE GREAT

WOMAN AND THE SEA: A BOOK OF POEMS

X-15 DIARY

Other JMFdeA Press Books

CHASING THE SURGE

THE ENERGY INSIDE VALSIN'S CHOICES

PERSIGUIENDO LA OLEADA

SASSY FOOD

CPSIA information can be obtained
at www.ICGtesting.com
Printed in the USA
LVHW051939160222
711308LV00015B/2111